The
EVERYTHING®
Self-Esteem Book

Dear Reader:

I ran away from home on a Monday. I left the South and ran to D.C., to New York City, and further north. Sadly, I did not find happiness or joy at any stop. I didn't find validation and I didn't find any place that made me feel any better about myself. *Where is my happiness?* I questioned. *Why is no one here to rescue me? Why? Why? Why?*

I did not have happiness in my heart, my work, my relationships, my home, or my life. I didn't like me, and I traveled for days trying to lose myself. I was twenty-seven years old. It took me twenty-seven years to realize that we cannot run from ourselves. That trip taught me that self-esteem isn't about running; it's about stopping.

In this book, I share the advice and activities that have helped others, and me, over the years. I provide a framework so that *you can begin your work* to better understand your worth, carve a path to your happiness, uncover your purpose in life, and move toward an inner peace about the gifts and challenges bestowed on you as a human being.

All the best to you,

The EVERYTHING® Series

Editorial

Publishing Director	Gary M. Krebs
Managing Editor	Kate McBride
Copy Chief	Laura MacLaughlin
Acquisitions Editor	Bethany Brown
Development Editor	Karen Johnson Jacot
Production Editor	Khrysti Nazzaro
	Jamie Wielgus

Production

Production Director	Susan Beale
Production Manager	Michelle Roy Kelly
Series Designers	Daria Perreault
	Colleen Cunningham
Cover Design	Paul Beatrice
	Frank Rivera
Layout and Graphics	Colleen Cunningham
	Rachael Eiben
	Michelle Roy Kelly
	Daria Perreault
	Erin Ring
Series Cover Artist	Barry Littmann

Visit the entire Everything® Series at everything.com

THE
EVERYTHING®
SELF-ESTEEM
BOOK

Boost your confidence, achieve inner
strength, and learn to love yourself

Robert M. Sherfield, Ph.D.

Adams Media
Avon, Massachusetts

Dedication

To Rhonda Montgomery, Patricia Moody,
Sande Johnson, and Nancy Forsyth

Acknowledgments

My earnest thanks to Barb Doyen of Doyen Literary Services,
Karen MacDowall Jones, Steve Spearman, Brian Epps, Leo Borges,
Tina Eliopulos, Todd Moffett, Lynn Forkos, Debi McCandrew, Bill Clayton,
Meg Galliano, Dr. James Williamson, Dr. Charles Mosely, Dr. Don Smith,
Dr. Robert Palinchak, and Dr. Ron Remington.

An Everything® Series Book.
Everything® and everything.com® are registered trademarks of F+W Publications, Inc.

Published by Adams Media, an F+W Publications Company
57 Littlefield Street, Avon, MA 02322 U.S.A.
www.adamsmedia.com

ISBN: 1-58062-976-8
Printed in the United States of America.

J   I   H   G   F   E   D   C   B   A

Library of Congress Cataloging-in-Publication Data
Sherfield, Robert M.
The everything self-esteem book / Robert M. Sherfield.
p.   cm.
(An everything series book) ISBN: 1-58062-976-8
1. Self-esteem. 2. Self-actualization (Psychology) I. Title. II. Series: Everything series.

BF697.5.S46 S52
158.1–dc22

2003017008

This book is available at quantity discounts for bulk purchases.
For information, call 1-800-872-5627.

Contents

Top Ten Benefits
of Having Healthy Self-Esteem

1. You are more secure in who you are and what you have to offer the world.
2. You are able to see the good in others and in the world around you.
3. You are able to move on from the past and experience joy in the present.
4. Your are able to overcome adversity and setbacks more easily.
5. You are able to forgive yourself and others.
6. You have a clear sense of your own values, worth, integrity, and character.
7. You take better care of your physical and mental health.
8. You are able to develop a positive philosophy of life and live by that philosophy.
9. You are more optimistic, happier, and able to give of yourself to others.
10. You are able to take responsibility for your own thoughts, actions, and indeed, your life.

Introduction

▶WELCOME! AND CONGRATULATIONS! It may have taken a great deal of courage to meander over to this book, but in the words of an ancient Chinese philosopher, "The journey of a thousand miles begins with a singe step." You are to be commended for taking that step. If you are reading these words because you feel a need to improve your self-esteem, you need to know that you are among the millions of people who suffer from self-doubt, fears of inadequacy, feelings of worthlessness, and unhealthy self-criticism. You are not alone in your journey. *The Everything® Self-Esteem Book* is written to help you gain a new perspective on your life, your actions, your thoughts, and your personal success.

This book is about reflection, personal and professional goals, growth, renewal, and results. It is not a book for simply browsing through or just flipping through page after page. This is a book to be used, dog-eared, marked in, talked about, and used over and over. This book is about you and your journey. This book is about work! Changing the way that you look at yourself is not an easy task, but it is possible—very possible.

Simply put, your search for healthier self-esteem is essential for your life. Yes, your life may depend on how well you think of yourself. Your self-esteem determines how well you treat yourself, how well you treat others, how you view the world, how you view yourself in the world, how you act in the world, and how you take care of your basic needs that are required for survival. The renowned psychologist Abraham Maslow identified a series of needs that exists in every living human being. Among those listed, in addition to your need for safety and love, are esteem needs. He suggested that until your basic needs of air, water, safety, love, and esteem, are met, you can't fulfill your needs for intellectual achievement, the appreciation of beauty, and self-actualization or fulfillment.

Many experts believe that moving toward healthier self-esteem requires two things: setting high, realistic goals, and acting in some fashion to have a degree of success in reaching those goals. This book gives you not only self-esteem theory and thought, but also a series of practical, useful exercises and thought-provoking suggestions to help you help yourself in reaching your goals of healthy self-esteem.

As you begin working toward healthier self-esteem, think of it as a daily goal. Choose some task each day that will help you more clearly see what you have to offer to yourself and the world. Once you have begun to realize the gifts that you possess, you can begin to concentrate on finding positive self-esteem through laughter, spiritual thought, exercise, risk taking, contemplation, positive visualization, forgiveness, creativity, and personal integrity.

This book is useless without your total commitment and unbridled passion for improving your self-esteem. You, and only you, have the power to change your life. Know, however, before you begin the journey, that the path to healthier self-esteem will not be completed instantaneously. Just as your self-esteem was not shaped overnight, it will not be reshaped overnight. Honesty, patience, work, and need are the tools required for this journey.

Before you begin reading the chapters in this book, turn to Appendix A and take the Self-Esteem Assessment. This will give you a better understanding of your present thoughts and ideas about yourself before you begin. (E)

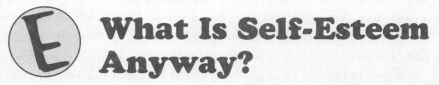

Chapter 1

What Is Self-Esteem Anyway?

Self-esteem is one of the most elusive concepts in the world. Some people call it the "eternal elixir for happiness," while others call it "useless psychobabble." You will need to decide how important self-esteem is to your life and what steps you need to take to acquire a healthier self-esteem.

Finding Your True Self

Who are you really? When you are at home at the end of the day and you are alone for a moment, who are you? It has been suggested that your true self is who you are when no one else is looking. Are you the bright, energetic person you portrayed at work today, or are you the shy, sullen person you portrayed at a meeting last week? Only you can answer that question. You may not even be able to answer it right now, but rest assured, true self is personal, true self is deep, true self is complex, and true self is important.

When is the last time that you stood before a mirror and honestly, truthfully, completely looked yourself in the face and read the story of your own life? It's not something that you do every day, but have you ever done it? Have you ever realized that you have more than one "self"? This is not to say that you have multiple personalities, which is a rare condition. But everyone has more than one self. Your selves may include the roles of a mother/father, a daughter/son, a wife/husband, an aunt/uncle, a friend, a traveler, a searcher, a teacher, a learner, a leader, and/or a follower. You may not act the same way in every role or "self." Deeper still, you have a public self and a private self. This complicates the issue of self-esteem further. You sometimes see yourself as a public mother and a private mother, a public son and a private son. Your history, your environment, and your own value system shape your different selves. Even without you realizing it, this duality can be very costly. Portraying two selves can cost you in terms of stress, energy, honesty, and self-esteem.

FACT

Many psychologists suggest that while we may have multiple selves, that we should focus on being one self instead of many selves.

The Public Self versus the Private Self

People may see you as bright, youthful, happy, carefree, and helpful. Are these really true depictions of yourself, or are they pictures you have painted for them to view? Your public self may sometimes be very different from your private self.

You may be afraid to let "the public" see who you really are for fear of being criticized or embarrassed. You may pretend to be something that you are not just to fit in or, at the very least, to avoid standing out. People with healthy self-esteem have found the way to blend the public and private self to form a close partnership so that the two are not diabolically juxtaposed to each other. That is to say that as a private mother or father, you would not do something that you would not consider doing as a public mother or father.

Two as One

Are you your true self, or are you the self that others want you to be? Do you behave so that others will accept you, love you, invite you places, and call you, or do you behave so that you are happy with yourself? Your self-esteem is damaged when you try to be someone or do something for the sake of others. When you do something that goes against your inner grain, you know the internal struggle that brews. You know that your true self lost out and your "public self" or "persona" won. Self-esteem is aided when you learn to take the best of every self you have and work to make that your one self, the self to whom you are true.

Formal Definitions of Self-Esteem

There are as many definitions, assumptions, and revelations about self-esteem as there are people who write about it, research it, and long for it. Two of the earliest theorists on self-esteem were William James and Stanley Coopersmith.

The "Sum Total"

William James is usually identified as the earliest psychologist to investigate the concept of "self." He defined the self as "the sum total of all that a person can call their own." He divided the self into three parts: the "Material Me," the "Social Me," and the "Spiritual Me." Most importantly, Smith argued that self-esteem is largely dependent on the goals we have for ourselves and the degree to which we reach those goals. He believed that if something is important to you and you achieve it, your self-esteem grows. Conversely, he suggested that if something is not important to you and you do not achieve it, it does not damage your self-esteem. Self-esteem is weakened or damaged only by negating or failing at the things that are important to you.

The Material Me

The Material Me refers to all that you have that gives you harmony and unity, such as your body, your family, your possessions, and material belongings. James stated that as a human, you have a need to protect your body and your material things, and to have others notice them and look on them favorably. He suggested that your material "things" such as your home, your clothes, your car, and your furniture are all extensions of your self.

The Social Me

The Social Me is about recognition and even acceptance from others. You show different sides of yourself to different people depending on the situation. James suggested that you have as many "social selves" as you do people, or groups of people, for whom you care, because you need to be recognized positively by this group of people. He believed that your relationships with other people played a great role in your identity.

"Nobody gets to live life backward. Look ahead—that's where your future lies."

—Ann Landers

The Spiritual Me

The Spiritual Me relates to the feelings and emotions you have about yourself—your innermost thoughts, desires, dreams, and feelings. This "spiritual" me has little to do with formal or organized religion; it has more to do with the relationship with and knowledge about your self.

James suggested that we have a tendency to seek honor and favorable praise for ourselves. This is tied to the need for self-preservation.

A Judgment of Worth

Stanley Coopersmith defined self-esteem as "a personal judgment of worthiness that is expressed in the attitudes we hold about ourselves." His landmark self-esteem assessment instrument The Coopersmith Self-Esteem Inventory (CSEI) remains one of the most widely used and reliable tools in self-esteem research.

Most psychologist, therapists, and self-esteem experts agree on a basic level that self-esteem is the picture we hold of ourselves in our own mind and the value we place on ourselves. Healthy self-esteem is having a positive, affirmative, and constructive view of yourself. These words suggest that you believe in your capabilities; accept your strengths and limitations; set and work toward realistic goals; develop positive, rewarding relationships; and discover comfort in the world around you.

Unhealthy self-esteem is having a negative, pessimistic, disapproving view of yourself and the inability to see beyond your limitations and problems. Low self-esteem *is* a mental health problem. Low self-esteem can cause you to lose sight of your goals, weaken your motivation, deprive you of meaningful relationships, and cause you to focus only on your limitations.

FACT

Psychologist Charles Cooely likened self-esteem to a "looking glass." He believed that you define your self by what is reflected back to you from others, using what others think of you to build your own concept of self.

I Will Survive

A more recent theorist and psychologist, Nathaniel Branden, defines self-esteem as "confidence in our ability to think, confidence in our ability to cope with the basic challenges of life, and confidence in our right to be successful and happy, the feeling of being worthy, deserving, entitled to assert our needs and wants, achieve our values, and enjoy the fruits of our effort." He sums this statement up in a formal definition: "Self-esteem is the disposition to experience oneself as competent to cope with the basic challenges of life and as worthy of happiness."

Taking this definition to its basic core and using everyday language, you could say that people with healthy self-esteem hold the following motto in earnest: "Happiness is possible and I will survive."

Self-Esteem Takes a Bad Rap!

Thomas Sowell, a columnist for *Forbes* magazine and a Senior Fellow at the Hoover Institution at Stanford University, calls the theory of self-esteem "useless psychobabble." Michael Edelstein, psychologist and writer, finds that studies "not only cast doubt on the benefits of high self-esteem but suggest that it might even be harmful." Roy Baumeister—noted professor, researcher, and self-esteem expert—concludes, "the enthusiastic claims of the self-esteem movement mostly range from fantasy to hogwash." Dr. Onkar Ghate, researcher and writer, categorizes some teachers who use self-esteem theories as "pushers of pseudo self-esteem" and calls their ideas "a disease." In a *Newsweek* article, Sharon Begley cites research to support her assertion that "unjustified self-esteem can trigger hostility and aggression, and may even underlie violence like the recent school shootings."

Why So Bad?

Why is self-esteem taking such a bad rap? Why do these noted professionals have negative remarks and theories about acquiring healthy self-esteem, and if they are correct, why is healthy self-esteem pursued by millions, and why are there books, tapes, articles, psychologists, therapists, and educators advocating that you lift your spirits and elevate your self-esteem to unprecedented heights?

Honestly, many others agree with their views! *What?* you ask. How can people agree that healthy self-esteem can be "hogwash," "harmful," "psychobabble," or even dangerous?

The answer is quite simple. In the past decade, acquiring healthy self-esteem has taken a frightening turn toward the ridiculous. Scores of well-meaning individuals including teachers, parents, and counselors have turned the quest for positive, healthy self-esteem into something that would make Stanley Coopersmith, Abraham Maslow, William James, and countless other pioneering psychologists whirl in their graves! In the past ten to fifteen years, self-esteem theory has moved away from the concept that well-planned goals, hard work, and achievement brings healthy self-esteem and rushed toward the notion that self-esteem comes from a series of meaningless phrases and inappropriate praise.

QUESTION?

What is a self-affirmation?
A self-affirmation is when you use phrases such as "I am okay," or "I am good at my work," or "I am a great baseball player" to help you feel better without doing any work to make yourself better.

Self-esteem is not about chanting phrases or unwarranted praise. To simply state, "I love myself!" or "I'm okay!" or "I am smart!" or "I am pretty!" is as useless as saying, "I am a great pilot!" never having taken a flying lesson. Unless you do something today to "love yourself more" or make yourself more "okay" or "smarter" or "prettier," your position in life will be unchanged. Acquiring healthy self-esteem is more than saying, "I'm great," it is about setting goals and *doing* things to make yourself great.

It Takes Action

With all of the feel-good propaganda surrounding self-esteem, many people are mistakenly led to believe that there is not that much to gaining healthy self-esteem other than chanting a few phrases and receiving passing approval from others. This is not to suggest that thinking positive thoughts and receiving warranted praise can't aid you in your quest; they may. But acquiring healthy self-esteem is arduous work, and without *action* on your part, true self-esteem will remain elusive.

Let's say that you are feeling down because your weight is out of control. Someone comes along, a friend perhaps, and tells you that you look nice today. For a moment, your spirits are lifted—you feel better. However, you know that you have made no effort to control your weight, that you gained two pounds this week, and that you don't believe that you look nice. The good feeling that the praise gave you is fleeting.

However, if you have worked all week on a new wellness program, eaten healthier, walked two miles each night, and have lost four pounds this week and that same friend comments about your appearance, the feeling brought on by that positive comment will last—because you did something to deserve it. You worked toward a goal, achieved it, and you were recognized for it. This is the stuff of true self-esteem.

One of the most exciting ways to begin to build healthy self-esteem is to set a small, short-term, realistic goal and work toward that goal with passion. Once that goal is reached, you begin to understand what achievement means to healthy self-esteem.

Feeling Good versus Feeling Right

Self-esteem has less to do with "feeling good" than it has to do with "feeling right." There is a substantial difference between the two. Feeling good cannot make you feel right, but feeling right can make you feel good. Now, do not be mistaken here. This "right" has nothing to do with "right versus wrong." This feeling of right has to do with feeling authentic and genuine inside. Healthy self-esteem is much like your old, comfortable recliner. When you sit down in it, you feel at home. It's like the chair knows you. Other chairs are okay and may even be comfortable, but nothing feels like *your* chair. Your chair feels beyond good to you, it feels right. It fits you well.

The Luck of Larry

Take the case of Larry, for example. Larry works for Cooper Industries. He likes his job as an advertisement layout artist, but it is not the career of his dreams. His real love is painting. He works steady and does well, but usually he does just enough to get by. However, Larry's "getting by work" is much better than some people's "best work." Larry continually receives compliments from his supervisor and colleagues. These compliments make Larry feel good and give him a boost, but deep inside, Larry knows the truth. His work just happens to please a few key people. Larry knows that he is not really even trying. He knows that his heart is in his artwork, not in his ad designs. The praise feels good for a while, but it does not feel right. However, whenever Larry receives a compliment on a painting that took weeks to conceive and much creative energy to paint, the praise feels right. The feeling lasts.

Continually doing things that go against who you are as a person and what you know is right can cause immense damage to your self-esteem. Imagine yourself in this situation for a moment so that you can fully understand Larry's situation. You may have experienced a similar situation in your own work or life. If so, you know that feeling good is temporary while feeling right is long lasting.

Such is the case with self-esteem. Simply having people compliment you on something for which you did not work may make you feel good for a moment, but deep inside, you know the truth just as Larry does. You know that if you do nothing tangible to deserve the compliment, the "good" feeling quickly disappears. However, if you actually do something to deserve the praise, the right feeling lasts.

The Magic Wand

If a magic wand could be waved to give you positive, healthy self-esteem, there would be many more happy people in the world. But there is no magic wand; there are no phrases of praise that can come from anyone that can give you meaningful, lasting, self-esteem. And finally, there are no words, exercises, or suggestions in this book that can help you . . . unless you want them to help you. There is no magic fix. Reading this book without doing the work suggested (and it *is* work) is a waste of time.

Recognizing What's Right

You may be thinking to yourself, *I haven't felt "right" in ages.* How do I find "right" in my life? Perhaps the best way to find "right" is to think about when you did not feel "right." The answer may be in the negative more than the positive.

For example, suppose for a moment that you went to the post office and one of the clerks was very rude and unhelpful to you. During your conversation with him, you made several rude comments back to him and also made several remarks about his job performance. It felt great to get that off your chest. You feel good! *He deserved it,* you were thinking at the moment. Later in the evening or maybe in the car on the way home, you begin to regret what you did. You know that those comments did not help the situation. You know that you may have hurt someone. You begin to feel "less good" about what you did. Why? Because that action was not "right" with who you are as a person. That action went against the grain of your personal fabric. This is a perfect case of how "good" and "right" are very different. This is also a perfect scenario of how our self-esteem becomes damaged when we forego "right" to have a momentary "good" feeling.

"Sometimes a person hits upon a place to which he or she mysteriously feels that he or she belongs."

—S. Maugham

Self-esteem is as complex as the heavens, as vast as the desert, as deep as the oceans, and as fleeting as the wind. But, self-esteem is also as simple as setting a personal goal, working toward that goal with passion, focusing on the positive aspects of your life, and adhering to your personal sense of "right" as you move through the days. (E)

Chapter 2

When Self-Esteem Is Unhealthy

The beast of unhealthy self-esteem knows no prejudice; it does not discriminate based on race, age, sex, religion, or any other social or economic category. It does not work on a time clock and approach when it is convenient. It does not tap on your door and ask your permission to enter.

Recognizing Unhealthy Self-Esteem

The beast of unhealthy self-esteem wanders into your life at the time and place of its choosing. It sometimes masks itself as depression, fear, anxiety, or feelings of utter worthlessness. The beast knows no boundaries and has a mind all its own. It is relentless unless you learn how to recognize its approach, distinguish its footsteps on your porch, and deny its entrance into your life.

There are those who think that people who suffer with self-esteem issues are introverts who never leave home; individuals who are submissive and oppressed; or people who fail at family, career, and friendships; and people who are always involved in self-destructive, self-sabotaging activities. This simply is not true. Granted, a lack of self-esteem certainly causes many people to be introverted or have poor relationships, but generally speaking, the downtrodden are not the only people who have self-esteem issues. People with self-esteem issues come from every walk of life; they are lawyers, auto mechanics, hospitality professionals, teachers, swimmers, construction workers, and investment brokers.

QUESTION?

What is self-sabotage?
Self-sabotage is consciously or unconsciously doing things to obstruct your success. This includes lying, cheating, closing off your emotions, attacking others, refusing to participate in activities, and procrastinating.

Phillip and the Good Life

A compelling example of this is a young man named Phillip, who worked as an accountant for a major firm. He drove a new Viper, owned his own home, and seemed to be as happy as anyone could be. He often spoke of going out with friends and taking vacations. The good life was his.

But Phillip revealed to a friend that he was totally miserable. His friend was completely shocked. He had gone into accounting because his parents pressured him by refusing to pay for his college education unless he majored in a business field that "offered lucrative employment." The car and home were purchases aimed at making him happier in a job he hated. When he assessed his friendships honestly, he admitted that he had only one real friend; the rest were merely acquaintances. He confided, "I don't contribute anything to anybody or any purpose. I feel useless and I'm miserable."

In order for Phillip to be happy, he had to change his life. He had to make adjustments so that his own personality could begin to blossom. On his own dime, and on his own terms, he returned to school to study what he loved most, drawing and painting.

Today, Phillip owns his own art supply store. His accounting background comes in quite handy, but he is using his skill as an accountant to augment his passion, his "calling" in life. He makes time to draw and paint now, and he is surrounded by artists on a daily basis.

The Moral of Phillip's Tale

Much of Phillip's self-esteem was tied to his work. Research suggests that this is usually true for men, while women tend to tie their self-esteem to family and home. You may be thinking, *Well good for Phillip, but I can't just up and quit my job; I have to make a living somehow.* You might even be thinking, *My career is not the problem; I love my work. I'm just not happy with X or Y or Z.*

FACT

Research shows that people spend less than thirty hours over their entire lifetime thinking about and researching their career choices. If you begin work at twenty years of age, work forty hours per week, and retire at sixty-five, you will have worked 93,600 hours in a job that may not have been your calling.

The moral of the story about Phillip is varied. Phillip was quite successful in the eyes of many people, but inside, he was in agony. He was unhappy and suffering from diminished self-esteem for several reasons, the most essential one being that he was working in a job that did not match his purpose in life. This is a real-life example of someone who did something to change his life and improve his self-esteem. There is no positive affirmation that could have changed his life. He could have repeated, "I am successful," "I am happy," "I love my job," 10,000 times, and at the end of the day, he would still have known the truth. He took action and found his fervor, his purpose. You can, too.

What Self-Esteem Isn't

Sometimes it is easier to understand what self-esteem really is by looking at what it is not. You may recognize many of the following traits from experiencing them yourself or by witnessing them in other people.

There Is No Bandwagon

First, self-esteem is not a group activity. There is no "we" in self-esteem. You never hear people talking about "our" self-esteem. In this voyage, you are on your own. Yes, you can seek the advice of loved ones, you can share your dreams and struggles, and you can talk about your advances and setbacks; I encourage that. But ultimately, there is only you. It is essential to your journey that you understand this concept. No one can give you self-esteem.

"I want to know if you can be alone with yourself, and if you truly like the company you keep in the empty moments."
—Oriah Mountain Dreamer, Native American Elder

Leave the Magic to Merlin

Self-esteem is not an illusion. It is abstract and intangible at times, but it is not an illusion. Healthy self-esteem is possible and real. Many people give up on self-esteem because they have never tried to improve it, used incorrect techniques and advice, and/or allowed themselves to believe that it is a myth postulated by "mystical healers." Self-esteem is real, and your journey will be real, also.

I'm Too Sexy for My Shirt

Self-esteem is not arrogance. Arrogance is an overabundance of false pride that is used as a defense when a person feels his or her actions or character are being attacked. Arrogance aligns itself with egocentrism, a belief that your worth and importance is greater than John Doe's worth and importance. People with healthy self-esteem find joy in recognizing others' worth as well. Self-esteem is about finding one's inner beauties, strengths, and gifts and using them to the fullest advantage. It is not about bragging and making yourself more than you are. As you well know, few things turn people off more than the unabated arrogance of a person.

"Tell me what you brag about and I'll tell you what you lack."
—Spanish proverb

Could You Stamp This Please?

Self-esteem is not validation. There are those who believe that if they can get a few people to love them (or to like them), they will be validated as a person of worth. Self-esteem is about only one type of validation—self-validation. It means that you have come to terms with your worth and merit and that is the only stamp of approval that you need to survive.

Some people seek validation through detrimental avenues. They believe that self-esteem will come if they can get validation through whom they know ("Guess who *I* went out to dinner with last night?"), what they have ("You'll just have to come with us on our new boat . . . we bought a larger one!"), how they look ("Brandon told me I was beautiful"), where they've been ("It's nice, but not nearly as nice as when we were in Florence!"), or what they do ("I'm the executive vice president to the CEO of the owner"). There is absolutely nothing wrong with being proud of what you have and where you've been, but it will not validate your existence.

Wallowing in the Mire

Self-esteem is not about "if only." Yes, you may have to revisit the past and make reparations for pain and hurt, but the road to healthy self-esteem does not involve a vocabulary filled with "if only . . ." The past is done. You can never change it.

The most you can hope for from the past are lessons learned and possibly forgiveness. Nothing can be gained from "if only-ing" yourself to tears. You know the drill: If only I had worked harder. If only I had been more self-sufficient. If only I had foreseen. If only I had loved him or her more. If only I had not been afraid. If only I had been stronger, quicker, braver, happier, healthier, friendlier, sexier, thinner, prettier, less selfish, richer, smarter, more outgoing, sportier, more powerful . . . yaddah, yaddah, yaddah. Aren't you tired? "If only" is one of the worst enemies of healthy self-esteem. Move on!

Characteristics of Unhealthy Self-Esteem

Debilitating. That is a powerful and scary word, but it is a fact of life for scores of people who suffer from low, unhealthy self-esteem. It is amazing how many people still joke about self-esteem as if it were a word made up to explain away a hangnail. Unhealthy self-esteem has ramifications that reach into your career, your relationships, your behaviors, and your psychological well-being.

Your personal attitude is as visible as the clothes you wear. People see the attitude that you wear and they treat you accordingly. People with positive attitudes and an upbeat way of thinking are greeted with positive feedback. People who have negative viewpoints and constantly act downtrodden are treated as such. Your attitude is a self-fulfilling prophecy.

Self-esteem is not a panacea for world peace and total bliss, but it definitely has its benefits. This list includes some of the negative behaviors and attitudes associated with unhealthy, poor self-esteem. You decide if these attitudes or behavior have ever crippled you in some way or if you recognize these characteristics in yourself or other people.

Generally speaking, people with self-esteem issues may have a tendency to:

- Act immature and have poor interpersonal skills.
- Participate in self-destructive behaviors.
- Become angry and lose their tempers quickly.
- Sacrifice their identity for the sake of "fitting in."
- Dodge reality and unpleasant situations.
- Enjoy the demise or humiliation of others.
- Criticize themselves and others frequently.
- Act superior and brag incessantly.
- Overreact when criticized in any manner.
- Engage in self-sabotage.

This list may be just the entrance to the mine. Deeper and darker characteristics appear in countless people who leave their esteem unattended.

Looking for Love in the Wrong Faces

Another unhealthy characteristic of people with low self-esteem is looking for "love" or affection or even sex from anyone because you do not feel you deserve real love or affection. *I'll take what I can get,* you convince yourself. *He's better than nothing,* you say on those lonely nights. These feelings come from years and years of convincing yourself that you are not really worthy of true, authentic love because there is something wrong with you. Stop for a moment and think how totally debilitating, thoroughly devastating, and downright tragic that thought is: "I am not worthy of love. I am not worthy of love."

So in that unworthy state, you search for anyone who shows you the least bit of attention. You take "love" in any form you can get it. You give of yourself emotionally, financially, and yes, sexually just so you can have another person hold you for a few moments. Does any of this sound familiar? If it does, then you know how demoralizing these actions are to you and how damaging they are to your self-esteem.

The psychologist Abraham Maslow detailed the basic need for every human being to feel love. It is innate. It is a part of our genetic makeup. It is as necessary as air and water, and our need to feel love can sometimes be overwhelming. The relationship of this need to your self-esteem is this—if you feel badly about yourself and feel that you are not truly worthy of something so wonderful, you will either deny yourself this treasure, or you will take it from the first person that offers it, even if it is false and not genuine.

When you wake up in the morning with one more "bad love experience," this only deepens the feeling and belief that you are not worthy. It is only when you can begin to understand that you do deserve honest love, and that you don't have to take the first thing that comes along (because you believe it may never come again), that you begin to know your worth. Unhealthy self-esteem inhibits us from seeing that authentic, legitimate love is out there for us. It forbids us from being able to welcome, understand, or appreciate the real thing when it comes along.

The Effects of Unhealthy Self-Esteem

Unhealthy self-esteem can worm its way into every facet of your life. Sometimes, many of your problems may be tied to unhealthy self-esteem and you don't even know it. People with unhealthy self-esteem tend to be pessimistic and then push that pessimistic view on the world. If you are a pessimistic person, this affects the way you see yourself moving and working in the world.

People with unhealthy self-esteem also often display anger toward others inappropriately. If you are filled with rage and anger, you have a hard time controlling it and a harder time still of knowing where to focus that anger. Tied to this anger, people with unhealthy self-esteem also become aggressive for no apparent reason. The smallest remarks or criticism can send them into a tirade. They begin to blame others for their lot in life and refuse to accept responsibility for their own actions and the consequences. They tend to have very little compassion for their own lives, and thus, they have very little compassion for others. If they have nothing to live for, they can't see that other people do.

"The point of the journey is not just healing. It's also recovering the truest, most spontaneous, joyful, and creative core of ourselves."
—Gloria Steinem

Ironically, it has even been suggested that people with unhealthy self-esteem tend to be more promiscuous and participate in unhealthy sexual behavior at a greater rate than those with healthy self-esteem.

More Bad News

Following are further examples of how unhealthy self-esteem affects people from every walk of life. People with low self-esteem tend to:

*   Pressure people and become overbearing.
*   Be devastated by simple mistakes.
*   Have few resources.
*   Provoke domestic and social violence.
*   Concentrate on their failures, weaknesses, and setbacks.
*   Put themselves down either in a joking fashion or seriously.

Give Me All You've Got

It is interesting to note that people with unhealthy self-esteem are prone to engage in obsessive activities such as overeating, overdrinking, or binge drinking. They tend to develop addictions to legal and illegal mood-altering substances at a greater rate than people with healthy self-esteem. Perhaps this phenomenon has something to do with searching for peace outside the body. When you feel that you have no control over what is happening in your mind and soul, you try other outlets to ease the pain and erase the hurt.

Does unhealthy self-esteem cause drug addiction and alcoholism? There is no proof of this and the answer is probably no, but when you are in pain, you search for what brings relief. You search for what helps you forget. You search for what helps you escape. Once again, the beast of unhealthy self-esteem has ramifications that reach further than most people care to admit.

As you can see, poor self-esteem left unattended can have devastating and far-reaching effects on the person who suffers and the society in which they live. Can possessing a healthy self-esteem erase all of the bad things that happen in your life and all of the negative aspects of your personality? No. But left unattended, unhealthy, low self-esteem can take over your life as quickly and completely as kudzu in a vegetable garden.

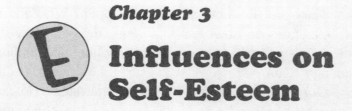

Chapter 3

E Influences on Self-Esteem

How did I get to this place in my life? you may ask yourself from time to time. What made me who I am? Why am I afraid of X and yet Y doesn't bother me at all? Why do I get so upset at A, when B has never caused me to think twice? Why do I feel the way I do about myself and my abilities?

The Past Matters

You may catch yourself saying, "I don't remember ever making a conscious decision to like or dislike something, to be comfortable around some things and uncomfortable around others. I don't ever remember saying to myself, I'm going to have positive, healthy self-esteem or negative, unhealthy self-esteem." So, how does it all happen? Who and what are the greatest influences on how you think, feel, and act? How do you get to the places in your life that are sometimes wonderfully familiar and sometimes stunningly alien?

In the movie *Out of Africa*, the main character narrates, "He gave me a compass to steer by, because he knew, as I did not, that the world was made round so that we could not see too far down the road." Depending on whom you ask, the concept of the future, of seeing "down the road," is paramount. Some, however, feel it is not nearly as important as seeing the past more clearly. Some people truly want to know where they are going, and others simply want to know from where they came.

In your quest for healthy self-esteem, it can be vitally important to "look back" in order to understand some of the habits, customs, and yes, quirks that are with you today.

Your Family

There are countless influences on your life as you grow and mature. Your parents, certainly, make impressions, but influences also come from other people in the home, such as siblings, grandparents, cousins, and so on. Some parents are keenly aware that they are shaping your future, while others don't have a clue that what they say and do leave indelible marks on your soul forever. Even small things like gestures, vocal tone, smiles, frowns, and silence influence your development.

You often don't even realize all the little things that have influence on you. As children learn, they pick up cues from their parents about how to act and feel. A study was conducted where children played with toys while their mothers watched. If the mother smiled at the child as he or she played, the child played with the toy longer than if the mother frowned. Also, when given the opportunity to play with the toy again at a later time, the children who had seen their mother frown earlier tended to shy away from the toy even when the mothers remained neutral during the later play period.

FACT

Children are deeply influenced by what they see and hear. Those who are exposed to and witness moral behavior, caring and loving parents, generosity, support, and compassion have a propensity to be more tuned in to the feelings and well-being of others.

In later years, these same influences can wreak havoc on your self-esteem. You begin to rely on the approval of others, either verbally or nonverbally, to tell or show you how to act or react. You may do this unconsciously and not even know that you are being "controlled" by something that stems back to your infancy. This can negatively affect your self-esteem as you internalize feelings you pick up from external cues.

During infancy, you also begin to experience attachment. This is important to you and the development of your self-esteem because the degree to which you feel attachments to special people in your early life affects the way you relate to people for the rest of your life.

As a child, your identity and self-esteem are tied not only to what you hear from your parents and family members, but also to what you see and feel. Perhaps your family has the greatest influence in the development of your self-esteem and in the way you develop over a lifetime. People who come from a family structure that is not supportive, unresponsive to needs, lacking in communication, and detached from everyday emotion tend to develop unhealthy characteristics such as:

- Grave insecurities
- Victim mentality
- Lack of respect for self and others

- Irresponsibility
- Uncaring and unable to give or receive love
- Feelings of loneliness, fear, and immense anxiety
- Unsure of their own true identity
- Untrusting of other people
- The need to control and sometimes manipulate

It is unfair to blame every problem or give credit for every success to your family members. However, it is important to understand their influence on your development so that you can better determine the validity of your own feelings.

Your Friends

As you move from the sole influence of your parents, you begin to be influenced by the friends you have. If you think back, your self-esteem has been prejudiced by your friendly relationships from childhood to the present moment. They play a vital and crucial role in your life, your beliefs, and most importantly, in your actions.

A Source of Development

During your developing years, one of the most important attributes of friendship is proximity. This has two definitions: that you are close enough geographically to keep the relationship alive, and that you have beliefs, interests, and desires that are closely related. If you scrutinize the friends you have had in the past and the friends that currently surround you, you may begin to see a pattern—they are like you. You seldom have friends who are diabolically juxtaposed to your own beliefs and values. Sure, you have friends who do different things, have different religions, and espouse different ideas, but at the core, your friends, more often than not, are much like you.

As you grow older, your friends become your primary source of support and guidance. This changes when you become involved in intimate love relationships, but for many years, your friends are your supporters, aids, and champions.

Here's to the Life

Friends help shape your self-esteem and friends aid in good health and long life. In California, over 7,000 people were studied over a nine-year period. The people who had the best health, lived longer, avoided disease more often, and dealt with life's difficulties better were the people with strong social support.

FACT

Divorced men are more likely to suffer from heart disease, cancer, strokes, stress, and hypertension than married men. They are also more likely to commit suicide and die earlier than men with close relationships.

Conversely, people who were isolated did not enjoy these benefits. When you are in caring relationships, you are not lonely, and the less lonely you are, the longer you live and the better you feel about yourself. On the other hand, when you see others in caring, loving friendships and you do not have them, your self-esteem and health suffer. This can affect you over the course of your life.

If you do not have the relationships that you see others enjoying, you may negate your own beliefs and values so that you can "fit in" to a group and be socially accepted. This, too, is detrimental to your self-esteem. Countless people are in "friendships" to combat loneliness only to find that the relationships are abusive, controlling, and unhealthy. These people are called *toxic* or *contaminated*. They infect the way you act, think, and feel. They bring poison into your life and it takes a great deal of work to cleanse yourself of the debris. It also takes time for your self-esteem to heal because of these relationships.

Your Teachers

Teachers are among your earliest influences, along with parents and childhood friends. For many, you spent more time with your teachers than you spent with your family. Not only did they have monumental influence over your acquisition of knowledge, but over your self-esteem as well.

"For eager teachers seized my youth, pruned my faith and trimmed my fire. Showed me the high, white star of truth, there bade me gaze and there aspire."

—Matthew Arnold

You remember the great teachers who nurtured you, encouraged you, challenged you, and led you to understand the world in healthy terms. Their names come to you immediately. If only they all could have been this way. Conversely, you also remember the teachers who embarrassed you, humiliated you, and made you feel as if you did not deserve life. Whether you knew it then or not, they were shaping many of the beliefs about yourself that you carry with you to this day.

Television, Movies, and Music

As if you did not have enough influencing your self-esteem, along comes America's pastimes—television, videos, movies, and music. What does the Roadrunner, Andy and Opie, Superman, *The Bridges of Madison County,* Tom Cruise, and Sade have to do with your self-esteem? Much! It is estimated that children watch over forty hours of television a week and adults watch over twenty hours per week. Cable radio, DVDs, and CDs bring pleasure by the hours to children and adults alike. You see and hear things twenty-four hours a day, from spy dramas to emergency room reality shows, from love stories to murders, from family comedies to prison dramas, from rap to soul, from Glen Campbell to Snoop Dog.

So many mixed messages can blur the line between reality and fiction. Countless people inadvertently compare their lives to the lives of television, movie, and music personae. You sometimes catch yourself saying, "Why can't my partner be more like X?" "Why can't my life be as good as Y?" "Why can't I be a Wichita Lineman?" These questions begin to play a role in how you see yourself and how you function in the world. Subconsciously, you begin to ask yourself, by way of comparison, "If Johnboy Walton can have parents who are so loving and supportive, why can't I?" "If Will can have a great friend like Grace, why can't I?" "Why can't I be as sexy-in-the-city as Carrie Bradshaw?" Why can't I build my own home like Bob Vila?" and "*Why* oh why can't I wiggle my nose and make my mother-in-law disappear!!?" Over the years, these comparisons begin to impair your judgment and wear away your self-esteem.

QUESTION?

Are we shaped more by our genetics or our environment? Psychologists still argue this point. Some say that our genetic makeup is the number one attribute to our personality. Others say that our environment is most important. It is called the "nature-nurture" controversy. It is suggested that our genes play a major role in our development, but our changing scenery plays a role in how our lives progress.

Letting Go of Old Ways

You call it spring-cleaning. You clean your closets, your pantries, and your garage. You scour your linens, shampoo your carpets, and scrub your windows. You like things to be clean. But when it comes to cleaning the cobwebs and badly blemished mirrors of your own mind, you are less likely to do so. You allow dirty self-criticism, stained images, and soiled decisions to linger for years and years, sometimes until it is nearly impossible to clear them away. Healthy self-esteem enjoys a home that is cleaned of our polluted past decisions and actions.

Why is it so hard to move beyond what you have thought about yourself for years? Why is it so hard to believe that you can, and have, changed? The primary reason is repetition. You have heard the same old song in your mind for so long that you have come to believe the lyrics about yourself. Sometimes, you even catch yourself (you negative self-talk) remembering things that you said about yourself in high school. How can that be? How can you still remember what you thought about yourself twenty-five years ago and you have trouble remembering what you ate for dinner last night? Again, repetition is the answer. The truth is, you have never let go of your past negative self-talk. You have given it safe harbor in the back of your mind and it knows exactly when to appear.

"The voice" appears when you are afraid. It appears when you are sad, depressed, and lonely. It stalks you when you have faced a challenge unsuccessfully. It comes around like an old acquaintance that you'd just as soon never see again. But, because you never had the courage to tell it to leave, it continues to come back and remind you of all the negative things you believe about yourself. This voice makes it difficult to move past decisions that you made long ago. This voice embodies what Robert Frost wrote almost 100 years ago: "And nothing to look backward to with pride, and nothing to look forward to with hope." Given the chance to survive, this voice is incapacitating.

"We do not see things as *they* are, we see things as *we* are."

—Anais Nin

For healthy self-esteem, you must move toward a state of self-forgiveness. You must move toward eradicating the negative voice that lives in you. You must work on the optimistic part of your soul that says, "Look only at the goodness you have. Look only at the joy you give. Look only at the work you do. Look only at the love you share. For once, look only at the harvest and not the loss." Ⓔ

Chapter 4

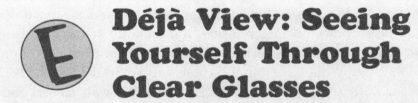

Déjà View: Seeing Yourself Through Clear Glasses

It can be hard to take an honest look at yourself. So much of what we believe about ourselves is tied up in how others perceive us. But it's important to learn how to see yourself for who you really are, and not to let anyone convince you otherwise.

The Pitfalls of Comparisons

Why does everyone dread reunions? Few people ever express elation and joy over going to reunions. Why?

The answer to why reunions are not at the top of the entertainment list is found in one word—comparison. Comparing your life and accomplishments to the lives and accomplishments of others is sometimes an uneasy task. Somewhere deep inside, you dread to see what Penelope "Most Likely to Have a Perfect Life Running a Major Computer Firm in New York City While Living in the Hamptons with Kent Randolph Windsor IX in a 16,753 Square Foot English Tudor with Jacuzzi and Maid" Madrigal has been up to.

Self-comparison is the age-old, hellish self-esteem question of "Will I measure up?" "Am I as good as Penelope?" "Why can't I . . ." Self-comparison involves two seemingly simple but highly complex words: worth and uniqueness.

"Ninety percent of the world's woe comes from people not knowing themselves, their abilities, their frailties, and even their real virtues. Most of us go almost all the way through life as complete strangers to ourselves."

—Sydney Harris

Self-Worth

Comparing yourself to others can be one of the most detrimental and fundamental roadblocks to healthy self-esteem. When you compare yourself to other people, you are, in essence, questioning your own worth. You are either consciously or subconsciously saying to yourself:

- "I'm not as _____ as he or she is."
- "I don't have the same _____ as he or she has."
- "I'm not as good at _____ as he or she is."
- "I've never had _____ like he or she had."
- "I don't look like _____ ."

If you make these statements aloud, you begin to hear a lack of self-respect. You are questioning your own value as a human being and as a deserving person in the world. Imagine what this is doing to your self-esteem.

Comparisons like these can turn into self-fulfilling prophecies. The more you say something, the more you believe something; the more you trust that something is right, the more likely it is that it will happen, positively or negatively. When you continue to question your worth with statements such as the previous ones, you begin to believe those statements, and in time, you live out what you believe.

The problem with worth is that there is no universal definition for it. For some, worth means money. For others, worth means possessions, children, marriage, talent, virtue, honesty, love, respect, or education. Worth is extraordinarily different for everyone. Counting your worth is as difficult as trying to count money when you have dollars, yens, pesos, euros, and pounds all on the counter together. Which is more valuable at the moment? Which one will suit you best on your journey? Just as it is useless to try to buy corn in Iowa with yen, it is useless to have possessions on a sinking ship. It all depends on the journey.

The most important thing that you can do for your self-esteem is to understand that worth is something that is subjective at best, and it must be viewed in its social or individual context. You are the only person on earth who can define your worth. To let another person do it is self-esteem suicide.

Your Uniqueness

If you try to place a value (worth) on your life based on other people, you are denying your uniqueness, your rareness. You are saying to your-self, *It is of no importance to have qualities that belong exclusively to me.* You are saying to yourself, *I am not a miracle. I am not a marvel. I have no specific purpose for being here.* Think of the tragedy in those statements.

Think about your life at this very moment. What is your miracle? What have you done that no other human on earth could have done?

You may say, "Nothing." Wrong! "I've never invented a vaccine to cure polio," you might say. "I've never painted a canvas that will hang in a museum." "I've never saved a life on the operating table." This may be true, but maybe those things are not your purpose. Those things are not your rareness. They are not your gifts.

QUESTION?

How does self-concept develop?
We look to others to answer the question, "How am I doing?" We search for their verbal and nonverbal reactions to our actions, our words, and our behaviors. The reactions that we get shape our behaviors and judgments.

Your Miracle

Your miracle might be that on a rainy day last winter, you answered the phone and on the other end of the line was an old friend in pain who needed your ear. You were the only person on earth to whom he or she wanted to speak. Your miracle is that you listened and eased your friend's pain. A life breathed easier because of you.

Your miracle might be that last Wednesday you left work early and went home to do a few badly needed house repairs, but instead, you chose to have a tea party with your daughter. No other human on earth could have done what you did last Wednesday.

If you insist on measuring yourself against others, at least measure yourself correctly.

Rocket Boys

The movie *October Sky* is based on the autobiographical novel *Rocket Boys* by Homer Hickam Jr. He grew up in the very rural backwoods coal-mining town of Coalwood, West Virginia. His father and his father's father were miners and he was expected to be a miner as well. Homer was not doing very well in school, so it came as a complete and total shock to his family when, upon seeing the Russian orbiter Sputnik, he announced that he was going to be a rocket engineer. The year was 1957.

Can you imagine telling your parents that you were going to be a rocket engineer in 1957 when the rocket and space program in the United States was in its infancy? Can you imagine believing that you could be a part of something that most people were sure had no future at all? By 1960, Homer and his friends had won the National Science Fair for their project "A Study of Amateur Rocketry Techniques."

In three short years, he and his friends went from a sure future in mining to National Science Fair winners. Homer went on to the Virginia Polytechnic Institute and eventually became a NASA engineer at the Marshall Space Flight Center in Huntsville, Alabama.

How did Homer Hickam know what his miracle was? How did he find his unique talent that helped change the face of America? How can someone from such humble beginnings see themselves as a major player on the world stage? How can someone like Homer, whose father offered little to no support for his dreams, amass the courage to believe that he was worthy and capable?

Sometimes it takes just one other person, like Homer's teacher, to help you see your miracle. More often than not, however, it will come from what you believe about yourself and from what you allow to become a part of your psyche.

Believing What Others Say

Phil was completing graduate school and one of his last professors was
_____s the first openly gay professor Phil had
garded faculty member, a writer, a speaker,
curriculum design and gay studies. Phil lis-
students in various study groups discussed
n. Most had no problem, but some people
While in a workshop one day, someone asked
Wright made the following statement: "What
of my business." Let me give that to you
again. *What you think about me is none of my business.* Profound.

When you think about Dr. Wright's statement, you realize just how brave that statement is and how much self-esteem one has to have to ever think it, much less say it out loud. He went on to discuss the fact that the students present did not know him as a private citizen, as a son, a brother, a partner, an uncle, or a friend. When you think about it, how many people know us in every capacity? Dr. Wright's statement is prophetic. He was right. Others' opinions of you are none of your business, because they don't really know you.

"Nothing splendid has ever been achieved except by those who dared believe that something inside them was superior to circumstance."

—Bruce Barton

If you can get past others' opinions, you can have the level of self-esteem that Dr. Wright has. So often, it is too easy to become consumed by what others think, what will be said, and what might "get out" about you; you become paralyzed by other people's opinions. You're letting others' opinions influence your actions, your beliefs, your behaviors, and most importantly, those opinions affect how you see yourself.

Has there ever been a time in your life when you chose to do or not do something simply because of what people thought of you? When you succumb to this type of behavior, you can't help but damage your self-esteem. When you seek the approval of others to this degree, you suffer, and your psyche suffers.

A Dream Terminated

When Samuel was in the tenth grade, he was interested in the medical field. One day while driving by the local hospital, Samuel stopped to ask about volunteer work. The volunteer coordinator was enthusiastic about his interest because as she put it, "We can always use volunteers, but we especially need men to assist with lifting and turning patients." He was excited about this opportunity. It was one of the very first things in which he had ever had any real interest.

When Samuel went to school and told a few people that he was going to volunteer at the hospital, everyone began calling him a candy striper, a term used exclusively for female volunteers. "Men don't volunteer as candy stripers," he heard time and time again, even from some of his teachers. He heard it so often and was so worried about what people were saying that he called the volunteer coordinator and withdrew his name. Years later, Samuel still wonders what that volunteer work might have led to. Could it have changed the course of his life? Could it have given him a sense of belonging and purpose much earlier? He'll never know, because he was too afraid of what others thought of him. This fear damaged his self-esteem in more ways than can be listed on this page. If only Samuel had heard Dr. Wright's statement early in his life.

Truth versus Opinion: Testing Your Beliefs

When you have a belief, you are essentially saying that you think something is true and accurate. A belief is the act of having confidence in something. As you work toward healthier self-esteem and begin to evaluate your beliefs, you will need to determine if they are truths or opinions. Opinions are unproven statements that are held as truths but can't be proved or substantiated. Truths are statements that can be proved scientifically.

Some beliefs are rational; some are irrational. Rational beliefs are logical, and at some point can be proved. They are based on more than innuendo. An irrational belief is a belief that is based on unreliable, unreasonable, illogical, and incorrect information. Think for a moment about some of your beliefs. Do you believe that you are a nice and friendly person or a person who is rude and insensitive? Do you believe that you have capabilities and talents, or do you believe that you are not good at many things? Do you believe that you are nice looking, or do you believe that you are unattractive? Do you believe that you have worth as a human being, or do you believe that you are worthless?

You need to look at your belief system to determine if what you hold as true really is true or if you have just convinced yourself of it over the years. Perhaps others convinced you of the belief and you never bothered to prove them wrong.

Myrtle was a wonderful woman, a kind and giving soul who worked hard to be a productive citizen, a supportive mother, and a loving grandmother. She had always wanted to drive a car so that she would not be so dependent on her children. However, if you ever asked Myrtle why she did not get her driver's license, she would tell you in an instant that she was not smart enough to drive. "I'm just plain stupid when it comes to cars. I'd never pass the test."

To change an irrational belief, you must first fully understand what the belief is and why you came to believe it in the first place. Then, you must work steadily to unlearn this belief through disputing this belief with yourself. Make a list and confront yourself with the real facts about the matter.

One day, Myrtle made the comment to some friends about *driving* her mother to the grocery store in her teens. When queried further, Myrtle revealed that she had her driver's license when she was younger. After she got married, her husband continually told her that she was a bad driver. Then, her friends and children chimed in over the years until she finally let her license expire and stopped driving. She firmly believed that she was an awful driver because she had heard it so often from family members. This is a perfect example of how others' beliefs can cloud your own judgment and play a major role in what you believe about yourself.

Handling Criticism and Praise

Most people enjoy praise and appreciate helpful, constructive criticism. Few, if any, enjoy condemnation and harsh, vindictive criticism. Unfortunately, both influence your self-esteem. There are those who would say, "Ignore the criticism and bask in the praise." This is not a healthy attitude. You either have to accept both praise *and* criticism as a learning tool or reject both as un-useful to your life.

If you only accept the praise, then you are cheating yourself out of valuable lessons that can be learned from *constructive* criticism. Constructive criticism is advice that is useful, practical, and valid. It is criticism that is backed up with facts, experience, and knowledge. An example of constructive criticism is when someone says, "Your presentation was well written and verbally sound. However, next time, try using a PowerPoint graph slide to show the audience how much growth the company has experienced." An example of harsh, vindictive criticism is, "I don't know who told you that you were a speaker or who let you make the address, but you embarrassed us all." There is nothing to be learned or gained from the latter.

But It Hurts

Why must you accept constructive criticism? Because if you only accept praise, you stunt your growth and you become complacent with mediocrity. This does nothing to help you build healthy self-esteem. A person with truly healthy self-esteem welcomes the constructive criticism as much as the praise, because together, they are a part of our learning process.

"I forgive myself for having believed for so long that I was never good enough to have, get, or be what I wanted."

—Ceanne DeRohan

You have to be very careful, however, not to overlook the praise and wallow in the criticism. So many people with unhealthy self-esteem have taken this route. You can receive 100 accolades and one criticism and you go home thinking about the one piece of criticism. You let it overwhelm you. You let it consume your thoughts and actions.

The best way to deal with constructive criticism is to own it and learn from it. If it is vindictive criticism, ignore it and move on. Depending on the circumstance, you have to choose which is most appropriate.

How Do I Know It's Right?

If your supervisor constructively criticizes your work, ask yourself, is his or her criticism valid and truthful? Look inside your heart and mind and answer that question truthfully. It is only when you refuse to answer that question truthfully that you run into problems. Did you do your best work? Did you follow procedure? Did you get it in on time? Was it formatted correctly? Were there any mistakes? You must own your truth here. If the truth is that you did not do your very best and you were constructively criticized for it, then accept it, learn from it, and move on. There is nothing more that can be done with it. It is finished.

On the other hand, if you are criticized for your work and you know in the deepest reaches of your being that you did exactly what was expected, met the deadlines, formatted the document correctly, met all of the other specifications, and your boss is just being vindictive, then the only alternative is to ignore the criticism and move on. Dwelling on it will only damage your self-esteem.

There seems to be as many influences on our self-esteem as there are stars in the heavens. From parents to friends, from music to teachers, from criticism to past mistakes and glories, all play a major part in who you are today and how you choose to live your life. These influences are like a closet full of clothing. When you approach the closet to decide your daily apparel, you have a choice. You can either choose a ragged, torn, damaged, dirty outfit tired from the wear, or you can choose a crisp, starched, brightly colored outfit ready for a new day. You can't choose or change your past, but you can choose what you allow to influence your decisions, your thoughts, and your actions. You can choose chains or wings. This is the essence of healthy self-esteem. Choice! Ⓔ

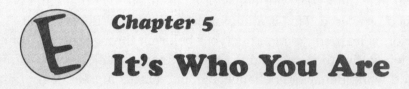

Chapter 5

It's Who You Are

The far-reaching effects of healthy or unhealthy self-esteem are astronomical. Even those with healthy self-esteem pay little attention to the fact that how you see yourself and how you treat yourself is the road map to how you see and treat others. Your level of self-esteem mirrors the goings and comings of your personal life such as your behavior and relationships.

How You Behave

Your behavior toward yourself is paramount in determining your behavior toward those you love, those with whom you work, those with whom you study, and those with whom you play. Your self-esteem is a driving factor in how you behave—yet so few people make that connection.

You may think that your behavior is an innate trait that can't be changed or altered. This is an incorrect assumption. Behavior, all behavior, is learned. You learned your behavior through the environment in which you were raised and the environment in which you continue to live and work. Behavior is changeable, but it takes a great deal of time and effort to change an ingrained behavior.

FACT

Any behavior that is reinforced time and time again usually becomes a part of your personality, and once imbedded there, it is difficult to change.

Many psychologists feel that behavior is most commonly learned from modeling. This term refers to the fact that "what you see is what you do." Your parents may have had good communication techniques—you saw how they talked through any disagreements without accusing or blaming the other. So you learned how to model your behavior after them to handle disagreements in a healthy manner. If you work in an environment where a strong work ethic is highly valued and rewarded, you will model your behavior to fit that environment. Conversely, if you were reared in a home where manners, respect, and good behavior did not matter, your behavior, more than likely, models this environment.

They Made Me Do It

Have you ever blamed your behavior on another person? Have you ever used the line, "She/he made me do it?" It sounds childish, but many adults still use the line to explain away their poor behavioral patterns.

How often do you read stories in the paper about adults refusing to accept responsibility for their behaviors? "They served me hot coffee, and

I burned myself." "They allowed me to gamble my money away, and I'm broke now." "They served me biggie French fries, and I gained fifty-eight pounds" This behavioral pattern is a clear and present sign of no personal responsibility based in unhealthy self-esteem.

It is the people who have so little faith in their own abilities, competencies, and actions who continue to blame others for all that happens—including things that happen under their watch and by their hands. Unhealthy self-esteem can have devastating results on the way you behave toward yourself and toward others.

Changing Behaviors—Changing Your Life

If you are interested in changing some of your negative or unhealthy behaviors, keep the following tips in mind:

- Make a list of the behaviors you wish to change.
- Talk to your friends and family about these behaviors.
- Think about why the behavior is unhealthy.
- Make a list of how the behavior can (or has) cost you.
- Make a list of how the behavior has affected others in your life.
- Make a list of alternative behaviors or actions.
- Use one of the alternative behaviors on a daily basis.
- Seek professional counseling to assist you with the change.

FACT

According to a survey in the *Journal of Personality and Social Psychology*, the categories that bring most people joy are: autonomy (the feeling of independence), competence (the feeling of knowing that you are effective), relatedness (the feeling that you have positive relationships), and self-esteem (the feeling of self-worth).

Finding Happiness

Happiness. Now, there's a word! Just the sound or sight of the word makes you feel a little better, unless you don't have it and can't find it.

Happiness is perhaps the most sought after passion on earth. Some people find it in money, some find it in possessions, some find it in other people, and some find it in nature and the earth's bounty. What brings you happiness?

What Is Happiness Anyway?

In the landmark book, *The Prophet*, Kahlil Gibran discusses happiness and joy. He says that the same thing that brings you joy is the same thing that brings you pain. Think about that for a moment. If you love a person or thing and that person or thing brings you great happiness, it is the fear or actuality of losing that person or thing that brings you immense pain. So, he concludes that pain and joy are one in the same.

The way that you feel about yourself largely determines the amount of joy and happiness that you let into your life. If you don't feel worthy of happiness, you won't allow any to come to you. If you constantly feel as if your happiness is a lost cause, you are going to stop looking for it and will not be able to recognize it when it is right before you.

Often, people are confused by the notion that they deserve happiness and that it should come to them with no effort or action. Some people believe that happiness is their right, that they are entitled to happiness simply because they were born. As Benjamin Franklin once said, the U.S. Constitution offers you the pursuit of happiness, not the acquisition of it.

"Happiness requires that we give up a worldly orientation—not worldly things, but a worldly attachment to things. We have to surrender all outcomes. We have to live here but appreciate the joke."
—Marianne Williamson

Happiness is like love; it is intangible. It cannot be touched. You can't put your fingers on it and hold it or caress it. You can't put it in a box and store it for a later date. Sometimes, when you can't see something, you tend to give it up. This can be the case with happiness. A certainty about happiness is that you know when you feel it and you know when you don't.

Unrealistic Expectations

Unhappiness can come from several issues, the forerunner being unrealistic expectations. Setting your goals high and dreaming big are healthy, very healthy at times, but every dream and every hope has its limitation. Setting unrealistic expectations for yourself is the menu for a huge serving of unhappiness.

Sonya wanted to be a nurse. She entered the community college to begin a two-year nursing program. She had her sights set on obtaining her nursing degree in two years, two and a half at the most. Sonya had never excelled in math or science, but she felt that her true calling was helping others. During registration, she took the math placement test and was devastated to find that she had placed in the lowest-level math course offered. She was stunned to find out that it would take her four semesters—two years—just to complete the math courses needed to upgrade her skills to even enter the nursing program.

While her desire and dream to be a nurse was not unrealistic, her timeline was. She may very well be able to complete the math and science classes needed to become a nurse, but her unrealistic expectations that it would happen in two years brought her much unhappiness.

Negative Thinking

Negative thinking is another cause of persistent unhappiness. It is a by-product of unhealthy self-esteem. Negative thinking clouds the way you think about yourself, your life, and your possibilities for happiness.

Nathan had suffered from unhealthy self-esteem for so long that he did not even realize that his every word, every thought, and most of his actions were negative. It was not until a coworker confronted him about his negative attitude that he even realized how it was affecting his life. Nathan began to talk with his acquaintances and family members and asked them if they saw this trait in him. When they agreed with the coworker, he began to listen to himself more carefully. He began to hear, for the first time, how negative his words were, how negative his thoughts were, and how all of this was tied to the way he felt about himself.

Looking to Others

Looking to others for happiness is the next major issue surrounding unhappiness. Just as other people can't give you self-esteem, other people can't bring you lasting happiness. Sure, others play a vital role in our esteem and happiness, but to rely on others for the delivery of either will result in ultimate unhappiness.

"The essence of philosophy is that a man should so live that his happiness shall depend as little as possible on external things."
—Epictetus

People who are unhappy often seek relief from friends, family, or strangers. You can find temporary relief, but lasting happiness comes from knowing that you are worthy of it, knowing that you like yourself, and knowing that you are making a difference in the world in some way.

The problem with looking for happiness in others, or relying on others to give you happiness, is that when that person leaves, they take the happiness with them. You are then left with only one thing—who you are. And if you are not happy with who you are when you meet them, you won't be happy when they leave.

Find Yourself, Find Happiness

In your pursuit of happiness, consider the following unusual tips that you may not have considered before:

- Surround yourself with happy people.
- Look for uncomplicated pleasures like a walk in the woods, a hayride, or window-shopping.
- Read a book of poetry, uplifting quotes, or positive stories.
- Give someone something (a flower, candy, a book, etc.).
- Listen to your favorite music.
- Go to a museum, library, gallery, or bookstore to expand your horizons.

- Cook something you love . . . just for you.
- Take a calculated risk that forces you to be brave.
- Do something totally out of character for you.

Forging Relationships

Unhealthy self-esteem can do one of two things to your relationships. It can cheat you out of relationships that could greatly enhance the quality of your life, or it can place you in relationships that are abusive, unloving, damaging, and even deadly.

First, if your self-image is damaged and unhealthy, you feel as if you don't deserve to have a relationship (intimate, friendship, or otherwise) or that you would not be able to "convince" anyone to have a relationship with you. You see yourself as unworthy of attention and affection. This can result in a variety of emotional and physical problems.

Second, if your self-esteem is unhealthy, you sometimes tend to "hook up" with people who are not good for you—toxic or contaminated people. These are people who do not care for you and your dreams or goals; they only want to be around you for what you can do for them, not for what they can give to you. Unhealthy self-esteem is one of the leading causes for people staying in abusive and deadly relationships. *At least I have someone,* you convince yourself. *I'm not alone.*

People with healthy self-esteem would much rather be alone with themselves than be around a person who causes paramount emotional, physical, mental, and financial damage. They understand that toxic people are the fuel that feeds the fire of unhealthy self-esteem.

Healthy Relationships

A relationship is about moving from "I" to "we." Any relationship, be it intimate, work, or friendship, is about understanding that you do not exist in the world alone. It is about choosing to share yourself with another person on levels that acquaintances and strangers never know.

Truly healthy relationships are about bringing out the best in each other. That idea sounds so simple and you've probably heard it for years, but the truth is that it is one of the most important aspects of healthy relationships. At its deepest, it means that every time you are around the other person, you are bringing the best of you, the total sum of you, to that moment. This *does not* mean that you have to be happy and joyful around that person all the time. What it does mean is that whether you are in complete bliss or complete pain, you bring that emotion in total to the other person so that he or she can bask in your joy or help you through your pain. It means that you are willing to bring your total self into that relationship and help the other person do the same.

"Help thy brother's boat across and lo! Thine own has reached the shore."

—Hindu proverb

Bringing out the best in others means that you support them and they support you. It means that you forego jealousy and competition and take pride in their successes. It means that you push them along to help them reach their potential as human beings, and it means that you get all of this back from them.

Working Toward a Healthy Relationship

As you begin to open up and give of yourself to another person in a love or friendly relationship, consider the following tips:

- Be clear and direct in your communication.
- Be forgiving and understanding.
- Work hard to create a positive, constructive place for both of you.
- Be willing to admit your mistakes and shortcomings.
- Be constructive and supportive.
- Have the courage to be warm and sensitive.
- Don't be afraid to talk about your differences.
- Never be afraid or too strong to be held.

Your Values and Spirituality

Self-esteem helps determine what you value, and in turn, what you value determines how you act and what you protect. Your value system helps determine how you treat others. If you identify yourself as a kind, caring, compassionate person, this aura will surround you as you interact with others. If you see yourself as cold, calculating, and rude, this aura surrounds you and guides your treatment of others as well.

What you value affects how you behave toward others. If you believe that education and learning are very important, you will react positively to your friend's announcement that she is going back to school to get her master's degree. You'll give her support and help her deal with the changes that this brings to her life. But if you think school is a waste of time, hearing your friend's news might cause you to react negatively— focusing on the money she's giving up by quitting her job or how much less time she'll have to spend with you now that she'll have tests to study for.

Closely tied to your value system is your own spirituality. Your self-esteem often plays a role in how you see yourself in the spiritual world. If you suffer from unhealthy self-esteem, you may feel that you do not deserve any rewards that spirituality can offer. But spirituality is about hope, and growing in your spiritual life can help you improve your self-esteem.

Spirituality and religion play vital roles in the way you live. Both have been proved to affect your health by lowering your stress level, lowering your blood pressure, increasing your tolerance of others, increasing your levels of joy and happiness, decreasing your use of controlled substances, and accentuating your wellness in general.

QUESTION?

What is the difference between religion and spirituality?
Religion is the belief in a supernatural power that is often tied to an organization such as Catholicism or Judaism. Spirituality tends to be more personal and individualized, not tied to one particular set of beliefs.

A strong sense of spirituality can also affect you in the following ways:

- A higher quality of life in general
- A greater sense of peace, purpose, and belonging
- A higher degree of hope and optimism
- A sense of personal empowerment to help others
- A more determined commitment to ethics and morality

Achieving Your Aspirations

Giving up on yourself is, in essence, giving up on your future—your dreams, your aspirations, your hopes, and your desire to move forward. Unhealthy self-esteem can cause you to lose sight of tomorrow. It can cause you to stop believing that things can, and will, get better. It can cause you to stop living even though you are still alive.

Most everyone has to have something to which they look forward. It can be as simple as a good meal or as complex as obtaining a Ph.D. Unhealthy self-esteem, left unattended, can cost you this life-pleasure. It can convince you that you are not worthy of a future and that your dreams are not as important as the next person's.

Perhaps one of the most powerful ways to combat unhealthy self-esteem is to begin planning simple goals and working toward them with unfettered passion and fervor. Begin by letting your negative self-talk know that it is not in control and that you've had enough of just getting by. Goal setting is a powerful tool to begin anew.

From happiness to home, work to wonder, spirituality to self-appreciation, unhealthy self-esteem can be a damaging force in your life. As you begin to work on each area, remember that you have the power to change any aspect of your life that you choose. You are worthy of happiness, spirituality, relationships, and aspirations. They are yours for the taking. Ⓔ

Chapter 6

It's Not Just a Job

Beyond your personal life, self-esteem matters in your professional life as well. Three of the top ten characteristics that employers look for in employees are topnotch communication skills, problem-solving abilities, and creative-thinking skills. Each of these qualities is greatly influenced by your self-esteem.

Change and Growth

Your ability to change and adapt is directly tied to how you feel about yourself and how secure you are with your own abilities. In this fast-paced, ever-changing world of technology, change occurs so rapidly that you scarcely have time to learn one thing before it is outdated and the world has moved on. Employers are looking for people who are not afraid to change, grow, learn, and take risks. Employers are looking for people who have the courage to get up and get on. This attitude has a direct link to how secure you feel about yourself.

Your professional life can be hampered or accentuated by your belief in your abilities to change and grow. If an employer sees you as a person who adapts well, is accustomed to growth and new challenges, and as a person who is willing to help others grow and change, your possibilities for promotion, raises, and additional responsibilities can be increased.

It Takes Courage

Change is never easy. Even good or positive change can be difficult and trying. The hardest part about change is that when change occurs, everyone returns to the bottom of the ladder—and no one likes to be at the bottom.

"The first step toward change is acceptance. Once you accept yourself, you open the door to change. That's all you have to do. Change is not something you do, it's something you allow."

—Will Garcia

Take as an example the case of John, whose company recently installed a new computer database. John had been working on the old database for ten years. Jane was recently hired and works with John. John has more to lose with this change because he has more invested in the old system. He has farther to "fall" than Jane. At the beginning of the day, John is ahead of Jane in terms of seniority, experience, and time spent with the old system. At the end of the day, John and Jane are in the same place; they are working on a system that is one day old and their experience with the system is one day old. Change takes you to the beginning.

Getting Secure on Unfamiliar Ground

In your quest to become more comfortable with change, keep the following tips in mind:

- Ask for help and assistance.
- Become a part of the change.
- Think about the end result.
- Look at the change as a growth and learning possibility.
- Keep the lines of communication open.
- Keep an open mind toward the change and the people involved.
- Ditch the "I can't," "Let someone else do it" attitudes.

Problem-Solving Skills

Your ability to solve problems is tied to your perception of yourself. If you perceive yourself as a person who has no solid answers, no useful information, and no practical experiences to share, your ability to solve problems effectively is going to be greatly reduced. Conversely, if you feel good about yourself and have a healthy self-esteem, you will be glad to share your ideas, your experiences, and your advice to change issues and solve simple and complex problems at work, at home, and in the community.

Unhealthy self-esteem can interfere with your problem-solving abilities because of ineffective communication. People with unhealthy self-esteem sometimes need to have the spotlight shine on them alone. They need to know that they have something that no one else has in order to protect their importance. Because of this need, they withhold information that could be essential to the problem-solving process. They see it as necessary for their personal survival, when in essence, the withholding of that information may be costly to the company, the community, and them personally.

Another problem with communication and self-esteem is that if you feel that your information is useless or arcane, you may not feel like you need to share it. In every problem-solving situation, there is information that is generally known, information that is known only by a few, and information that is known by you alone. Your information may be the key to the solution, but without your confidence to share it, it can't be used.

Going through a major life change can cause the same emotional reactions as going through a death. You may have to deal with stages of immobilization, denial, anger, bargaining, depression, testing, and acceptance. It is normal and natural to experience these emotions when major change occurs.

Critical and Creative Thinking Skills

Critical and creative thinking are both life-altering tools. They both allow you to survive where others have failed. People with unhealthy self-esteem may have a hard time realizing that their ideas, suggestions, and proposals have merit, and they simply shut off the critical and creative parts of their existence. They begin to be followers instead of leaders. They tend to take the word of others instead of finding their own voice. They tend to walk on the path instead of tromping down grass and making their own road.

In improving your self-esteem, you begin to see that your ideas, suggestions, and creative voice are as important as the next person's. You begin to realize that the more creative and critical you are in your approach to life, the more your self-esteem improves, because you are charting your own course and not just walking in the shadows. Creative and critical thinking give you more alternatives.

Critical Thinking at Work

As the world continues to move from jobs that require labor and toil to intelligence and thinking, critical-thinking skills are becoming essential to the modern-day workplace. No longer can a person move into management and upper-level positions without this ability. Self-esteem plays a great role in the development of critical thinking. It takes a person confident in their abilities, their potential, and their competencies to master the skills for critical thinking.

Critical thinking involves the ability to conduct research and do statistical analysis. It involves the ability to sort your emotions and use restraint when making judgments. It involves the ability to recognize fallacies or false arguments and make heads or tails of what is right and wrong. A person with unhealthy self-esteem would not be able to do these tasks because they would be filled with self-doubt and second-guess their every decision.

Creative Thinking at Work

Creative thinking is just as important as critical thinking because it moves humanity forward. Creative thinking involves a great deal of courage. It means that you are unafraid to try new things and implement new actions. Creative thinking requires that you be innovative and find new solutions to old problems.

QUESTION?

What is the difference between critical and creative thinking?
Critical thinking is thinking that is based in reason, logic, and research. It is thinking that is used for formulating inferences, calculations, decisions, and solutions. Creative thinking is thinking that is directed toward new ideas, innovative techniques, novel strategies, and uncharted territories.

Creative thinking means that you assert your individuality and that you are not afraid of criticism. Creative thinkers are not happy with being carbon copies of others. They have their own style. Creative thinking involves a great deal of curiosity and the desire to know more and know differently. Finally, creative thinking involves more persistence than most people can endure. It is only the people with healthy self-esteem who can manage these characteristics and take the company, and themselves, to new heights.

Your Personal Economy

Your ability to obtain employment, keep employment, and advance in your chosen field is a derivative of your self-esteem. If you have healthy self-esteem, you are going to be interested in and willing to re-educate yourself to keep up with the changing markets. You will be more willing to learn the skills necessary to make yourself competitive, and staying competitive is essential in your ability to maintain your personal financial well-being.

Do I Go or Stay?

Have you ever thought of starting your own business? People who have self-esteem issues are less likely to branch out on their own for fear of failure, lack of confidence in their own abilities to succeed, and their inability to see themselves as leaders and visionaries.

Another effect of self-esteem on your personal economy is the decisions you make about where you work, how you work, and for whom you work. If you suffer from unhealthy self-esteem, you may have a tendency to allow others to avoid recognizing you and your accomplishments, either financially or verbally. This could cost you dearly in the long run. People with unhealthy self-esteem are more likely to stay in a job that they are unsatisfied with, without taking the necessary personal growth steps to obtain something more satisfying.

The Worst Type of Financial Worry

Also affecting your personal economy is the use of credit cards. You may find yourself charging things that you perceive will bring you happiness and peace (even if they really don't). You finance that new car, charge that new outfit, and sign on the dotted line for that new furniture in hopes that it will make your life better—only to realize, after the damage is done, that possessions can't bring you inner joy. And to add to the misery, you've now charged items that put a strain on your financial situation. Overspending, overcharging, and purchasing items that you really don't need are all signs of unhealthy self-esteem and are self-destructive.

FACT

A person with a bachelor's degree earns approximately $16,000 more per year than a person without a degree. A person with a master's degree earns approximately $27,000 more, and a person with a professional degree earns approximately $50,000 more per year than a person without a degree.

As you begin to look differently at your self-esteem and how it plays a role in your personal finances, consider the following:

- A raise lost one year is seldom ever recovered in subsequent years.
- It pays to have a college degree.
- Credit card debt is the worst type of debt.
- Possessions will not heal the pain and end your suffering.

Dealing with Mistakes

When you look at a yard that needs to be mowed, do you see a dreaded chore or do you say a little "thank you" that your area of the world is not involved in a drought? Is the glass half full or half empty? It all depends on how you look at things. Your self-esteem plays a role in how you look at the world.

Your self-esteem also plays a role in how your deal with misfortune, whether by another's hand or your own. Making mistakes is a part of life, and many people use the mistakes they make as learning tools. However, people with unhealthy self-esteem can find mistakes crippling. They see them as failures, not as growth opportunities. They see them as the end, not a new beginning.

If you view mistakes as failure, this attitude hampers you from ever trying new avenues for problem solving, personal growth, or professional success. By viewing a mistake as something that cannot be overcome, you are less likely to try to do anything new or out of the ordinary. You become stagnant from fear of failure or fear of mishap. This is a direct by-product of unhealthy self-esteem.

People with healthy self-esteem understand that mistakes are merely great feedback for the next go-round. They see mistakes as a sign that they are trying new things and growing. They see them as a human quality possessed by all. Mistakes can even help you reclaim that part of yourself that forgot that it's okay not to be perfect.

Just as self-esteem plays a monumental role in your personal life, it plays just as great a role in your professional life. Healthy self-esteem can help you become more successful, assist you in achieving raises and promotions, help you have greater financial stability, and help you understand that every mistake is just a lesson to be learned.

Chapter 7

Getting Ready for the Journey

"Seek and ye shall find." The quote is as old as time it seems, but still bears weight and significance. The search for healthy self-esteem can be a long and treacherous road. It can also be a road filled with unparalleled pleasures, unique surprises, and an outcome that will take your breath away.

Developing a Positive Mindset

Negative self-talk, previously discussed, is the little voice in your head telling you that you can't, that you're not good enough, that you aren't smart enough, that you can't succeed, that you're ugly, fragile, weak, and fearful. The voice must be stopped. The voice must be silenced if your self-esteem is to ever flower.

You are the only person on earth who can stop negative self-talk, your inner critic. No friend, family member, coworker, or advocate can stop the voice, because it is in your mind. It is there, haunting you with pathological statements that cause great damage. A positive mindset will remain elusive until the voice is silenced.

"Do not attempt to do a thing unless you are sure of yourself; but do not relinquish it simply because someone else is not sure of you."

—Stewart White

Voice of the Critic

Your inner critic or negative self-talk is a direct consequence of your unhealthy self-esteem. Everyone has an inner critic, but people with unhealthy self-esteem are more likely to give the critic validation. Your negative self-talk damages your ability to function in many ways. Most specifically, it damages your ability to take constructive criticism without suffering a complete meltdown. It clouds your ability to learn from your mistakes. It limits your growth possibility because it continually tells you that you are not worthy of growth or change. It continually compares you to others that it perceives as better, smarter, kinder, prettier, and so on. The voice incapacitates you with "You should have . . ." You've heard them all: "You should have been more loving," "You should have been more forceful," "You should have exercised more," "You should have studied more in school." The "shoulds" are the primary ally of your negative self-talk.

The voice is a powerful force and a pollutant in your life. Sometimes, it is more powerful than your own voice or the voice of those who love and support you. However, you can learn to make the voice stop, or at least learn how to tune out the voice so that it does not exterminate your ability to have healthy self-esteem.

Shut Up!

It's not rude. Say it out loud. "Shut Up!" Say it again. Sometimes, this is the way to silence your inner critic—by simply letting it know that you are not going to take it anymore. It sounds crazy, but in actuality, it may be the sanest thing you do all day. The next time you hear your inner critic begin to drag you down with negative thoughts, acknowledge it. Let it know that you hear it and that you disagree with it and that you are not going to listen. This is the first step in silencing the critic. Ignoring the inner critic will not make it go away.

The next step in silencing the critic is to make a conscious commitment to yourself that the next time you allow the inner critic to have a voice, you are going to fight back with five tangible, provable, true facts about yourself. You are not going to use abstracts or false praise about you, but you are going to fight back with weapons of truth.

If the inner critic says that you are just a fat slob, you will find five ways to prove the voice wrong. "I am on an exercise program." "I have lost twelve pounds." "I am a very clean person." "I am exercising every day." "I have cut my food intake in half."

Another important step in the battle of the critic is to let it know that you know what it is up to. It is okay to let your inner critic know that you know it is trying to manipulate you and take advantage of you. It is okay to let it know that you know it is speaking so that it can live. Without your permission, the critic dies. Its motives are to keep you down so that you will keep it alive. So, the next time the voice arises, even the playing field by saying to the critic, "I know you have ulterior motives."

Acknowledge Shortcomings

Next, to silence the critic, you will need to take the power away from the critic. This means that you are going to acknowledge the negative traits on which the critic feeds. "I am overweight." "I am not perfect." "I am not good at relationships." "I did not finish college." "I lose my temper sometimes."

This is a strategy that many politicians could use if they were smarter. If you acknowledge that you have shortcomings, as everyone does, then you disarm the critic and make its use of these statements ineffectual. You have taken the power away from the critic by being the first to admit the shortcoming; as a result, it can't be used against you.

Finally, you can silence the critic by beginning to work on the negative aspects of your life that you wish to change. If you admitted that you are overweight, have a temper, and are not good at relationships and want to improve these attributes, goal setting is the best way to begin the journey.

Setting Goals That Work

Research supports the view that healthy self-esteem can be acquired more effectively and has more positive results by setting realistic goals and working toward those goals than by chanting affirmations and seeking praise from others. The remainder of this book is activity and goal intensive. Each of the following chapters offers an activity to help you find your self-esteem.

FACT

In 1953, a goal-setting study was conduced at Yale University. Students were asked if they had a goal and a plan. Only 3 percent replied yes. In 1973, a follow-up study was conducted and it was found that the 3 percent who had goals and a plan had a combined net worth that was greater than the remaining 97 percent of the class.

Getting What You Want and Wanting What You Get

Goal setting sounds so simple because we do it in our heads and "off the cuff" on an hourly basis. However, goal setting is serious business if you are serious about changing some negative qualities about your life, working toward positive outcomes, and acquiring healthier self-esteem.

It is the road map that can take you to places few people even dream of, much less actually get to visit.

A goal is anything that you can have, be, or do. Goals can be financial, spiritual, health-related, educational, social, family, professional, or personal. They can range from short-term goals to long-term goals. They can be as simple as a daily goal of clearing your desk of incoming work or as lofty as starting your own business.

Goals need to have a few guidelines, however. They need to be realistic and believable. They do not need to be realistic and believable to others, only to you. They need to be internal. This means that you want the goal for you and not someone else. Goals need to be measurable so that you can gauge your progress, and goals need to be controllable. Controllable means that you are in charge of the outcome, not another person. You can't have a goal that professes to change another person or a goal that relies on others for completion.

One goal should not contradict another goal. For example, if you have set a goal to spend more time with your children or spouse or friends, and you have set a goal to work as many hours as is humanly possible to get a promotion, you've set goals that are at odds with each other. Neither will be reached.

This also means that a minor goal must not contradict an overriding life goal. For example: Your overriding life goal, the goal that drives everything in your life, may be this: "I will never betray, hurt, or malign another human being to achieve any possession, success, or status." Now, if you had another goal that stated, "I will succeed as a nurse (or designer or teacher or writer or engineer) at any cost," this goal would be in opposition to your overriding life goal.

The Verb Is the Thing . . . and So Is the Date

Goals should be written with an action verb. You should not begin a goal statement with phrases such as "I want to . . ." or "I plan to . . ." These are goals that will never be reached, because they have no punch, no conviction! Begin with terms such as, "I am going to . . ." or "I will . . ." Notice the difference between the two? The first two are indecisive, while the last two are determined.

A goal must have a completion date. Without setting a time frame in which to achieve the goal, there is no push, no immediacy, and no sense of willpower for that goal to be reached. Without a completion date, you are saying that you really do not have a commitment to that goal.

QUESTION?

What factors contribute to the failure of my goals?
People fail at their goals for many reasons. They procrastinate and don't take any positive actions, they do not plan their objectives well, they do not have all of the information needed to be successful in the goal, the goal is not realistic or believable to them, and lastly, goals can fail because people are not committed to the changes that a goal can bring.

Making Personal Commitments

In order for your goal to ever come to fruition, you need to make a drastic personal commitment to that goal. You will need to think through the goal from beginning to end. You will need to look at how it is written, how long you have given yourself to reach the goal, and you must take a look at what this goal can do for your life.

The narrative statement is a picture, a visual image you are creating in your mind's eye of how your life will look, feel, and be when this goal or aspiration is reached. If your goal is to lose forty-five pounds, how will your life change because of reaching this goal? How will your life be different? What will you be able to do that you have not done in years? What will losing forty-five pounds bring to your life? If your goal is to become a better public speaker, how will this help your life? How will reaching this goal change your future? This is one of the most monumental parts of goal setting and it is a part that few people ever complete. The narrative statement helps you see the future.

You Deserve the Best

The "I deserve" statement asks you to do some soul searching. This statement asks you to look inside your life and truthfully answer the question, why do I deserve to lose forty-five pounds? Why do I deserve to become a better public speaker? Why? For those of you who have self-esteem issues, this may be the hardest part of this exercise. That is perfectly fine. If you look hard enough and are honest with yourself, you will find why you deserve this goal . . . and much more.

Picture This

If at all possible, a picture should accompany a goal. For example, if your goal is to buy a home for you and your family, make a collage of homes and post this picture next to your goal statement. This helps you visualize your goals on a daily basis.

If your goal states, "I will concentrate on my positive qualities and continue to find ways to contribute to my community," then you might make a collage of pictures (from magazine clippings, clip art, real photos, etc.) that shows what you think your positive qualities are and pictures of what you would like to do to contribute more. This collage may be abstract to others, but remember, this is not for them; it is for you.

Without visualization, goals can quickly fade from your mind's eye and your grasp. Pictures, photos, and clippings help you establish a visual of the outcome.

You are encouraged to post your goal pages in a place where you can see them daily—perhaps in your day planner, over your computer, on your bathroom mirror, on the refrigerator door, or on the door you exit from home. By posting your goals and pictures of your goals, you see them on a daily basis. You are reminded of them and they become a part of your daily routine.

Because It Is My Name

A goal must have your signature. Your signature is symbolic of your commitment to this goal. It means that you are signing your name to this pledge and making a commitment to yourself with your name. It means that you plan to work on this goal with all of your might in order to move closer to healthier self-esteem.

Developing a Plan of Action

A goal must have an action plan. The action plan is usually called objectives. This is the meat and potatoes of your goal. This is where you figure out how you are going to get what you want and need. If your goal is saving $1,000, how do you plan to do it? Are you going to get a part-time job? Are you going to open a savings account? Are you going to cut back on expenses elsewhere? How are you going to save this money? What is your plan?

This is the place in your goal-setting process where you use very specific statements. These statements will need to be realistic and doable to you. You may need to start simple and work toward complex, or start small and work toward big.

"If you are not out there creating your own future, you have no right to complain about the one that is handed to you."

—Unknown

Getting the Job Done

If your goal is to find employment that offers you more security, and your goal is to do this by getting a two-year degree, your action plan should include specific details that are realistic. Your action plan would not begin with "I'm going to go to college and take five classes per semester." Your action plan should look something like this:

- I will make an appointment with a counselor at Kodiac College.
- I will research careers of interest.
- I will decide on my major.
- I will apply to college.
- I will apply for financial aid and scholarships.
- I will meet with a college advisor to plan my first semester.
- I will register for two classes for the first semester.
- I will buy my textbooks early so that I can begin to study early.
- I will attend every class meeting.
- I will seek tutorial assistance if I feel that I am getting behind.

With this type of goal setting and action planning, your goal is more likely to come to fruition. It is detailed, simple, doable, and reasonable. To say, "I'm going to go to college next semester" is a recipe for doing nothing next semester.

The goal-planning sheet at the end of this chapter will help you create a workable goal. Appendix C provides you with an additional worksheet that you can duplicate and use time and time again.

Change can be exciting, rewarding, and helpful. However, change can also be dangerous, frightening, and complicated. If you have made a decision to change something in your life, make sure that you are committed to the change and that you have the tools necessary to see the change to fruition.

Preparing for success and optimism are not easy. You don't usually plan for the good in life; you plan for disasters, setbacks, and mistakes. However, with a positive mindset, an inner critic that has been silenced, and workable goals, you can begin to plan for the abundance that is yours.

Sample Goal-Planning Worksheet

Goal Statement: I will (Notice the action verb *will*. Never write a goal that states, "I want to . . ." or "I plan to . . ."; always begin with "I will" or "I am going to.") --

----

----

by ----------------, 20 ---------------- . (You must set a deadline for reaching this goal.)

I plan to do this by (These are your *action* steps. How do you plan to set this goal into action?)

1. --

----

2. --

----

3. --

----

4. --

----

5. --

Use another sheet if necessary.

Sample Goal-Planning Worksheet

Narrative Statement: (The picture of what your life will look like when this change is made) --

----

Use another sheet if necessary.

I deserve this change in my life because --------------------------------------

----

I commit to this change in my life this ---------------------------- day of

---------------------------- , 20 ------------

Signature (This is an important step in this process. Your signature binds you to this goal.)

Chapter 8

Work

Deep within the ancient Sanskrit language lies the word *dharma*. This word, at its core, means "purpose in life." According to this word, you have a specific reason for being here, a unique talent, a "gift." What is your purpose? What is your talent? What is your gift?

A Job versus a Career

In Buddhism, *dharma* means that as an individual you are living a life in which you accept responsibility for your actions so that you are led to self-fulfillment. As you can see, the quest for purpose in life spans religions and cultures, and is as old as civilization itself. It seems that for eternity, people have searched for meaning in their lives and in their work, for dharma.

Almost every person who wants a job can have a job. Not everyone who wants a career or vocation has one, however. A job is a place where you go on a daily basis to perform a task. A career or vocation is work that is a part of who you are. Your vocation involves your purpose.

Doing versus Being

There are tens of thousands of teachers in the world, but not all are really teachers. Some go through the motions and show up for work, but those who long for the chance to teach every day are rare. It is the rarest breed that carries teaching in his or her heart. Many people do the work of teaching, but there are fewer real teachers. Many people do the work of medicine, but there are few who hold medicine in their souls. Many people do the work of law enforcement, but few are motivated by their innate, purposeful desire to do the work of the law.

"You are what your deep, driving desire is. As your desire is, so is your will. As your will is, so is your deed. As your deed is, so is your destiny."

—The Upanishads

Being and *doing* are two totally different things. If you have ever gone to work and gone through the motions only to come home at the end of the day feeling empty, barren, and tired, you are probably just "doing." However, if you have ever gone to work and the joy in your heart is overwhelming just because you have the privilege of being involved in this work, then you know the wonderful feeling of "being."

What You Get from Work

When you go to bed at night, are you filled with delight that when you wake up you will get to go to work? Do you look forward to the next day of work? Or, do you dread getting up and going to work the next day?

These feelings can be a perfect indicator of whether you are doing or being, whether you are in the right vocation or not. Your vocation enhances your life both personally and professionally. If you are in the right vocation, you know it in your heart.

If you have a vocation where you are "being" and not just "doing," you should be enjoying the following rewards:

- You feel that your work matters to you and others.
- You know that you make a difference.
- You know that you are contributing to the good of humanity.
- You are eager to go to work.
- Your work brings you energy and excitement.
- You make the most of your time at work.
- You enjoy your colleagues and respect them.

Who Are You, Anyway?

Your personality plays a great role in your happiness at work. Understanding your personality can make the difference between being and doing. If you don't have a clear understanding of what you like or enjoy, what you value, where you perform best, how you like to be treated, and whether you work best alone or with others, then you may never find peace or self-esteem through your work.

Personality typology has been around for many years helping people understand more about their unique traits and qualities. The Myers-Briggs Type Indicator (MBTI) is one of the most widely used assessments in the world. There are many other assessment instruments based on the Myers-Briggs available online and in bookstores. The MBTI indicates whether you are more introverted or extroverted, more sensing or intuitive, more thinking or feeling, or more judging or perceiving.

The introvert/extrovert trait deals with how you interact with the world. An introvert draws strength from internal sources whereas an extrovert draws strength from external sources. The sensing/intuitive trait deals with how you learn. The sensing person learns by seeing, touching, smelling, and hearing information. People who are more intuitive rely on the sixth sense, intuition, for knowledge. They are people who look beyond the obvious for meaning.

If you want to do something that you see others doing, spend some time with those people. Ask them questions; volunteer to do some unpaid work (no matter how basic) in that environment so that you can be around your passion full-time for a few days. It'll give you a better idea of whether or not it's really something you want.

The thinking/feeling trait deals with the way you make decisions. The thinkers are very logical people and make their decision based on logic and reasoning. The feelers are more concerned with what they feel is right or what they care for deeply, and they make their decisions based on that mindset. Finally, the judging/perceiving trait deals with the way we live and move in the world. Judgers are very orderly people and perceivers are more spontaneous and carefree.

So, what does all of this have to do with self-esteem or purpose or work? Much! If you have no real understanding of your personality traits, you may be working in a job that is opposite to who you are as a person. If you are an extrovert and a feeler, and you are working as an accountant behind a desk where you don't get to make creative decisions, you are probably miserable. Conversely, if you are an introvert who is forced to make presentations and interact with others all day, this can be torture to you. To make matters worse, because you are unhappy in your work, your self-esteem suffers.

Understanding more about your intricacies, quirks, desires, and innate gifts can help you make career and vocation decisions that work in harmony with your dharma, not against it. In turn, you feel better about who you are and what you are contributing to the world.

More Than the Money

It is true. Some people work just for the money, and it is not just people who have no other choice; there are countless wealthy people who work just for the payday. Their self-esteem seems to be tied to how much they make and what can be bought with it.

Often, people who work just for the money do so because they have not found their purpose, their passion, their dharma. Finding your purpose means asking, *"Why* am I here?"

Finding Meaning

Many psychologists, Carl Jung included, found that many of the people they treated (sometimes as many as half) did not suffer from neurosis, or psychosis, but from aimlessness and meaninglessness. People who work to find meaning and purpose, and live their lives making decisions and choices based on their purpose, are the people with the healthiest self-esteem.

FACT

Brainstorming can be one of the most effective ways to look at different professions and to examine your purpose in life. Sit down alone and begin to write down ideas, truths, wishes, hopes, dreams, and fears about your future and your life of work. This gives you a starting place to begin making your transition plan.

Finding your purpose is best explained by Parker Palmer as finding the thing that you cannot *not* do. That statement may sound some-what abstract, but it means that you have found the talent, the passion, the miracle inside you that must come out. For some, it is music or medicine or repairing things or being around people. For others, it is surfing or writing or teaching or working with animals. It is the thing that pulls you so tautly toward your bliss that you can't resist it, though scores of people do! It is sometimes described as "your calling."

Listening to Your Life

Listening to what your life is telling you is as important as you deciding what direction your life should take. Perhaps you have been in a situation where you did not listen to your life, your true self, and your decisions, actions, and choices went against your internal purpose. When you do this, you are usually unhappy and feel unfulfilled. Your self-esteem suffers as a result. This is why purpose is one of the cornerstones of healthy self-esteem. Without a clear understanding of "Why am I here," "What is my calling," and "What does my life want from me," you will not have the healthy self-esteem that you seek, regardless of how much money you make.

Living purposefully means that you have found your calling, your passion, and all of your efforts, desires, goals, and actions are directed by this purpose. For example, Lynda found that her purpose in life is to help other people by being a social worker for the elderly. This is something that she cannot *not* do. Even if there were no pay for social work, she would have to do it to feel right about herself. Therefore, her life's goals, desires, and actions are directed by that purpose. She would not consider moving in another direction unless something fundamental and colossal happened in her life that altered this innate purpose. She does not act in any fashion that might jeopardize her ability to continue working with the elderly. Her purpose guides her actions, her beliefs, and her life. For Lynda, to live a life not being able to draw on her internal strengths (her purpose) would be a meaningless existence.

Meaning in Life

Countless people stake their purpose or meaning in life on jobs; other people focus on material belongings or accomplishments. Purpose is deeper than a job. It is stronger than another person and more resilient than possessions. Purpose does not leave you. You may leave your purpose, but it does not happen the other way around. Purpose is as necessary as a vital organ but as elusive as the soul. Perhaps this is why so few people spend time discovering their purpose, listening to their purpose, or answering the call of their purpose.

One way to begin your journey toward purpose in life is to take stock of what is happening in your life. Are you happy with the results of your actions? Do your efforts give you the outcomes you desire? Are you constantly asking yourself, *When are things going to get better?* Do you try harder and harder and success remains elusive? If so, you may not be living purposefully. You may be on a road that is not in alignment with your life's mission, and this may be one of the reasons for unhealthy self-esteem.

There is an old quote that says, "Insanity is doing the same thing over and over and over again and expecting a different result." The same is true with the relationship between self-esteem and purpose. If you continue to ignore your purpose, or refuse to acknowledge that you have a purpose, and persist in doing the same things over and over and over, self-esteem will remain a mystery to you.

"To put meaning in one's life may end in madness, but life without meaning is the torture of restlessness and vague desire. It is a boat longing for the sea and yet afraid to sail."

—Edgar L. Masters

Working for Others

"Working for others" does not mean what you think it means. We all work for others on some level, even those who are self-employed and own their own businesses work for their customers. "Working for others" refers to work that is done without the reward of monetary compensation. It refers to doing the work of the heart.

The work of the heart may very well be your vocation, but for many, it is not. You may have to find your work of the heart outside your place of employment. If you are lucky, and if you are living your life's purpose, the two may well exist in one place.

Volunteering

Volunteering is about working for others. It is about giving your time and efforts to formal organizations. It is one of the mainstays of compassion and caring in this nation. There are countless organizations that need your time and efforts. From Meals on Wheels to soup kitchens to the American Red Cross to local libraries, there is always a need for human-touch interaction and assistance.

You may be asking, "Why would I volunteer? I can barely do all that needs to be done now." The answer is quite simple. Volunteering can help other people, and it can help you find a part of yourself that may have been dormant until now. Volunteering can be the creative, expressive, human-touch outlet that brings you delight, comfort, and a peace within your own soul.

FACT

Americans of all ages, including teens, are volunteering more. Volunteers are giving an average of five hours per week and most are not associated with a "formal" organization, but rather volunteer as an individual.

Following are some of the places that you might consider formally volunteering:

- A group that does tax preparation for the poor or elderly
- AARP 55 Alive (driving program)
- Museums and performing arts venues
- Environmental organizations that assist with cleanup efforts
- Voter registration and Election Day assistance
- Organizations such as Meals on Wheels, Red Cross, Earthwatch, Habitat for Humanity, Peace Corps, etc.

Helping Those in Need

There are many avenues to working for others beyond the formal volunteer organizations. You need not become a part of the United Way or Meals on Wheels to offer true, genuine, needed assistance.

Following are some seldom-thought-of, informal ways that you can help others and your surrounding community:

- Cook a meal for a family that you see struggling.
- Recycle and try to get others to do it as well.
- Volunteer to read to children at the library.
- Serve meals at a soup kitchen.
- Be a model of good manners and polite behavior.
- Sit with an Alzheimer's patient so the family can have a night off.
- Send out one "thank you" or "I'm thinking of you" every day.

Doing the work of the heart isn't about money or status; it is about your innate desire to move humanity forward. It is about helping others understand that there is still goodness and kindness in the world. In return, you'll be utterly amazed at how quickly and easily your own world and view begins to change.

Givin' It All You've Got

In order to find your voice or vocation, you may need to look at every area available to you. Your self-esteem can be assisted by moving to a healthier work environment, formally volunteering, informally volunteering, discovering more about your own personality and gifts, and taking an all-out stance to find a place, your place, in the world of work. It may take time and energy, but finding your voice and place will be one of the most rewarding endeavors of your life.

Leaving the Moment—Thinking Backward

Sometimes, our future lies in the past. It is the best indicator of what works and what does not. It is a great teacher. You can freely look back to see where you made a wrong turn, where you made a bad decision, where you did something that worked wonderfully, and where you did something that made yourself (and others) feel alive and vibrant.

Thinking backward can help you find your vocation, your joy in work. Think back to the first thing you ever wanted to be. Was it a firefighter, a law enforcement officer, a doctor, an astronaut? Why did you want to be that? If you aren't doing it now, what stopped you? Think back to a job where you were truly happy and felt that you were making a difference. Is it still true? Does your current work bring you peace? If not, why? What did you have in the past that you do not have now? Looking back can be an important step in working forward.

Leaving the Moment—Thinking Forward

Leaving the moment also asks that you move to tomorrow and beyond. While the past is a great teacher, the future is where promise lives. Where do you want to be next month, in a year, in five years? What do you want your legacy to be? What are your pages in human history going to read? These questions are not only a part of the past, but are also a part of the future.

The worst job that you ever had can be the most important time of your life. The worst job can be the most effective, the clearest, and the most meaningful teacher of all. The worst job of your life, properly examined, lets you know what you don't want ever again.

An interesting but often scary thing to do is to consider the end of your life. Pretend for a moment that you have just passed away at the old age of ninety. What do you want people to say about you? What do you want your life to have meant? What do you want written in your obituary? This may seem morbid and strange, but thinking about this can help you clarify what really is most important to you.

If you seriously listen to your heart, examine what your strengths and weaknesses are, study your past, and make vocational decisions based on these things and based on your overriding life goals, the future can start at any moment of your choosing.

Working for money and working from the heart are very different, but carry several major common traits—to be successful in either, they both require your full-out talent, dedication, and energy. They both require that you understand your own role in the world, and they both can tremendously intensify your plan for healthy self-esteem.

Activity: Stretching the Limits

Directions: This journey asks you to think beyond what you do, feel, and have at the moment. The acclaimed minister Dr. Robert Schuller asked the following question: "What would you attempt to do if you knew you could not fail?" For this journey, list at least ten things that you would do if you knew you could not fail.

1. _____

2. _____

3. _____

4. _____

5. _____

6. _____

7. _____

8. _____

9. _____

10. _____

Did you have trouble listing ten things?   ❐ Yes   ❐ No
Why? _____

Activity: Stretching the Limits (continued)

Choose one of the things you listed above that you would attempt to do if you knew you would not fail.

That thing is _____

Why are you not doing it? _____

_____

_____

_____

What joy or happiness would doing this thing bring to your life?

_____

_____

_____

How would doing this thing aid your self-esteem?

_____

_____

_____

On a scale of 1 to 10, how important could this act be to your sense of accomplishment and purpose in life? (1 = low and 10 = high)

1   2   3   4   5   6   7   8   9   10

List five ways that you could begin to do this thing either alone or with someone else.

1. _____

2. _____

3. _____

4. _____

5. _____

Using the goal sheet from the back of the book, devise a goal plan to bring this ability into your life.

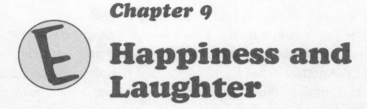

Chapter 9

Happiness and Laughter

Researchers have found that happiness does not come from income, intelligence, prestige, good looks, or nice weather. What brings you happiness? Is it marriage? Friends? Family? Food? Vices? What role does your self-esteem play in your overall happiness?

Defining Your Personal Happiness

In order to know what brings you happiness, you first must understand what happiness is. Dr. Martin Seligman defines happiness as the emotion that arises when we do something that stems from our strengths and virtues. Other definitions suggest that happiness is when all of your physical, mental, emotional, and spiritual needs have been met.

The self-help program called *A Course in Happiness* defines it as a natural state of mind arising from an understanding and acceptance of life exactly as it is. Another definition suggests that happiness is being in love with living. And finally, Ruut Veenhoven defines happiness as how much a person likes the life he or she leads.

Surely, happiness is a slippery and elusive creature. It is hard to define something that is so subjective. Some psychologists believe that happiness is not linked to one or two very intense moments of elation, but rather tied to a steady, more frequent flow of smaller joys into your life. This would mean that lasting happiness comes not from a few moments, but many moments. Further, happiness is directly related to the degree of optimism that you possess in all walks of life.

FACT

The quality of life for U.S. citizens has risen steadily since the 1950s, while people report that their level of happiness is no greater since World War II. According to a report in *U.S. News and World Report,* people today are ten times as likely to suffer depression as those born two generations ago.

The one thing that is known for sure by researchers, psychologists, therapist, educators, and practitioners is this: You have to work to find happiness. Happiness does not just walk up to you; you have to walk to it.

Types of Happiness

Researchers such as Steve Taylor—researcher and author of the article "Where Is Happiness?"—view happiness in several contexts: materialistic happiness, hedonistic happiness, ego-based happiness, future-based happiness, need-satisfaction happiness, event-based happiness, and circumstance-changing happiness.

Materialistic happiness is the type of happiness that you get from having things—material possessions like cars, boats, homes, clothes, fine jewelry, silver, or things that bring your personal joy. This type of happiness is strong, but it does not last long. After we get used to having the "thing" that we wanted for so long, we're ready to move on to our next "materialistically happy" experience.

Hedonistic happiness is happiness that comes from pleasure and pleasurable situations and stimuli. These pleasures can be food, sex, alcohol, a comfortable home, dancing in a wild nightclub, sailing on a clear lake, driving through the mountains, or listening to incredible music. These pleasures are very subjective because while food and dancing in a nightclub may be the biggest pleasures in life for some, they can be low on the list of pleasures for others.

Ego-based happiness is the happiness we get from success, self-esteem, status, praise, power, and fame. Ego-based happiness can originate from a compliment from a coworker on the quality of your performance, your partner telling you that you are beautiful, or receiving a standing ovation for a performance. These things feed your ego and bring you joy.

FACT

Researchers have found that women in their mid-forties to mid-fifties describe themselves as "happier" more often than women in their late teens to mid-twenties.

Future-based happiness comes from knowing that you have something to which you can look forward, joy on the horizon. Future-based happiness is associated with optimism and hope. It has its ties in plans that you assume are going to bring you joy on some level. It can be as simple as dinner tonight or that Alaskan cruise you're planning for next summer. Future-based happiness is a stimulus that keeps you going.

Need-satisfaction happiness is happiness that comes to you when you have had a need met. It can be as complex as the happiness you feel once a major problem has been solved or a health issue has been resolved, or as simple as the happiness you feel once you have slept or eaten.

Event-based happiness is happiness that comes to you when you have witnessed or participated in a pleasurable event such as a party, a marriage, obtaining employment, getting accepted into college, or watching your child hit her first home run.

Circumstance-changing happiness occurs when you change a part of your life with which you were displeased. You may have moved to a new home, lost weight, moved to another job from one that was not rewarding, or found a better way to do something that had been troublesome before.

Is It Enough? Will It Last?

Each of these types of happiness may bring you joy for a while, maybe even a long while, but each has its drawback and each has its "time limit." Future-based happiness is wonderful, until that point in your life when there may not be anything on the horizon. Materialistic happiness is great, until you run out of money. Ego-based happiness is wonderful, but what happens when people stop praising you and lavishing you with kind words? Where is happiness then?

One of the most important things about happiness is that it does not exist outside of yourself. You must bring happiness into your life and not expect happiness to be brought to you by an external force.

Researchers on happiness have found that enjoyment assists in good physical health, positive mental health, reduces stress, protects against illness, and combats negative mental activity.

There are several major ways to keep lasting happiness in your life. First is by setting goals and working to reach them. Next is by having an optimistic attitude about the world and the way in which the world moves and turns. Happiness is also best retained by understanding your spirituality and having a close circle of friends in whom you can confide and disclose important things about your life. Happiness can exist in your life when you remove things such as stress, anger, fear, and negative thinking.

The Habits of Happiness

Happiness is not a birthright. It is not owed to you. But, it is not a pipe dream and it is not impossible. Happiness is a habit that can be obtained just as you obtain the habit of having caffeine, or the habit of dessert after a meal, or the habit of saying, "bless you" when someone sneezes.

It has been said that if you do something for twenty-one days, without fail, it will become a habit, a ritual in your life. Most people spend time trying to change or break habits. You may not have spent time practicing obtaining a habit, but the habit of happiness is one that is worth practicing.

The Habit of Counting Blessings

Yes, bad things happen. But some of your happiness is determined by being able to look at the good things that still exist in your life, such as your family, your friends, your pets, flowers on the windowsill, rain, sunshine, the ocean, your health, love, passion, and other pleasures large and small.

It can be hard to count a blessing when tragedy strikes. Sometimes it is hard to even face the morning, let alone another day or month or year. However, learning to look at the good that remains will help you with your healthy self-esteem plan and will help you find joy once again.

There is an old Chinese story that tells of a poor farmer who depended on his horse for plowing and getting around. One day the horse left. The neighbors approached him with sadness and talked about how bad it was. The poor farmer said, "Maybe."

The next day, the horse returned with two other horses. The neighbors approached him with happiness and talked about how wonderful it was. The poor farmer said, "Maybe."

The next day, the poor farmer's son tried to ride one of the horses and it threw him and broke his leg, rendering him unable to work. The neighbors approached him with sadness to talk about how bad it was. The poor farmer said, "Maybe."

The next day, the army called on the boy to serve. They rejected him because of his broken leg.

The Habit of Spinning

You've heard of the "spin room" in politics. This is where politicians go to put a "spin" on what has been said. Spinning means that you take the information that you have and make it work for you. Spinning is important to your self-esteem and happiness because it teaches you to take the unpleasant, the bad, the ugly and find good in it. You look at the car accident in which you were involved and you don't see the accident, you see that it was a wake-up call to drive more carefully. You look at the divorce that you just survived and instead of seeing the pain and loneliness of being left, you become thankful that you did not spend one, five, or thirty *more* years *and then* find out that love was not really yours. This is the magic of spin.

"Our real blessings often appear to us in the shape of pain, loss, and disappointment."

—Joseph Addison

The Habit of Helping

Helping a person in need is surely one of the most magnificent offerings you can give another person—and yourself. The feeling is beyond measure when you know that you helped alleviate someone else's suffering. Helping another person can be as simple as offering a listening ear, to helping someone with car trouble, to pulling him or her from a burning home. Not all of your efforts need be monumental. Sometimes, the simplest acts are the ones that mean the most and help the most.

The Habit of Being in Control

When you are in control of your own destiny, your life begins to change and you begin to feel happiness, a joy and peace that you have never known. Allowing others to control your life, your actions, your thoughts, your desires, and your needs is quite damaging to your self-esteem and keeps happiness at bay. Starting small, begin to take control of your life. Set a goal and work toward it on your own. Arrange your own schedule. Take time for yourself and your needs. Being in control of your life is paramount to happiness.

The Habit of Empathy

It has been said that "empathy is your pain in my heart." Empathy means that you have allowed yourself to listen to and become involved in another person's life. They may be in pain, but your happiness comes from knowing that your ear, your smile, your voice, and your presence are helping.

Empathy means that you try to put yourself in the other person's shoes. It means that you look at their life and problems from their perspective, not yours. When you have empathy for others, you begin to understand just how connected we all are and how much joy can come from the feeling of "oneness."

The Habit of Self-Disclosure

Self-disclosure means that you allow yourself to be open. It means that you have enough trust and faith in others that you can share your life, your dreams, your pains, your desire, your frustrations, loves, goals, and passions with another human being. In doing so, you are opening yourself up for great happiness. You are also opening yourself up for great pain. Self-disclosure is a double-edged sword. You should, and need, to be open with people, but you have to choose the people whom you trust enough to let into your life.

The Habit of Fitness

The simple act of walking can reduce stress and depression. The lack of activity in your life can be causing you unhappiness. Everyday you need to walk or exercise or jog or run or roller-skate or swim—something to get your energy level up. Fitness involves more than physical fitness, it involves emotional and mental fitness as well. Get into the habit of taking care of your body and in turn, your body will take care of you.

FACT

Pleasure leads to a reduction in stress hormones and leads to a better immune response, and therefore, more resistance to illness. Happiness tends to be greater among people in good physical shape and who have an abundance of energy.

Finding Happiness

"I've looked, I've searched, I've explored every mountain and rummaged every valley, and I can't find happiness. I just can't find it," you might say. Maybe, just maybe, you've been looking in the wrong places. Remember that happiness is something that you have to bring to yourself; it will not come looking for you. Following, you will find some places that you may have failed to look.

Happiness Through Leisure

If you've never tried sitting in the sun or having a glass of wine under a shade tree or walking on the beach or hiking in the fall-colored mountains, you have cheated yourself out of moments of happiness and joy. People are sometime so obsessed with "finding" happiness that they do not take a quiet moment to enjoy the happiness that leisure can bring.

Happiness Through Travel

There is a great old saying that the two greatest teachers on earth are time and travel. Happiness can be found in going to places where you have never been. It does not have to be an expensive vacation to Switzerland; it can be a day-trip to the countryside or a ride into the city for a play and dinner. Look for places within a day's drive where you could spend a weekend and explore a new place. Travel opens your horizons and allows you to see how others live and move in the world.

Happiness Through Education and Discovery

The joy of learning something new, of discovering another way to do a task that is easier and quicker, of completing a course in baking or computer troubleshooting can flood you with happiness like you've never known. Education and discovery are important to happiness because you are not only working on finding happiness, you are directly working on building your self-esteem as well.

Happiness Through Small Pleasures

Petting your cat. Listening to Rachmaninoff's Symphony no. 1 in D Minor. Watching the sun make a rainbow through a cut-glass bowl. Sitting on the curb eating cotton candy while watching a parade. Telling the best joke you've ever heard. Watching the squirrels eat acorns. Calling an old friend with whom you've not spoken in years. Listening to wind chimes on a cool afternoon while sipping apple cider. Sound far-fetched? Out of reach for you? Hopeless in the wake of that new job? Then find your own small pleasures and bask in the glory they can bring. You'll be amazed.

Sharing Happiness with Others

While it is not healthy to rely on others for your sole happiness, others can play a vital and necessary role in your quest for happiness. Isolation from people can be a detriment to your health and it can be a deterrent to happiness. Family and friends are two of the top factors in guiding happiness into your life.

You can bring happiness to other people just by being around, and in turn, you can increase your own happiness by just being with them.

Following, you will find some simple ways that you can bring happiness to, and find happiness in, others:

- Go to a movie together.
- Exercise together.
- Make Thursday night TV watching a weekly appointment.
- Take up a new hobby together.
- Join a social, educational, spiritual, or meditation group together.

Turning Away Misery

The less misery you have, the more likely happiness, joy, and laughter are to appear in your life. Following, you will find a few tips to usher misery out of your life:

- Face your problems head-on and don't ignore them.
- Put a positive spin on your unfortunate situations.
- Get out and live among happy people.
- Move away from miserable people who love miserable company.
- Reach out to people.
- Accept that some of life is misery and some is glory—choose glory.
- Choose your battles wisely—you can't win them all.

Whether happiness comes from your strength and virtues; the meeting of your physical, mental, and emotional needs; your acceptance of life as it is; or the satisfactions with the life you lead; happiness can be yours. With a clear understanding that happiness is an internal characteristic and not an external force, you can change your life and move toward joy. Good luck.

FACT

Most habits are formed because we gain something from the action. If you have a habit of thinking negatively about yourself, it is a condition that you found worked at some place, for some reason, and you have repeated it so often, it became a habit. All habits can be broken.

Activity: Daily Happiness

Directions: In the space following, list at least three things that bring you happiness in each of the categories listed. List the happiness even if you have not experienced it in a while.

ENTERTAINMENT

_____

_____

_____

SOCIAL

_____

_____

_____

FAMILY

_____

_____

_____

EDUCATION/GROWTH

_____

_____

_____

CAREER

_____

_____

_____

FRIENDS

_____

_____

_____

PEOPLE IN GENERAL

_____

_____

_____

IN GENERAL

_____

_____

_____

Review your list. Select a happiness you listed that you _have not_ experienced in a while or the one that you experience less frequently than the others.

That happiness is _____

What role does this happiness play in adding to your self-esteem?

_____

_____

_____

Use the goal sheet in the back of the book and develop a plan to bring this happiness into or back into your life.

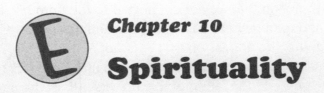

Chapter 10

Spirituality

Spirituality is so profoundly personal and individualized that it can scarcely be defined or explained. Is spirituality a feeling of wonderment? Is it awe of the universe's powers? Is it the basis for religion? Is it the opposite of religion? Is it the foundation for healing and trust? Does it have anything at all to do with your self-esteem?

What Does It All Mean?

Spirituality comes from the Latin word *spiritus*, which means "breath," as in "breath of life." Spirituality and religion differ in that religion is more concerned with rules, policy, codes, and laws. Spirituality is more personalized and free; it moves beyond policy.

Spirituality is the notion that we are connected to the universe, to nature, to others, and to ourselves. It is an understanding and acceptance of the unexplained. It is the admission of, "I am not alone."

Spirituality is the complete acknowledgment and understanding that you are indelibly woven into the fabric of this universe—that whether you die tonight or 10,000 nights from now, it is the insight that, because of your birth, you are a part of human history. It is the total awareness that you can never change that fact.

It is the wisdom that there is purpose and meaning even if you can't see it and don't understand it. It means that you accept the notion that that there is an energy that moves about you that can't be seen or touched or captured. Spirituality means that you are open to divine guidance.

Moreover, your spiritual nature guides your character, your ethical behavior, and has a profound effect on the development of your self-esteem. It is the internal map that guides you toward peace.

FACT

Spiritual activities such as prayer, contemplation, and meditation can reduce stress, promote a healthier lifestyle, and intensify your sense of belonging. Spirituality can also have a positive effect on brain activity.

Why Spirituality Matters

If religion is more concerned with rules, policies, and codes than spirituality, your self-esteem may actually suffer because of these guidelines. If you are involved in an organized religion, your self-esteem may suffer because of the feeling that you do not really fit in or believe every tenet of that religion. You may begin to have self-doubts because you actually disagree with some of that religion's teachings. This can cause damage to your self-esteem.

Your self-esteem may suffer because you do not believe every code or policy practiced by that religion and you begin to feel guilty. If you are involved with a formal religion and you do not attend every service, you may begin to feel pressure and more guilt, even if it is self-imposed.

Conversely, spirituality is about caring for yourself, understanding yourself, examining your gifts and strengths, and looking inside yourself for peace and understanding. Spirituality is concerned with self-determination and being able to face problems without going to pieces. It is about learning to solve problems and learning to come to conclusions that are positive for you, others, and the earth.

Spirituality helps you appreciate yourself and the space in which you live, breathe, and work. It helps you understand the ebb and flow of life and what part you play in the grand scheme of things.

These things serve to strengthen self-esteem, whereas a formal religion with its guidelines and policies may in some cases serve to damage your self-esteem.

The Power of Beliefs

Spirituality is one of the guiding factors in what you believe and how those beliefs preside over your life. As your spirituality guides your beliefs, your beliefs guide your actions and behaviors. Your behavior, positive or negative, affects how you think and feel about yourself.

Your spiritual beliefs guide how you feel about issues ranging from living, death and dying, to understanding the meaning of life, to faith and trust. Among all beliefs, your spiritual beliefs are usually the strongest indicators of your actions and behaviors.

"Fear imprisons, faith liberates; fear paralyzes, faith empowers; fear disheartens, faith encourages; fear sickens, faith heals."

—Harry Emerson Fosdick

Your self-esteem is tied to your spiritual beliefs in that your esteem soars when you have acted in a way that is harmonious with your belief system and it is damaged when you act in a way that is detrimental to your belief system.

The Placebo Effect

Countless studies have been done on the placebo effect. Patients who are suffering from various conditions are given either a "real" drug treatment or a placebo, a "false" drug treatment commonly called a sugar pill.

The power of the placebo effect is that people do not know they are receiving a placebo (the nonmedicine), and their belief in the real drug and their confidence that they are going to improve is so powerful that it actually works, even though they did not receive the real drug.

Placebos were recently used by groups of scientists to treat Parkinson's disease, depression, and pain. In every study, the placebo worked as well as the actual treatment. In a study on depression, cited in *Chemistry and Industry*, the placebo worked as well, or *better* than, Prozac, Paxil, and Zoloft. The antidepressants worked as well, but the placebo did, too. Why? Because of the power of belief!

Believing in Yourself

Imagine how powerful the brain is if it can actually begin to heal the body and mind with a sugar pill. Can you imagine the changes that could occur in your life if you gave yourself a self-esteem placebo? For one day, imagine taking a self-esteem pill and believing that you are the very best that you can be. Imagine that all of your innate gifts are shining and ready for use. Imagine that your advice and information is the most powerful thing on earth. Imagine, for one day, that the pill helps you see your self-image so clearly that you can see your purpose, your reason for living, and you can help heal yourself and the world.

Of course, it isn't possible to take a self-esteem placebo, but it is possible to trick your brain into believing in yourself. It is possible to convince yourself that you are okay and that you have worth. It is possible to include yourself in your belief system. In believing that you are okay, you begin to be so.

Why are beliefs so hard to change?
Tradition and fear are perhaps the most common reasons that people do not change their beliefs. You've heard people say, "We've always done it that way." Many people are afraid of the unknown and lack the self-confidence needed to make a major life change such as changing a belief, a custom, or a tradition.

The Role of Spirituality in Character

Spirituality and self-esteem play major roles in character development. They are the road maps that guide you as you act and move with others in the world. People with strong spiritual beliefs understand and practice the deep convictions of character. It has been said, "character is who you are when no one is looking."

Character can also be described as how we act when there are no policies and guidelines for behavior. If you were able to treat anyone any way without any culpability or responsibility, how would you respond? If you could do what you wanted to do with that person who just cut you off on the interstate, what would you do? If you could say anything to that nasty person at work, what would you say? If you could get your hands on the person who stole your wallet and then your identity, what would you do to them? You character is the guiding force for how you act, and your character is a direct product of your spirituality and spiritual nature.

Broken Character

Almost every person can point to someone they personally know and suggest that his or her character is less than sterling. Is it the person who steals from work? Is it the person who cheats on his or her spouse? Is it the person who can never be trusted with anything? What causes you to look at people and label them "bad characters"?

It is generally held that people with flawed character are people who make decisions based solely on how the outcome affects them. People with flawed character can't be trusted with secrets and fail to keep their word and their promises.

They are people who do not tell the truth and who continually backstab others to get ahead. They are people who bend the truth or cover parts of the truth to get what they want or need without consideration for others' wants or needs.

People with flawed character tend to have an egotistical view of the world. They see it only through their eyes. They make decisions, rules, and design courses of action based on a myopic view of the universe.

A Person of Character

What are the qualities of a person with strong character? Who is a person in your own life that you perceive as having virtuous ethics and character? Most people would say that a person of character is trustworthy, someone whom you can rely on in times of need and times of joy. A person of character is someone who is respectful of others, their values, their customs, and their traditions.

A person of character is someone who always accepts responsibility for his or her actions. Such a person does not place blame on others and he or she does not take the glory from others. A person of character acts in a fair and equitable fashion toward everyone, and he or she does not single out individuals or groups of people and treat them differently.

"Good character consists of knowing the good, desiring the good, and doing the good habits of the mind, habits of the heart, and habits of action."

—Thomas Lickona

A person of character is open-minded and willing to listen to every side of the story and understands that every story has two or more sides. A person of character is a good citizen in the world and understands his or her role in the progression of humankind.

Character is one of the most monumental forces in building healthy self-esteem. When you know beyond doubt that your actions, and indeed your life, are guided by moral and ethical standards, you can't help but have a sense of pride in your own life.

The Role of Spirituality in Ethics

Ethics and character are closely related. Ethics are the code or principals on which one's character depends. Ethics develop at an early age and can be instrumental to building character.

Consider Matt. He is a thirteen-year-old young man who is beginning his first job as a paperboy. He is excited to be able to earn his own spending money for the first time in his life. His parents have coached him about the safety issues of the job, and they spent the weekend walking him through his route. Monday evening comes and Matt is excited to begin his job.

Matt enters the printing room of the local newspaper and is greeted by the delivery supervisor. He tells Matt that he will be delivering 127 papers daily. He also tells Matt that if he runs out of papers, he should go to the local 7-Eleven store on his route, put a quarter in the outside paper box, and take as many papers as he needs from the box. "We do it all the time, son," he tells Matt. "That's a different account, and our division is not charged for those papers. It helps us out in the long run, buddy."

Matt is deeply concerned over what his boss has instructed him to do. He has feelings of guilt and confusion. Matt is struggling with his ethics.

Even at thirteen or younger, people have a code of ethics and they know when they have gone against that code.

The Components of Ethics

Ethics have two components: belief and practice. Your beliefs and convictions are only the first part of ethics. These beliefs are rooted in your spiritual nature. You may believe that stealing is wrong. You may feel that lying is wrong or that hurting someone's feelings is unsuitable. These are beliefs.

The second part of ethics is how you act on your beliefs and convictions. Yes, stealing is wrong, but it is okay to take a few ink pens and a pack of Post-It notes home from work every week. Everyone does it. Yes, lying is wrong, but a little lie could save your job. What's the harm in that? The second part of ethics, how you practice, is the heart of ethical behavior.

Perhaps the most important word associated with ethics is betrayal. Is there a worse word or act? Ethics demand that you consider this word. When you are making a decision, evaluating whether to act or not, or when you consider the consequences of a decision or act, is there any betrayal? That one word can be your guiding force in ethical behavior.

Putting Ethics to Work

If you have concerns about whether a decision you are about to make is ethical or not, or if how you have treated someone is ethical or not, consider the following guidelines:

- Will this decision hurt your reputation or the reputation of others?
- Can you tell others about this decision or action with pride?
- Would you do it to your mother?
- Is it legal?
- Have you considered every angle and option?
- Is it right? (Yes, you do know!)
- Is it balanced and fair to others?
- Does your conscience approve?
- Have you betrayed anyone to make this decision?

These simple but important questions can help you learn to make ethical decisions that are in line with your spiritual nature. They can also help you build positive self-esteem, in that you know that you have done right by others.

Spirituality is as personal as your life itself. It contributes to the overall efforts and actions of your existence. It plays a role in your character, your beliefs, your treatment of others, and yes, in your overall self-esteem development. Spirituality is the guiding force that lets you know what is right and just in the world, and just what your part is in the master plan.

Activity: If It Is to Be, It Is Up to Me!

Directions: Following, you will find a list of positive qualities. Circle fifteen of the qualities that you feel you *do not* currently possess. The qualities that you circle should be qualities that you would like to obtain in your own life to help you develop a greater sense of spirituality and character.

HAPPY	LOVING	FUNNY	TRUSTWORTHY
RATIONAL	WARM	HONEST	AMBITIOUS
SUCCESSFUL	CANDID	KIND	CARING
OPEN-MINDED	INDUSTRIOUS	CREATIVE	DETERMINED
NURTURING	ORGANIZED	ATTRACTIVE	COOL
HOPEFUL	ENERGETIC	MUSICAL	ARTISTIC
ACCEPTING	TACTFUL	THOROUGH	EMPATHIC
ASSERTIVE	INTELLIGENT	HELPFUL	SOCIABLE
THANKFUL	SPIRITUAL	COURAGEOUS	INVENTIVE
PEACEFUL	PASSIONATE	CHARMING	TOLERANT
POSITIVE	HOPEFUL	HEALTHY	PURPOSEFUL
PATIENT	COMMITTED	FULFILLED	SERVICE-ORIENTED

Your own word(s):

_____   _____   _____   _____

Choose *two* of the words that you circled. They are:
_____ and _____

Word one: Why is this quality important to you

_____

_____

_____

How could you use this quality to help you spiritually?

_____

_____

_____

Activity: If It Is to Be, It Is Up to Me! (continued)

How could you use this quality to help you strengthen your character?

- -

- -

- -

How could you use this quality to help someone else?

- -

- -

- -

Word two: Why is this quality important to you?

- -

- -

- -

How could you use this quality to help you spiritually?

- -

- -

- -

How could you use this quality to help you strengthen your character?

- -

- -

- -

How could you use this quality to help someone else?

- -

- -

- -

Now, choose one of the words above and complete the goal sheet to help you bring this quality into your life. As you acquire this quality and move through this book (and beyond), you are encouraged to come back to this exercise and choose another quality.

Chapter 11

Wellness

Does the term "Wellness" conjure up images of monks kneeling for meditation on a foggy morning in a monastery? Does it extract images of perfectly shaped bodies doing tai chi on the beach in Southern California? Or does wellness trigger the likeness of a health nut who only eats the bark from certain trees found in the rain forest?

Wellness in the Body

Wellness is a relatively new word. For those who grew up in the 60s, 70s, and 80s, you will remember physical education in the school system. "Wellness" meant that you could run around the football field thirteen times and climb a knotted rope in the gym—while dressed out, of course.

Today, wellness encompasses much more than physical activity. It involves the entire body, mind, and soul. Physical strength and endurance are certainly included, but so is meditation, healthy eating habits, stress reduction, relaxation and reflection, attention to sleep, and a focus on mental well-being.

Wellness and self-esteem are closely tied. If you feel good about your body and your physical appearance, your self-esteem improves. If you feel well, meaning that you have an absence of physical illness, your self-esteem improves. If you are mentally relaxed and healthy, your self-esteem improves. If you are relatively stress-free, your self-esteem improves.

Get Up and Get Out

Daily exercise is one of the keys to wellness. Fitness experts, wellness gurus, TV infomercials, and even medical professionals tout the benefits of just twenty minutes of exercise daily.

Exercise can consist of working out in a gym, lifting weights, running, swimming, kickboxing, or simply walking briskly around the neighborhood. Exercise does not need to be something that is dreaded or something that costs you $123 a month, but it does need to happen in your life. Exercise improves your ability to fight illness and your ability to bounce back from an illness.

There are several types of exercise that can help you work on your physical and self-esteem health. The three leading types of exercise are strength exercise, stretch exercise, and cardio exercise.

Strength exercising involves concentrating on your muscles and muscle groups. This includes lifting weights and doing pushups, sit-ups, and exercises to strengthen the muscles in the stomach, arms, back, legs, and neck.

Stretch exercising concentrates on stretching the muscles in your body. Techniques such as yoga are in this category. Cardio exercising is working on strengthening your heart and lungs. Good cardio exercises include running, jogging, swimming, cycling, rowing, skating, aerobic dancing, kickboxing, and the like.

Finally, there is cross-training exercise—a workout that includes each of the three types of exercises—strength, stretch, and cardio. You might consider doing fifteen minutes of stretching exercises, thirty minutes of aerobic exercises, and twenty minutes of strength exercises to complete a well-rounded program. Always check with your physician before you begin an exercise regiment, especially if you are overweight, over sixty, smoke, and/or in generally poor health.

FACT

Exercise aids the body in many ways, but specifically, it helps the body to release endorphins (a natural body chemical) into the bloodstream. Endorphins help fight stress by calming the body.

Exercise does more than strengthen the body and keep you physically healthier; it also helps relieve stress, decreases the potential for depression, and subsequently, helps you build healthier self-esteem.

Start Simple

An exercise program can begin as a simple, brisk walk down the street. When you begin your program, keep the following tips in mind:

- Choose an activity that you like to do.
- Make exercise a daily routine.
- Do simple things like taking the steps and parking further from stores than usual.
- Exercise with a group of friends to help time pass more quickly.
- Don't do the same thing every day; vary your workout.
- Join a group at a fitness center (aerobics, kickboxing, tai chi, etc.).
- Work in the yard raking leaves or sweeping the sidewalk.
- Purchase an inexpensive treadmill and weight set for your home.

By keeping with your exercise program, you will not have to wait six months or a year to begin to feel and see the results; you'll begin to notice a change in your life in just a few weeks.

Eating Right, Feeling Right

Have you ever eaten a box of Krispy Kreme donuts because you were sad or stressed or because your craving for them was beyond control? If you have, then you know the guilt and anger associated with that binge. You also know how damaging it can be to your self-esteem to have so little control over your eating habits.

Not everyone suffers from an eating disorder, but few people understand the rituals of healthy eating and the effects on your body. The United States has been called the "Healthy Portion Country." We love our buffets, our biggie fries, our king-sized sodas, and our mammoth pastries. No other country on earth serves portions as large as in the United States.

Studies suggest that diets high in fat and sodium, such as the typical American diet, may influence the development of cardiovascular disease, certain cancers, and high blood pressure.

Some people use food as fuel for their bodies, while others use it as a social tool, a celebration tool, a "gotta get outta this funk" tool, or a recovery tool. Many people see food as something you eat, not as something you think about. If you've ever driven while eating, eaten while conducting a meeting, or eaten when doing another chore, you are, in effect, saying to yourself, "nutrition and healthy eating are not that important to me."

People with healthy eating habits have learned to treat food as a drug for the body. Not only do they know what to eat, they know how to eat, when to eat, and where to eat.

Nutritionists vary in their opinions, but overall they agree that breakfast should not be skipped. Many nutritionists suggest that you eat a healthy allowance of protein in the morning to give you energy. Many nutritionists also suggest that you move away from the three-meals-a-day idea and suggest that you consider "grazing"—eating a steady diet of healthy foods throughout the day. They suggest this controls hunger and assists in weight loss. Grazing could consist of eating raisins, grapes, berries, fibers, and some proteins throughout the day in place of unhealthy snacks such as candy, potato chips, or cookies.

Some nutritionists suggest that you eat up to six meals per day: breakfast, midmorning snack, lunch, midafternoon snack, dinner, and a late-night snack—all involving the appropriate healthy foods.

The following tips can help you get started on a healthier food management program:

- Eat a variety of foods.
- Be sure to include fiber and whole grains in your meals.
- Eat moderate portions (meat sizes no larger than a stack of playing cards).
- Drink at least eight to ten cups of water per day.
- Eat a portion of protein, carbohydrates, and vegetables at every meal.
- Plan your shopping list in advance.
- Eat what you really want, but in strict moderation.

Caffeine, Nicotine, Alcohol, and Drugs

Let's get this straight up front. Caffeine, nicotine, and alcohol are drugs; they just happen to be legal. Nicotine is one of the most addictive substances on earth. Caffeine and alcohol are not far behind.

Caffeine, Nicotine, and Alcohol

Caffeine is a controlling stimulant and can have many adverse effects on the body, such as anxiety and restlessness, and can contribute to sleep disorders.

Nicotine is another stimulant and is highly addictive. It acts as a pain reliever and as an anxiety suppressor. It is also poisonous and is used in insecticides. Long-term usage can result in bronchitis, emphysema, ulcers, high blood pressure, and can cause lung, throat, and mouth cancers.

FACT

According to the former Surgeon General C. Everett Koop, "Cigarette smoking is the single most preventable cause of death in the United States."

Alcohol is a depressant. Yes, a depressant! It can increase the risk of liver disease, impair your digestive system, destroy brain cells, cause damage to the central nervous system, and contribute to obesity among other health risks. However, alcohol, especially red wine, in moderation also has some health benefits. In some cases, it has reduced the risk of heart disease.

Other Drugs

No one can tell you what to do with your body. That is your business and your business alone. What you choose to put into it is a choice with which you live. However, in working toward healthier self-esteem, you will need to decide how each particle that goes into your body affects your wellness and your self-image.

Drug addiction is one of the most consuming problems in America today. Whether it is pot or heroine, crack, crank, roofies, GHB, ecstasy, mushrooms, glue, or cocaine, drugs are as easily obtained as a Hershey bar from the convenience store.

Drug abuse has a direct impact on the number of violent crimes, traffic deaths, domestic and child abuse cases, and self-inflicted injuries committed in the United States.

The questions you need to ask are these: What do you want from your body, your emotions, your health, and your life? Can you get it while using controlled substances? How have the substances listed earlier hindered your wellness and self-esteem in the past? Can a controlled substance help you in developing a positive feeling about yourself?

Eliminating harmful elements from your daily habits can assist you in having a healthier lifestyle and, in turn, help you feel better about yourself in general.

Sex-Esteem

When discussing wellness, it is important to take your sex life into consideration. Yes, it is personal and private. However, if you are genuinely interested in your wellness, you can't overlook the fact that sex plays a major role in your health.

One of the most staggering problems in America today is the use of drugs while participating in sex. Study after study have proved that the use of drugs and alcohol lowers your inhibitions and allows you to do things that you might not normally do. Dangerous sexual behavior is included in this. Unsafe sex can result in a plethora of negative events such as unwanted pregnancy, contracting an STD, contracting HIV, immense guilt, fear, self-doubt, and lowered self-esteem.

The way that you feel about yourself determines what types of situations you allow yourself to get involved in. If you have healthy self-esteem and value your body and your health, you will do whatever it takes to protect it. The less you like yourself, the more likely you are to get into situations that are unhealthy or even unsafe.

Good self-esteem includes looking out for your sexual health. You are in control of your body, and you should not let anyone try to convince you otherwise. How good you feel about yourself is directly affected by how you let other people treat you.

Wellness and Your Thoughts

Your thoughts, as previously discussed, play a significant role in how physically, mentally, emotionally, and spiritually fit you are. How many times have you sabotaged yourself simply because you talked yourself into believing that you were not good enough, strong enough, fit enough, or attractive enough? If you continually allow negativity to rule your thoughts, it will begin to rule your life. Think about the last time you walked into the post office (or any customer service driven area) and there was a lengthy line. Your brain automatically and immediately begins to think negatively because of the last line you had to wait in for over an hour. It does not know the difference between this line and the last line. Your automatic response kicks in and helps you bemoan your fate. You begin to think, *Long lines are a way of life for me,* or *I can't ever go anywhere anymore without a line,* or *I've going to draw my first social security check standing in this line!*

What is "thought magnification"?
Thought magnification is when you take a small situation and blow it up in your mind until it becomes an all-consuming event. For example, when someone pulls out in front of you while driving, your automatic thoughts may lead you to believe that this person did it on purpose, that he or she knows you and hates you and is trying to get back at you for something. This is how automatic thoughts can lead to situations such as road rage.

Before you know it, your automatic response and thoughts have ruined your day, ruined the moment, and ruined what could have been a pleasant conversation with the person in front of you. Your thoughts have caused unneeded and unhealthy stress.

It doesn't matter that the line moved quickly and that you only waited five minutes; what matters is that your automatic thought process took over the situation and made it negative. This is how powerful thoughts are to you and your mental and physical health.

If you find yourself seething and fuming about a negative situation because of your automatic thoughts, ask yourself the following questions:

- Are you jumping to conclusions?
- Is the situation really that dire?
- Is it life threatening?
- Are you being irrational?
- Have you magnified the situation in your mind?

- Is it really as bad as it seems?
- In ten years, will anyone know the difference?

Stress Reduction

There is not one certain thing that causes stress in your life. What you view as stressful may be relaxing to another person. Some of the common causes of stress are major life changes, being rushed, doing too many things at one time, your health or a family member's health, changes in your environment, facing and making critical decisions, worries about money and the future, and too many responsibilities. Stress is a major factor in the onset of illness as well as a major factor in job turnover, job dissatisfaction, decreased productivity, and other workplace ills. To more effectively cope with stress, you first have to make a decision that you want to do something about it. The first step is to make a list of what you perceive as stressful situations in your life. Write them down.

After you have identified the things in your life that are causing you stress, choose one or two of them and begin to develop a plan, a goal to remove or decrease that stress from your life. You can begin by taking charge of the stress-causing situation. Can it be changed? Can it be reduced? Look at it. Talk about it. Try to do it differently. Do not ignore it.

Next, try several other techniques that have been proved to reduce overall stress, such as meditation, relaxation tapes, and relaxing music. Talk to your friends and your support network about the situation and get their take on it. Ask them for their advice.

Here are some other suggestions for ways you can decrease stress: exercise; practice positive thinking and looking toward a healthy ending to situations; set a realistic goal for eliminating the stress-causing "thing" from your life; stay away from alcohol, drugs, caffeine, and other drugs that can make the situation worse; and surround yourself with positive, upbeat people.

Remember that you will never alleviate all stress from your life, and a certain degree of stress is actually good for you, but distress is when you begin to damage your body, your mind, and your soul.

Wellness as a Way of Life

Wellness is not a plan for the day, a plan for the week, or even a plan for a few years. Wellness is a total life-altering plan that can help you live longer, live stronger, live more abundantly, live more freely, and most of all, live a life of which you can be proud.

When designing your wellness program, be certain to include activities that work on the well-being of your mind, your thoughts, your body, and your stress level. Work to eliminate stimulants and depressants that can damage your body and your mind. Think about your actions such as drug usage and sexual behavior before you engage, and overall, think about how anything that you eat, drink, or do will affect your self-esteem.

Just as no one else can ever give you self-esteem, no one can ever give you wellness. It is a personal journey that you don't have to travel alone, but it is a journey that you must certainly personalize. If you have been unwell for years, start by seeing a physician. Then, start with small steps. Before you know it, you'll be on your way to a healthier body, mind, and soul.

Activity: Bury the Victim

Directions: It would be difficult to find wellness in your life if you surrender to a victim mentality. Building wellness and healthy self-esteem require that you move beyond "the victim" and begin to live to your fullest capacity. Following, you will find statements that an unhealthy "victim" might use. Read the statement carefully and devise an alternate statement that a person determined to be well and a person with healthy self-esteem might use.

EXAMPLE

Victim: You can't imagine what my childhood was like.

Healthy: *I had a very unhealthy childhood because my father left when I was three. However, I have forgiven him for leaving and I have forgiven my mother for going back to him so many times. I have moved on.*

Activity: Bury the Victim

Victim: I just can't do anything about my weight.

Healthy: _____

_____

_____

Victim: My friends got me hooked on drugs and now there's nothing I can do about it.

Healthy: _____

_____

_____

Victim: Alcoholism runs in my family and I'm just prone to drinking.

Healthy: _____

_____

_____

Victim: I've tried every type of diet and exercise in the book and there is no hope for me.

Healthy: _____

_____

_____

In the spaces following, list two victim statements that you have used. Then, turn those statements into healthy statements.

Victim: _____

_____

_____

Activity: Bury the Victim (continued)

Healthy: _____

_____

_____

Victim: _____

_____

_____

Healthy: _____

_____

_____

How does being a victim suppress your wellness?

_____

_____

_____

_____

How has the "victim mentality" hindered you from living life to the fullest in the past? Why and how?

_____

_____

_____

_____

Select one of your previous statements. Using the goal sheet in the back of the book, develop an action plan to eliminate this statement from your life.

Chapter 12

Expanding Your Comfort Zone

Your comfort zone is a place where you feel secure, safe, and confident. You know what to expect, what it's like. Getting out of your comfort zone can be scary, because you're facing new and different situations that aren't as familiar to you. But expanding your comfort zone is easier than you think, and once you've successfully done it, it will get easier and easier.

Getting Out, Getting On

Susan was filled with fear and anxiety as she picked up the phone. *I've made a thousand calls before,* she thinks to herself, *Why is this one so difficult?* She dials the number, hears the ring, and immediately slams the receiver down. *I can't,* she thinks. *I just can't!*

Susan was trying to call her supervisor to let her know that after years and years of verbal abuse and harassment, she would not be coming into work today, or ever again. Why was the call so difficult? It was so difficult because the call required Susan to move out of her comfort zone and into the unknown.

Comfort zone has two meanings. First, it is a place where we feel secure, safe, and confident. It is a place where we seldom have to worry about embarrassment or criticism. It is a wonderful place to many people. However, the word *comfort* can be confusing. It usually means nice and warm and cozy. *But* when speaking of the comfort zone, this term can also refer to a place that is "comfortable" to us just because we know it, not because we love it. This was the case with Susan.

Her comfort zone was not a comfortable or happy place, but it was a place with which she was familiar and a place where she knew she had a steady paycheck.

A comfort zone can be a prison. If we refuse to move beyond our comfort zone, we never grow. We become stagnant and life ceases to have any surprise or mystery. Stagnation does nothing to help you with self-esteem. You may say, "Every time I try something new, I just fail," or, "As long as I stay put, do only what I'm comfortable with, no one will criticize or yell at me." Those statements may be very true, but is that the essence of life?

What Is Your Comfort Zone?

Picture your comfort zone as a target on a wall. Each circle from the center is wider and encompasses a larger space than the one inside it. This is comparable to the comfort zones you experience in your own life. As a child, it is quite small. Your parents and surroundings protect you, and that is all you know.

As you get older, learn more, and have more life experiences, your comfort zone grows. For some people, the zone stops here because they refuse to be open to possibilities and new experiences. They are afraid to take risks.

FACT

Not taking risks can help you avoid suffering, disappointment, fear, and sorrow, but it also causes you to avoid learning, changing, loving, growing, or really living.

For those who are unafraid of change and new experiences in the world, the zone continues to grow wider and wider. They begin to be more comfortable in more places, around more events, and different people. They continue to expand their zones by travel, meeting new people, learning new things, trying new life experiences, and being unafraid of what others think, unafraid of embarrassment, and by embracing adventures that come only once in a lifetime. They are more comfortable in more places in the world. They are just as at home in Paris or in Des Moines.

Moving Beyond the Zone

Moving beyond your comfort zone requires that you take calculated risks, make uncommon decisions, and put courage before comfort. You don't have to do it all at once; you can take small steps until your zone or circle becomes larger.

Suppose that you are afraid of speaking before a group of people but you need to learn this skill for growth at work. You don't have to run to Carnegie Hall tomorrow. Rather, begin by volunteering to read to children at the library. When that becomes more comfortable, join a Toastmasters' group. When you are comfortable there, volunteer to speak before a small group, perhaps at a PTA meeting or a religious gathering.

Maybe you want to go back to school to earn a degree but you just can't face it because you think you're too old or that you've forgotten everything you learned twenty years ago. Start small. Go to the bookstore or library and check out a few books that interest you on the subject in which you might major.

Read them, study them, and then move on to more intensive materials. Then, go to your local college or university and audit a course. This means that you take it for no credit. You don't have to take the exams, but you can get a taste of what college is going to be like for you.

By taking these small steps, you begin to expand your zone. You begin to become more comfortable in more places in the world. You are able to have conversations with people you never had before. You begin to see the world through eyes that have been opened and expanded. You have more opportunities in this world and your self-esteem begins to flourish.

The Zone and Your Ability

A formal definition of ability is that you have the quality of being able to do something, a physical, mental, financial, or legal activity, and that you have a natural or acquired skill to perform. On a deeper level, ability involves stretching your limits and believing that you have the capacity to perform on some level, either innately or through learning. Ability also means that you are realistic about your competencies and your capacities.

It does not aid your self-esteem to pretend that you are brilliant at something at which you have little or no aptitude. This is not, however, to say that you can't develop an aptitude.

The Case of Stephanie

Ability does not mean that you have to have the talent or skill in hand; it means that you have some aptitude for a task, skill, trade, or vocation and are willing to overcome obstacles to master the talent or skill. Consider Stephanie.

Stephanie was an awful student in high school. She graduated with a D- average. Her SAT score was in the lowest 10 percent. However, due to immense pressure from her parents, Stephanie enrolled in the local community college and began taking basic-skills courses. After a few semesters in college, she knew that she wanted to be a college teacher. Certainly, she did not have the ability at that point in time to achieve the goal, but because she discovered that teaching was in her nature, that she had a true aptitude for explaining things, that it was who she was as a person, she was able to develop the ability to earn three college degrees. She found "her calling" and has been teaching college for fifteen years now. It is something that she "cannot *not* do."

She was lacking in ability, but found what she really wanted to do and worked hard to gain the ability to do it. She had to leave her comfort zone in order to do this. Stephanie reports that this was the single hardest thing that she ever did, but the one thing that truly changed her outlook on life and her image of herself.

Taking Positive Risks

Just as Stephanie had to take positive risks, you will, too. Healthy self-esteem is built on overcoming obstacles and moving beyond what is accepted or ordinary. It is built on overcoming your fears, insecurities, worries, and your own self-imposed limitations.

Most risk experts suggest that risk taking is at the heart of all creative endeavors, is responsible for worldly innovations, and has aided many people in their quest for success.

There is an old story about Thomas Edison. He was at a meeting when someone from a crowd yelled, "Mr. Edison, how does it feel to have failed over four hundred times at making the light bulb work?" Mr. Edison stopped, turned, and answered, "My dear sir, I have never failed at my attempts to make the light bulb work. I have successfully identified four hundred ways that it will not work." Risk taking involves this type of fearless, optimistic thinking.

 "Risk-taking is inherently failure-prone. Otherwise, it would be called sure-thing-taking."

—Tim McMahon

Risk—The Leap of Faith

The economy of risk taking grows more each year. From bungee jumping to level-four white-water rafting to skydiving to snake handling, the business of risk taking is huge. Risk taking does not have to involve imminent physical danger or climbing mountains, but it does involve a hefty degree of personal commitment, a willingness to move beyond what is known, a personal desire to grow, and a belief that you can accept the unknown.

There are several major benefits to risk taking. First, it increases your confidence about what can be done. Second, it can increase your sense of control about your life and help reduce feelings of victimization and helplessness. Next, risk taking decreases your anxieties and fears. It provides practice for, and participation in, decision-making, and finally, risk taking can increase your motivation level. It develops character and courage, extends creativity, boosts confidence, and helps establish a sense of both limitations and possibilities.

"T" Is for Too Wild for Me

The term *T-type personality* has been associated with risk taking for quite some time now. The *T* stands for "thrill seeker." It is used to describe people who love risks and will do almost anything to have adventure and excitement in their lives. Frank Farley, the man responsible for the term, says that the T-type personality will seek thrills in the physical and mental domain. T-type people are outstandingly creative but some with the T-type personality can also be destructive and criminal.

How can this be? The T-type personality must have adventures and thrills. Some may seek this through legal—albeit dangerous and extreme—methods, while others may seek the thrill through illegal activities such as robbery, invasion, and beyond.

While risk taking is a productive and, yes, necessary way to help develop your self-esteem and assist you in moving beyond your comfort zone, it does not have to paralyze you. Risk taking will come in small steps for some and larger steps for others. The most important thing about risk taking is that you must want the outcome *from the risk*. Risk taking is a private issue and others' opinions, judgments, and criticisms should not come into play. Risk taking is your decision.

Risk taking is naturally scary, but it is also one of the most important things you can do to move beyond your zone of comfort, reduce your anxieties about the future, and minimize your worries about stagnation. To take risks means that you are working toward growth and renewal.

Some tips on risk taking, large or small:

- Ignore your critics.
- Know and understand yourself and what you want from the risk.
- Be prepared to take the risk and expect the unexpected.
- Use your goal-setting skills to help you along.
- Don't give up or back down at the first sign of trouble or defeat.
- Realize that not all risks pay off immediately.
- Understand that risk taking is an investment in your future.
- Know that risk taking will help you build healthy self-esteem.

Holding Back the Fears

A major part of risk taking involves overcoming your intimate fears. Fear can be crippling. To some it is a motivator; to others it is a devastating de-motivator. It is the "thing" that keeps them from growing and experiencing life. Fear is one of the major factors in unhealthy self-esteem.

Fear, however, can be good for us as well. Fear can help keep us safe. It keeps us alert and arouses in us the notion that something is wrong, out of place, or askew. It warns us. However, irrational fear can cause us to become reclusive, stagnant, and steal our very desire to live.

The terms *fear* and *anxiety* are often used interchangeably, but they are different. Fear is an emotion of distress. Anxiety is a state of uneasiness about the future. You can also look at them in this light; fear is when you are afraid and you know what you are afraid of. Anxiety is when you are afraid and you don't know what you are afraid of.

Everyone has felt fear at one point or another. It is a normal human response. The fear may have been as simple as asking someone out on a date or as severe as giving a major speech in front of 700 people or handling a reptile.

However, you can overcome your fears by following one simple rule—face them. Yes, that is right; just face it, engage it, tackle it, touch it, get down in the dirt with it, and let it know that it will not rule your life any longer. Sometimes, just experiencing the fear is enough to get you over it.

By facing your fears and acting to overcome them, you begin to change your life in several ways. First, the fear that once paralyzed you is gone. Next, you feel better about yourself, and finally, your self-esteem begins to blossom. Facing your fears is a powerful tool in working toward healthier self-esteem.

When tackling your fears, think about the following:

- Fear is only as deep as you allow it to be.
- Fear must be faced head-on.
- You must own your own fear.
- Fear is not failure.
- Fear is not a mental illness.
- Fear is learned and can be unlearned.
- Fears take time to overcome, even if you go straight at them.
- Sometimes, fears get worse before they get better.

Dreaming Big

You've decided to move out of your comfort zone. You've made a personal commitment to your growth and your future. You've looked at your life and identified your fears and anxieties and are ready to do some risk taking.

One of the first ways to begin your new journey is to answer this question: "If I had *nothing to lose*, what would I do?" That's a powerful question but one that begs an answer.

What is the biggest thing you have ever dreamed of doing? Did you want to be a Broadway star? Did you want to write a bestselling novel? Did you want to be onstage singing a love ballad to thousands of adoring fans? Did you want to climb Mt. Everest? Did you want to become a space shuttle astronaut? What was it? Most importantly, however, why did the dream die? Was it fear? Was it the inability to take a risk? Was it anxiety over the future? What took the dream away?

What is your big dream? What is that innate destiny that has called you for years? As you think about this, remember, big is an opinion. Big is in the eye of the beholder. Big is personal. For the next few moments, stop reading this book. Keep the book open and just turn it upside down in your lap while you think about these questions.

What came to your mind? Before you go any further, write this big dream down. Scribble it on the side of this page, or in the back of the book, or on a paper towel. Just write it down.

As you begin to move beyond your comfort zone and take more chances with your life, take this dream out. Wash it off. Blow off the dust and look at it again. Hold it. Caress it. Feel it. Kiss it. Yell at it if you must, but let this dream become a part of your plan. Let this dream help you move beyond your comfort zone. Let this dream live again.

Motivation to Move On

You've got it all. You have made a decision to move out of your comfort zone. You're facing your fears and tackling your anxieties; you've assessed your abilities, rekindled an old dream, and you're ready to take some risks. Now, all you need is the "oomph," the push, the thrust, and the impetus to move.

Motivation is the force, the energy that drives you to action. Motivation is a compelling asset to reaching your big dream. There are two types of motivation—external and internal.

External Motivation

External motivation is the weakest motivation. It is motivation that comes from others to you. It is the motivation that comes from others pushing you and not you pushing yourself. It is motivation that is driven by external reward or punishments. External motivation is your husband or wife telling or asking you to lose weight. External motivation is your parents making you go to college. External motivation is your boss demanding you attend a meeting you'd rather skip. External motivation is forced and is not altruistic.

Most dreams and goals driven by external motivators are not reached. They are not reached because they are not your own. You did not initiate them. A dream must be *your dream* or it stands the grave likelihood that it will not be reached.

QUESTION?

What is altruistic motivation?
Altruistic motivation is when you are driven to do something for the good of doing it. There are no monetary rewards, no paydays, no congratulations, and no hero's welcome. Altruism is being intrinsically driven to do something good for someone or some cause just because it is the right and just thing to do.

Internal Motivation

Internal motivation is the strongest motivation because it is yours; it comes from your heart and it is driven by your desire to grow. Internal motivation is a force. It is the psychological power that demands that you get up and get out. It is energy unbridled.

You've felt it before. It is that indescribable feeling when you just can't help but do something. It is that unstoppable urge to "take the bull by the horns" and conquer the world. Most dreams, when fueled by internal motivation, are achievable.

Leaving your comfort zone involves the possibility of failure, but it also involves the possibility of winning, growing, succeeding, and changing your life for the better. It is not a simple or easy thing to do, but it is a thing you must do if you want to achieve a healthier sense of self-esteem.

Once you move out of your comfort zone just a little, it becomes almost addictive to find the answer to "What can I do next?" Only *you* will ever be able to answer that question, and that question can only be answered by moving out of your comfort zone.

Activity: Your Legacy

Directions: Sit back in your chair and imagine that you are ninety-five ~~years~~ old today. Play out in your mind all that you would like to do in your life. It may pertain to family, friends, career, travel, relationships, anything—whatever you want your life to be like and what memories you want to have. In the space following, write your obituary as if you died at the age of ninety-five. What do you want it to say? What would you like others to write or say about you? What do you want your legacy to be?

Look at this exercise as a long-term goal statement. Think big, but truthfully. Do you want people to say that you were a grand Broadway actor or a quiet, loving family man or woman? Think about this for a moment and begin to write.

Now that you have written your obituary, take a moment and select one thing written previously that you have not yet accomplished but that you consider the most important "legacy" of your life.

That one thing is _____

Activity: Your Legacy (continued)

Will you have to move out of your comfort zone to accomplish this?

❐ Yes   ❐ No

Why have you not done this thing?

_____

_____

_____

_____

What fears are involved in trying to accomplish this thing?

_____

_____

_____

_____

What risks will you have to take to accomplish this thing?

_____

_____

_____

_____

Using the goal sheet from the back of this book, write a goal that will help you begin bringing this legacy into your life. Good luck.

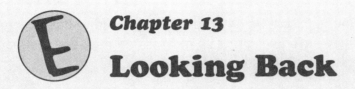

Chapter 13

Looking Back

The past can bring glorious memories or horrendous pain. It can be an exciting journey down memory lane or it can be a road filled with treacherous curves and unforgiving potholes. Either way, the past is perhaps the best teacher you will ever have.

Clearing Up the Past

Self-esteem is a strange thing. It lives in the present, it lives in the future, and yes, it lives in the past. How can it live in the past, you might ask? It lives there because, in many cases, you have forgotten, neglected, or refused to revisit unpleasant past events and they are holding your self-esteem hostage.

Clearing up the past is one way to begin the road to healthier self-esteem. This may include clearing up messes and mistakes you made or forgiving others for their messes and mistakes.

What the Past Means

The past is your history. It is your kindred spirit. It is your mirror. The past is what made you who you are at this very moment. You can refute it, ignore it, lie about it, and pretend to change it, but know the truth; the past is the reason that you are *who* you are and *where* you are at this moment in time.

The past is a compelling entity because it cannot be changed. We can forgive, forget, move on, even erase the memory, but the past is set. It is unalterable. However, just because the past is unalterable, this does not mean that the effects and ramifications of the past on your life and self-esteem are unalterable.

The unchecked past dictates how we act in certain situations, how we love, if we love, how we treat others, and how we view many life-altering challenges. It may be that your frustrations, denials, setbacks, and unfinished goals hang in the balance because of unresolved conflicts and issues from the past.

Conflicts and issues that you had in your childhood and early family relationships that are left unresolved will still exist in current relationships. The issues won't just go away.

Resolving issues from the past can help you alter the state of your self-esteem. It can help you eliminate the weight that has loaded you down for years. Resolution, or at least acknowledgment of the event, can help you move on.

One of the most important things about revisiting the past is the ability to reshape and recast your views of what happened. This is not to suggest that you got it all wrong the first time, but it is to say that with age and more experience, you may look at the unvisited event in a different light and see parts of it that were simply unnoticeable before.

The Danger of Living in the Past

Just as it is painful for many people to look back, some people cannot seem to get out of the past. The past, for them, is better than the present; therefore, they chose to live there instead.

You probably know several people who live in the past. They speak of it often, compare today to yesterday, and have a hard time accepting the fact that the past is never coming again. This can be paralyzing to healthy self-esteem.

At first thought, you may assume that most people who live in the past are older and have retired. This is not the case. Many young people live in the past as well. They are caught up with people and events of which they just can't seem to let go.

It is perfectly fine, even recommended, that you revisit your past to clear up unfinished business and even to remember and bask in the good times, but living there, as a rule, is unhealthy.

Jan loved her job as much as life itself it seemed. She was productive, admired, and had moved through the ranks with impressive speed. She was touted as being "the next CEO." Everything was working in her favor. She remembers vividly the Wednesday evening that her husband came home and broke the news: "I've been transferred." Bill was a successful banking executive and his company wanted to make him a regional vice president. After much discussion, Jan and Bill decided that it was a great offer that they could not turn down. Jan knew that she could easily find another job in her field of insurance.

Shortly after they moved, Jan began to look for employment. Finding the right job, or any job for that matter, was much more difficult than she had imagined. After several months, she accepted a position as an entry-level manager in a local insurance office.

"Living in the past is a dull and lonely business; looking back strains the neck muscles, causes you to bump into people not going your way."

—Edna Ferber

Jan was not passionate about the job, but it offered her the opportunity to be out of the house and on a career track again. Jan saw many problems with the local office and set out to correct them. One day, Jan overheard her coworkers talking about her. "That lady had better wake up and realize that she is just a manager, not the CEO," one said to the other. "Yeah, I'm so tired of hearing about how they did it back in Oakland."

Jan was devastated. She began to realize just how much of the past she had brought with her. Here skills and talents were still great, but she had failed to move beyond her past position. She realized that she was still living in her old job and working toward goals that were tied to her past position. She revisited her comments to her current peers and was shocked to remember how many times she had said, "Back in Oakland," or "We used to do it this way," or "When I was vice president . . ."

Running from the Past

Just as some people aid their unhealthy self-esteem by choosing to live in the past, others scamper to the other side. They choose to run from the past and all of the memories and pain it brings. Just as living in that past can harm you, running from it can, too.

Running away from things in your past that scared you, angered you, or caused you emotional distress will never bring you peace. The only way that the fear, anger, and distress can disappear is to revisit the situation and try to bring some clarity to the "now."

Unfinished Business

Think for a moment about your past. Do you have any unfinished business that is looming over you like a dark cloud? It may be something from last week, last year, or last decade. Having unfinished business is like leaving a movie before it is over; you never know the ending. You never know who survives or thrives.

Unfinished business can involve relationships, unfulfilled commitments, fragmented projects, lingering emotional problems, anger, fear, and guilt to name a few. Perhaps the most serious of unfinished business is that of tattered relationships left to decay. This can be one of the most serious types of unfinished business because it may be the cause of some of the other negative feelings you have from the past. Frayed relationships can involve those of old lovers, husbands, wives, friends, coworkers, partners, or even distant acquaintances. They can exist because of your neglect or the neglect of the other person.

Think back on a past relationship that just dissipated and you (or the other person) did nothing to bring the relationship to closure. The relationship could have been damaged over an argument, a misunderstanding, or simply because of geography or time.

QUESTION?

Why do relationships end?
Relationships end for a variety of reasons. Sometimes it is as simple as distance. Others end for more major reasons such as ethical and moral issues, value conflicts, miscommunication, no communication, or poor communication. Sometimes they end because the relationship has run its course and neither party has anything left to offer the other person.

Bringing closure to this unfinished relationship does not necessarily mean that you have to write the person, call them, or meet with them (although you may choose to, and in *some cases* you may have to); it means that you are going to take the necessary steps to bring this relationship to its natural end.

It can happen as simply as forgiving them in the privacy of your own mind and soul, or sending them an apology for the wrongs you committed. Regardless, the unfinished business of relationships can continue to cause damage to your self-esteem.

The Case of Mattie and Bob

Mattie and Bob worked at the same company. They did not work for each other or under the same supervisor, but they had to depend on each other because one portion of their jobs was tied together. Mattie performed a task that Bob relied on to get his job done. Over the course of time, the relationship became very confrontational and there was seldom a pleasant word exchanged between the two.

After a few years, Bob decided to leave the company. A few days before he left, he and Mattie had the worst verbal confrontation in all of their years together. Bob made some horrific comments to her and, in turn, she opened the floodgates as well.

Three years after Bob left the company, he still had issues with Mattie and that last conversation. He was surprised at the guilt he felt for having been so nasty and rude to her. The feeling followed him for another two years. Finally, five years later, Bob decided to write Mattie a letter and apologize for his behavior, his words, and for leaving the relationship in such a condition. He mailed the letter and did not hear anything back from Mattie.

Several months passed, and one day Bob went to the mailbox and noticed a familiar address, that of his old place of employment. He opened the letter to find a reply from Mattie.

In the letter she stated that she knew that they had not always seen eye-to-eye, but that she thought their relationship had been okay. Further, she confided in Bob that she did not even remember the verbal confrontation, but appreciated his honesty—and his apology. She further confided in him that the reason she had not responded was because she was in such a state of shock over getting the letter in the first place. She really did not know what to say.

They have never corresponded again, but with one simple letter, Bob was able to clear up this unfinished business, clear his conscience, make

Mattie's day, and put his soul at rest over this one issue.

Forgiveness is one of the many ways that you can assist in the development of your self-esteem. Forgiveness allows you to move beyond the anger and guilt and replace those feelings with peace and closure.

> "Anger makes you smaller, while forgiveness forces you to grow beyond what you were."
>
> —Cherie Carter-Scott

Yourself in the Past

While cleaning out the closets of past relationships, think about one more relationship—your relationship with yourself. How have your treated yourself in the past? Have you loved yourself? Have you respected you? Have you treated yourself as well as you've treated others?

There comes a time, *and it is now,* that you will need to apologize to yourself in order to move on. If you are truly committed to cleaning up the past, start with cleaning out your own skeletons and putting them to rest.

When is the last time you had a conversation with yourself about forgiveness? Has it ever happened? Have you ever written yourself a note just to say, "I'm sorry that I've treated you badly."

You are involved in your own past. You are as much a part of your history as your parents, your teachers, your siblings, your friends, and your neighbors. If you've made a commitment to forgive them, you will not be able to fulfill that commitment until you forgive yourself.

Sit quietly for a moment, put this book down, and have a conversation with yourself about the past, the now, and the future.

Learning from Mistakes

Mistakes can be looked upon in two ways. First, they can be looked at with negativity and disgust. They can be seen as stupid errors in judgment and failed attempts at triumph. Mistakes can also be looked upon as teachers, guides, and tutors for the future. Mistakes do not have to be brandings of shame and disgust; they can be looked upon optimistically as another chance at triumph.

If you are alive, you have two choices; you can sink in sadness over the mistake or you can rise up and rejoice that you lived through it. There is absolutely nothing wrong with saying to yourself and others, "Wow, I really flubbed up!"

"The only people who make no mistakes are dead people. I saw a man last week who has not made a mistake in four thousand years. He was a mummy in the Egyptian department of the British Museum."

—H. L. Wayland

Mistakes are proof that you are taking risks and not just sitting around waiting for the world to bring you something. Mistakes mean that you had a plan of some measure and you were working toward it. Yes, you may have fallen short, but at least you were doing something.

The True Cost of Mistakes

Think of the last time that you made a major mistake. Was it personal, professional, financial, educational, spiritual, health related? What was the cost of this mistake? What was the price (real or symbolic) that you paid for this mistake? What lessons did you learn?

Sometimes the costs are astronomical and involve real money. Sometimes the costs are not in dollars, but in pain, agony, suffering, and defeat. The cost of a mistake is easier to bear when you understand the lessons that come from it.

The Case of Rene

Rene thought his life was over. He had made the biggest mistake of his thirty years; he cheated on his wife. Looking back, he can scarcely even remember why it happened, but the mistake cost him dearly.

He now pays over $500 per month in alimony, is divorced, lives in a much smaller home due to finances, and most importantly, lost his soul mate. Not only did he lose his soul mate, he lost most of the friends that they had in common. He can't go to certain places for fear of running into them and having to face the shame. His loneliness is monumental and the pain of what he did to another human being, a human being that he loved, is fierce.

You may be asking, what good could come out of this mess? That mistake cost him his wife, his home, his livelihood, his dignity, his friends, and his way of life. What else could he lose because of this mistake? He's finished.

Not quite. This mistake changed his life. It changed the core of who Rene is as a person. This one catastrophic event in his history made a profound change in the way Rene looks at life, people, money, commitment, relationships, love, and endurance.

The real cost of a mistake is not making the error, but failing to learn and grow from it.

Embracing the Lessons

As you look back and begin to examine your life more closely, hopefully, you have decided that it is time to break up with the past and move on. Consider the following tips when embarking on this journey:

- Face every day as a new beginning.
- Draw on past experiences, but face every challenge as if it is brand new.
- Consciously think about your language and the terms you use.
- Plan ahead instead of looking back.
- Be aware of today; live in the "now."
- Make a list of the things you truly, honestly, want from "now."
- Remain open to change and transformation.
- Be willing to forgive others and yourself.

Clearing up the past can be one of the most important gifts that you give yourself in your quest for healthy self-esteem. The past, and all of the mistakes that go with it, are wonderful teachers. They are invaluable as you live in the moment and plan your future. But you can't live there, you can't go back, and you can't run. The best you can do is to atone your mistakes, learn from them, enjoy your successes, and realize that every second that passes becomes you past.

Activity: Digging Up Bones

Directions: In this exercise you will do two things. First, think about a person in your past who hurt you deeply. Someone who "did you wrong," whether deliberately or not; someone whom you have not forgiven for this act. Next, think of someone whom you hurt in the past, deliberately or not, and have never apologized to.

The person who hurt me is ....

What did this person do?

....

....

....

Why have you not forgiven her or him?

....

....

....

....

How could forgiving this person help you let go of the feelings you have about her or him?

....

....

....

....

Activity: Digging Up Bones

How could forgiving this person help your self-esteem?

_____

_____

_____

_____

The person that I hurt is _____

What did you do to this person?

_____

_____

_____

_____

Why have you not apologized to this person?

_____

_____

_____

_____

How could apologizing to this person help you let go of the feelings you have about the situation?

_____

_____

_____

How could apologizing to this person help your self-esteem?

_____

_____

_____

Now for the hard part, by letter, phone, e-mail, or in person, contact these two people and begin to clear up the past. Only you can make this decision and only you can make the effort. Good luck.

Chapter 14

E

Developing a Philosophy of Life

Why are you here? Why does your life matter? What is your purpose? Why do you exist? What are you here to do? Do you have the answers to these questions? Philosophers, religious leaders, education masters, and psychics have tried to answer these questions for centuries. Figuring out your own answers to these questions is important to healthy self-esteem.

What Is Your Purpose?

What are you looking for in these pages? Is your life's purpose here? Is it in your heart? Your family? Your home? Can it be found at all? Many experts on this topic agree that your purpose has been with you from the moment of conception. They feel that your purpose is as innate as your hair color or the hue of your skin.

Your purpose has been with you all along. If you have not found it, it is because you have not taken the time to listen to it. You have not taken the energy required to find "true self." Does your "true self" wait quietly, just beneath the skin? Is it there, waiting for you to caress it and bring it forward?

Your life's purpose plays a grand role in your quest for healthy self-esteem. It can point you in the direction of your dreams and goals, it is a guiding force in the way you behave toward others and yourself, and it is a determining factor in the work you do in this world.

Knowing What You Need

Finding your purpose in life may rest in that one question: What do you need—not what do you want, but what do you need? Your needs are quite powerful and they may hold the key to helping you discover your purpose.

There is a difference between need and want. To need is to require, to want is to desire something greatly. Needs are stronger than wants. Many people confuse the two.

Needs involve things that are required to actually help you live, but they also involve things that are required to help you live well. Psychologist Abraham Maslow identified several levels of needs in every human, including basic needs such as air, water, safety, love, and esteem, higher-level intellectual needs, and finally, the need for self-actualization or self-fulfillment.

So, what do you really need in your life? Do you need happiness? Do you need passion? Do you need love? Do you need caffeine? Do you need to have purpose?

"If you deliberately plan to be less than you are capable of being, then I want to warn you that you'll be deeply unhappy the rest of your life."

—Abraham Maslow

Stop reading for a moment and make two lists—one list should be the things you need to actually *survive,* and the other list should involve things you need to live *in true self.* Do not include wants. Make your list now.

Survival and True Self

Was that a hard task? Look at your list and see if there are any "wants" listed? Can you tell the difference? If you have listed things like a new car, a luxurious home, a supercomputer, you are listing "wants" instead of needs.

If your needs list for survival includes things like food, shelter, clothing, safety, and some money, you are on the right track. If your needs list for "true self" includes things like family, friends, passion, and intimacy, you are on the right track.

What is the lowest common denominator in the list of "true self" needs? It is people. So, it can be said that a part of your needs for "true self" is an association with people.

Take a moment and think about your list of needs for "true self." After you review your list, look for the common denominators such as people, power, the need to be outdoors, the need to have creative access, or the need to feel needed. This will help you begin to define and refine your purpose.

The Case of Gloria

Gloria felt lost, absolutely lost. She felt alone, empty, and unfulfilled in her home life, her career, and in her heart. She knew that her life was not in sync with her purpose, but she did not know what her purpose really was. She had tried to find her purpose while in college. She majored in office administration and had become a very successful executive assistant. While the people she worked with loved how she did her job, she did not love her career.

She sat down one weekend and tried to think about the things in her life that brought her joy. She listed her friends, her two cats, food, music, going to the movies, and reading. But she wondered how her purpose could be found in a hot dog and *Gone With the Wind*. She began to list the things that she really needed in her life. Her list revealed that she needed to feel loved and give love, she needed to feel safe, both in terms of physical safety and in terms of monetary safety, and she listed that she needed her two pets.

That was a very strange and unexpected thing for her to find on her list. She knew that she loved her pets and cared for them deeply, but she never dreamed that pets would appear on an honest list of basic "true self" needs. But there they were, larger than life.

What does this mean, she thought? So, she began to explore further and realized that she not only loved her pets dearly, but that she had always loved others' pets as well. She thought back across her life and realized that she had always taken in stray cats and dogs, and on occasion, she had volunteered to pet sit for friends going out of town.

"Happiness is the meaning and the purpose, the whole aim and end of human existence."

—Aristotle

She made a decision to take a step. She went to the computer, created several flyers and some business cards, and decided that on Monday, she would begin to let people know that she was available to "pet sit" on a limited basis. She wondered if she would enjoy it as much as she had in the past. She knew that she had the skills, knowledge, and desire to do it, but she wondered if this new part-time job would bring her joy.

She booked a few jobs and found that she was in love with being around animals and caring for them in their owner's absence. She was giving love and feeling love. She began to book more sitting jobs in the early mornings, walks during lunch, and feeding in the evening. She could not believe how much elation this had brought to her life.

Her friends could not believe it either and thought that she had gone overboard with the number of bookings. She knew that she had not. She knew that bigger things were on the horizon. She knew that in one month, she would quit her job and become a professional pet sitter. She had found her passion, her calling, and her joy. There it was written on a strange little list during a weekend of soul-searching. There it was, in the face of her two cats, her purpose.

Pursuing What You Want

Wants are completely different from needs. Wants, however, can play a part in your search for purpose in life. Wants do not have the innate power of needs, but they can be strong. Wants do not carry the profound truth that needs carry, but they can be a guiding force.

On the list that you created earlier, what were some of the wants that you listed? Were they things such as respect, pride, admiration, acceptance, happiness, and inner peace? Sometimes, our wants come from what we have experienced and from what we enjoy doing. Perhaps your list included things such as, "I want to watch TV more, sleep late, enjoy chocolate, or go to more sporting events."

As you try to find your purpose, consider your wants as well as your needs, but understand that your wants are not a part of your true self; they are learned.

Mick was trained as a chef. He taught at a local university and catered many outside functions. He enjoyed his work and earned a fine living for himself and his family. However, Mick wanted something else. He wanted to work for himself. He did not need to do it—that is to say that neither his life nor livelihood depended on it—but he wanted to do it.

Mick set out to learn how he might become self-employed. He attended seminars on small business management and talked to many people who owned their own businesses.

He surprised most people when he announced that he was starting his own business. The surprise was not so much that he was venturing out on his own, but that he was not opening a café or diner as everyone thought he would. Mick decided that those two operations would require much more of his time than he was willing to give, even to his own business. Mick studied his city, studied what businesses were effective, studied what people seemed to need and lack, and lastly, studied how he wanted to work. After all, the reason for starting his own business was not to be a slave to it, but the master of it. Mick found that a need existed to have private and home association clubhouses serviced and maintained. He found that the few people who performed the service were not very effective, and he knew that he could be.

FACT

To have healthy self-esteem, you must feel safe in your environment, have a connection to a community of people, feel as if you can "make it on your own," and have a strong sense of direction in your life.

He printed his own advertising materials, traveled to meet with association and club managers, and today, his business brings in over $200,000 per year. The most interesting thing is that Mick based his decision on what he wanted and, in turn, what helps other people; found his purpose; and still has four days off per week to volunteer to cook for a local homeless shelter.

Purpose can also be found in want!

Why Are You Here?

Do you sit around thinking of an answer to this question on a daily basis? Probably not. It is not a question that many people ponder on a daily or even yearly basis, but it is a question that needs to be examined when searching for purpose.

Earlier, the ancient Sanskrit word *dharma* was mentioned. Dharma means purpose in life. According to this word, you have a rare gift, a unique talent, and an uncommon way of bringing that gift to life.

Have you discovered your dharma? Have you given thought to why you are here? Discovering your gifts can very well lead you to your purpose, which in turn can lead you to healthier self-esteem.

Ask yourself a few questions. What are your unique talents? What are your unique abilities? What do you do that you don't see anyone else doing? What can you do that you see others doing but not as well as you do? What aptitudes and powers do you have that you simply don't see exercised every day? Answering these questions can help you find your purpose.

Let's turn this around for a moment and look at it from the negative side. Sometimes, finding your purpose, and indeed your esteem, comes from looking at what you do not do well, and then changing your actions accordingly.

"Everyone has a purpose in life . . . a unique gift or special talent to give others. And when we blend this unique talent with service to others, we experience the ecstasy and exultation of our own spirit, which is the ultimate goal of all goals."

—Deepak Chopra

So, what is it that you do on a daily basis that you do not do very well? What do you do on a daily basis that you do not enjoy doing? What do you do that does not bring you joy? What do you do that does not serve humanity and make the world a better place?

Answering those questions can help you better identify the things that you do well, enjoy doing, and the things that bring goodness into the world.

Where Are You Going?

A plan for life is important, but few people ever take the time to develop a real plan for getting to where they want to be. This plan can assist you in finding your purpose in life. Without a plan, the purpose may never come to fruition. As you think about what you love to do, want to do, and need to do with your life, think about where you want to do it, with whom you want to do it, and how you want to dress while you're doing it.

That may sound crazy, but think about it for a moment. If you detest suits and ties and scarves, will you ever be happy in a vocation that requires that you wear them on a daily basis? If you love to work indoors in the cool air-conditioned comforts of an office, but your vocation requires that you work on a tar roof somewhere, will you be happy?

A plan for purposeful living can help you see further down the road. It can help you look into the nuts and bolts of your life's work and make choices that are appropriate for you.

As you consider your purpose in vocation, think about the following:

- Do you prefer physical or mental work?
- Is it important to you to make a lot of money?
- Where do you want to live?
- Do you want to travel?
- How do you want to dress?
- What do you value in life?
- What are your motivators?
- What are your innate skills and talents?

Considering these questions can help you find out where you are going and assist you in developing a plan for purposeful living.

Getting There

Most books on motivation, leadership, change, personal effectiveness, and success suggest that successful people get to where they are by having a plan and having the help of others. How are you going to get to the point where you are living purposefully and living with healthy self-esteem? How are you going to find your purpose?

A Starting Point

"I'm not sure how to begin looking for my purpose," you might say. "I don't have a clue as to how to begin." The key to beginning is to simply begin. That sounds simple, but sometimes the first step is the most paralyzing step. To begin on your journey, start! That's right, get up out of the chair and take a symbolic step right now. As you take the step, say to yourself, "Today, I'm changing. Today, I begin living purposefully." Put this book down and do it.

See, that was not so hard—strange maybe, but not hard. You have taken the first symbolic step and now you can take the first real step to finding your purpose in life.

Mental Work

Mental preparation is an important step in beginning your journey. You will need to capture the power of your desires to make this work. You will need to tell yourself that the journey is going to be worth the trip. You will need to convince yourself that if others are not supporting you, they will not be invited on the journey. Mental preparation is essential in discovering and living your purpose.

Beat the Clock

Procrastination can be a huge problem in discovering and living your purpose. Many people say, "I'll begin tomorrow." For those people, tomorrow comes, but means nothing.

Some people seem to think that others have more time than they do, but that is a fallacy. We all have 24 hours a day, 168 hours a week, an average of 730 hours a month, and 8,760 hours a year—no more, no less. Time does not discriminate.

The reason it seems that others have more time is that they have learned to manage it better and they have learned that procrastination is the death of plans.

If you link your time management plan with your goals, you will see what an important correlation exists between the two. Without a commitment of time, your life goals will not be reached, your purpose will not be found, and your esteem will not be healthier.

Consider the following tips when planning time to find your purpose and change your life:

- Make a list and prioritize the list daily.
- Don't overbook your life with meaningless work.
- Plan time for your improvement before anything else.
- Plan time for solitude and reflection.
- Plan time for exploration and discovery.

Focus

For a moment, forget safety, forget fear, forget what others think, forget what happened in the past, forget your parents, your husband, your wife, your friends, your doubts, your inabilities, your responsibility— forget!

Let them go for a moment and focus on *one thing*. What would your life be like if you found your purpose and began to live it? How would your life change? What could you accomplish for yourself and humankind? What greatness would come to you? How would your self-esteem be affected? Focus on that one question and let go of anything holding you back.

Expect

Few people expect greatness. Few people expect abundance. Few people actually expect happiness, but you can buck the trend and expect great things.

So often, you focus on scarcity, not plenty. You focus on unhappiness, not joy. You focus on failure, not success. You focus on pain, not pleasure. You focus on aimlessness, not purpose. Today it is time to focus and look for what is rightfully yours, your purpose and mission in life.

Finding your purpose may not be easy, but it will be one of the most rewarding gifts you ever give yourself. If you truly examine your needs, your wants, your desire, examine your perception of why you were put here, where you want to go, how you want to get there, and who you want to be when you get there, purpose can be yours.

Activity: What Is Different?

Directions: This activity seems simple, but it is not. It may remind you of the old Jimmy Stewart movie *It's a Wonderful Life.*

Answer this one question: What is different because you are living? List at least ten things.

_____

_____

_____

_____

_____

_____

_____

_____

What is the most surprising thing on your list?

_____

_____

_____

_____

Why?

_____

_____

_____

_____

_____

Activity: What Is Different? (continued)

How is this item important to your Purpose in Life?

How is this item important to your self-esteem?

Chapter 15

Dealing with Contaminated People

Contaminated! The term itself conjures up images of something abominable, dirty, toxic, unhealthy, impure, corrupt, or vile. Contaminated people can conjure up the same images. If you've ever had one in your life, you know the damage such a person can do.

Identifying Contaminated People in Your Life

What makes certain people contaminated? What could they have done to be associated with words like toxic, abominable, and vile? They are associated with everything from backstabbing to betrayal, from hurt to anger, from causing emotional distress to lying. They can be your family, your coworkers, your friends, and *yes*, they can be your spouse or partner.

Do you have one in your life? How can you tell if a person is contaminated? Ask yourself the following questions:

- Does he put you in a bad mood?
- Do you feel emotionally numb or abused after being with her?
- Do you feel "dirty" after being with him?
- Do you feel tense, nervous, angry, or irritable around her?
- Does he make you feel disgusted?
- Does she sabotage you or herself?
- Is the person condescending, rude, or offensive to you?
- Do you fantasize about seeing them suffer or "pay"?

Contaminated people do not have to be contaminated around everyone. You may find that the person who is a contamination to your life is not a contamination to another person's life. This does not mean that the person is not contaminated to you.

Understand from the onset: Contaminated people do nothing to help you build your self-esteem. Their number one goal is to make you feel as badly about yourself as they feel about themselves.

Why Are People Contaminated?

People turn vile, ugly, mean, and corrupt for a variety of reasons. You never know what causes them to turn unless you have had a chance to walk in their shoes.

They could have been contaminated for years and years from events stemming from their childhood. They could have suffered a major loss from which they were never able to recover. They may have (and probably do have) significantly low, unhealthy self-esteem. They may have to treat others badly just so they can feel better about themselves.

Contaminated people feed off of jealousy. They see that you have something, physically, emotionally, financially, or socially; and their goal is to take that "thing" from you. They can't stand to see other people have positive possessions in their lives.

Types of Contaminants (A Baker's Dozen)

Contaminated people do not come in just one shape or size, they are many, they are varied, and they are armed with tricks. Contaminated people are out for the kill. They do not care about your desires, your dreams, and they certainly don't care about your feelings.

If contaminated people came in one or two forms, it would be easier for you to recognize them. It would be easier for you to rid them from your life. No such luck.

"If you do not tell the truth about yourself, you cannot tell it about other people."

—Virginia Woolf

The Two-Faced Foe

You know them, oh, do you know them. They are lovely to your face, supportive, encouraging, and helpful—until you turn your back. Then they go in for the kill. They talk about you to anyone who will give them an ear, even if you have given them no reason to soil your reputation. They will tell you one thing to your face and change the story quicker than lightning. The two-faced foe is dangerous because he or she can make you believe that you are at fault.

The Mean Manipulator

When you're around them, you feel as muddled as a jigsaw puzzle and Lincoln Logs mixed together. You don't know what is true or false, what is right or wrong, and what is real or fantasy. They like it that way. They use you and can turn any situation in their favor, usually at your expense. They seem on the up-and-up at times, but they are sly and coy and work late into the night thinking of ways to get something for nothing. They are dangerous because they can steal your time, energy, and talent and use it to their benefit.

The Laid-Back Liar

They should be in show business because they are so good at faking it and telling stories that are not true. The Laid-Back Liar can, and will, look you straight in the face and pretend that all is well and before you know it, you're a victim. You're a victim of receiving a lie, or you're a victim of a lie. Either way, the liar uses half-truths, untruths, and just plain false information to make the world slant his way. The liar is dangerous because he or she can make your life miserable and, in some instances, get you fired, cause you to lose friends, and produce havoc in your everyday life.

The Negative Pessimist

Could it be worse? Well, actually, yes! It can—and is—and it is never going to get any better! Just spend one hour in the presence of the Negative Pessimist and you'll see how gloomy and dark the universe can be. The pessimist is always negative and never finds the bright spot in anything. He or she can look at the most positive situation that has happened in years and turn it into doom instantaneously. The Negative Pessimist is dangerous because he or she can spread the feeling of darkness around, and you can catch it.

The Sexist, Racist, Ageist, Homophobic, Ethnocentrist

You know them. They are the ones who tell the off-color joke at the water cooler and then follow it up with, "You know I'm just kidding."

They never are. Secretly, they are "against" anyone not like them. They are dangerous because they can, and do, spread their venom around, usually cloaked as humor or someone else's opinion.

The Amoral Abomination

Nothing is sacred. The Amoral Abomination would sell the rubber tip off his or her grandmother's cane if it meant getting ahead or keeping himself out of trouble. They have no scruples, no values, no ethical guidelines, and no center of decent living. They are dangerous because they are weak and will use you in any way possible, morally or immorally, to get what they want.

"Patience in a moment of anger can save you a thousand days of pain."

—Chinese proverb

The Best Buddy Backstabber

With friends like these . . . you know the rest. He or she is your friend until something goes wrong. He or she will literally and figuratively stick a knife in your back and then swear that someone else was at fault. They work to undermine your progress and success. They are dangerous to you because of their high degree of betrayal.

The Mad, Angry Hatter

They are prone to temper fits, outbursts, and even physical rage. One moment things are fine and the next instant, they are in a violent rage. They not only have a temper, but they are temperamental. You never know what sets them off. One day they are fine with X and the next day, X is the thing that causes them to erupt. They are dangerous because of the physical violence and the threat they cause.

The Verbally Abusive, Demeaning Devil

We all know that you do not have to yell and scream to be verbally abusive. The abuse can come from a single, quiet word, but it can also come from uncontrollable rants. It can be as blatant as, "You're the stupidest person with whom I've ever worked," to something as subtle as, "You know, you almost did well with that presentation this afternoon." They are dangerous because if you are around them long enough, they can harm your self-esteem and make you doubt your own abilities.

The Jealous Joker

Jealously is at the heart of contaminated people. You have something that they want, and usually they want it so badly, they will destroy you in order to get it, or at least make sure you do not have it. They never understand that if they would work toward the goal, they might get it, too. They never see the work of others; they only see what others have and that drives them to blindness. They are not supportive of your efforts to better yourself. They are dangerous because they use almost any tactic in the book to get what they want.

The Cowardly Creep

This is the person that you may not have initially seen as contaminated because they are not bad or vindictive, they simply stand for nothing. They are contaminated because you can't count on them for anything. You can't rely on their constructive criticism, their judgment, or their advice because it changes with the wind. They are dangerous because they do not have enough courage to defend themselves or you.

"To avoid criticism, do nothing, say nothing, be nothing."

—Elbert Hubbard

The Superior Sick-O

No one on the earth, or in the universe for that matter, is better at anything than them. If you have a new Cadillac, they have a new Bentley. If you got a promotion at work to vice president, they were promoted to CEO. If you plant a new flower garden, they buy a flower shop. They always see themselves as better, more important, smarter, richer, and more worthy than you. They are dangerous because they can make you feel like you have to compete with them or make you feel as if you'll never measure up.

The Expert at Everything

They have a lot in common with the Superior Sick-O. Instead of having everything, they know everything. From brain surgery to nuclear rocketry, they are experts. You've probable worked with one or two of them over the years. Nothing you do, even if it is excellent, is as good as they could have done it. They are dangerous because if you are around them long enough, you will stop trying to be creative and ingenious because it never matters to the expert.

If you are involved with one or more of the types of people I've described, it is time to identify how they are contaminating your life and what steps you need to confront them or eliminate them from your life.

Confronting Contaminated People

If you have identified contaminated people in your life, it is time for you to do something about it. As you begin this journey, you must understand that you will never be able to change another human being. You can only change yourself. You can help others with advice and support, but you will never change another person.

The first step in confronting the contaminated person is to talk to them. Let them know that the relationship is not working and that things have to improve. It can be dangerous and unhealthy to give ultimatums at this point, but you need to be firm in your resolve to make your life better. Explain to them in detail just how you feel about the way they treat you. Let them know that you are suffering as a result of their attitudes, abuse, verbiage, or hostility.

Next, give them a chance to talk. Listen to them. It may be that they see you as the contaminated person in the relationship and there has been a misunderstanding. Listening is sometimes the best way to assess a situation.

Most people fail to realize that just communicating with a person in need can relieve suffering. The power of simply listening to a person in pain is monumental in the healing process. Not only does the person who is suffering benefit, you will, too.

When confronting the person, try to leave your emotions out of the picture, as they will only cloud the issues and make it harder for you to do the work that needs to be done.

Avoid yelling, screaming, demeaning language, and most of all, avoid any type of violence or altercation. If you see that the situation is becoming unproductive, leave, hang up the phone, get out of the chat room, and just leave. Nothing good will come from a negative confrontation. This may be the signal you need to move on.

Giving Them a Second Chance

After you have confronted the contaminated person, you will have to make the decision whether to give the relationship another chance. That decision should be yours alone. If they do not want another chance, move on. If you do not want another chance, move on. However, if you and the other party are willing to work—and it is work—then there is the possibility that the relationship with this person can be salvaged.

Before you go down this road, ask yourself the following questions:

- Do you truthfully see the relationship getting better?
- Why is the relationship worth saving?
- What does the relationship bring to your life?

- Can you honestly forgive the other person and move on?
- Will you always have lingering doubts about the other person?
- Can you ever trust the other person again?
- Do you foresee any future joy or happiness with the other person?
- Do all parties involved (direct and extended) support the attempted restoration?

If you have a positive feeling about these questions, it may be advantageous to move in the direction of restoration. As you move forward, the following suggestions can help you.

Communication

There are several methods to resolving conflict in relationships. The first step, of course, is to keep the lines of two-way communication open. This means that both parties will listen and speak. Few things will be accomplished if this does not happen.

Why is listening so important? Listening is a basic survival skill for any animal, humans included. Recognizing the difference between listening and hearing is essential to positive relationships. Without the skill of purposeful listening, most communication is shattered.

Communication can be the single most important step in identifying contaminated people, confronting contaminated people, restoring and refining relationships that were previously contaminated, or eliminating contaminated people from your life.

"I'd rather have people hate me for who I am than love me for who I am not."

—Unknown

Conflict and Issue Resolution

Now that you have decided on a second chance, a new start, and the lines of communication are open, you will need to understand that this will not be enough. If it were enough, you probably would not be in a contaminated relationship to begin with.

Second chances are most successful if you have a plan to resolve the issues that brought you to the mat in the first place. Consider the following steps:

- Identify all the problems involved.
- Find the root or central problem.
- Do not proceed until you have found the real problem.
- Discuss or even brainstorm solutions to the central problem.
- Talk about which solutions you want to try.
- Agree on which solution(s) you wish to try together.
- Test the solution(s) and establish a timeline for reviewing how things are going.

If you keep the lines of communication open and truly work to clean up the contaminated situation, there is a possibility that things will get better. Again, it depends on how much each person is willing to give and just how much effort, energy, and emotional toil you are willing to expend.

Eliminating Contaminated People

There are contaminated relationships that will not be restored. There are people that are so damaging to you and your self-esteem that you will have no choice but to eliminate them from your life.

One of the first personal characteristics that you will need to bring forward is assertiveness. Not aggression, but assertiveness. Assertiveness is when you hold tight to your decisions and needs. Assertiveness is when you defend your position with confidence and positive comments. Aggression is when you verbally or physically attack the other person. Aggression is never as effective as assertiveness.

When ending a contaminated relationship, try to avoid confrontations. However, do not avoid the contaminated person or the work that needs to be done. You may need to use a variety of methods to bring the relationships to closure, such as letters, phone, fax, e-mail, or in person. But do not avoid ending the relationship. Without closure, the contaminated person still has control over your life.

Some relationships are worth saving. They may be damaged, tattered, torn, and even broken beyond recognition, but some are definitely worth saving. Others are not. Sometimes love is not enough to save a relationship. Sometimes deep, committed friendship is not enough to save a relationship, but sometimes a simple phone call, five minutes of intense listening, or simply admitting that relationships transform takes the relationship to a healthier place. Only you can judge which relationships are worth saving.

Not every conflict can, or will, be resolved. Be extremely cautious of trying to resolve conflicts with people who are prone to anger and physical violence. You may need to have other people present when dealing with this type of contaminated person.

Activity: The Stupidest Person I Know

Directions: Pretend that a person you consider contaminated or not makes the following statement to you today.

"_____ , you're the stupidest person I know!"

What would happen to you? How would you feel? Does it make a difference who said it? Complete the following steps on analyzing your feelings and thoughts.

How would you feel if this remark came from your . . . Spouse/partner/significant other?

_____

_____

_____

_____

Activity: The Stupidest Person I Know (continued)

Best friend?

Supervisor/boss?

Spiritual leader/preacher/minister/rabbi/priest?

Parent(s)?

Stranger?

Review your responses. From which person would it be the most painful to hear this comment? Why?

Activity: The Stupidest Person I Know (continued)

Why is this person's image of you important?

_____

_____

_____

Review your responses. From which person would it be the least painful to hear this comment? Why?

_____

_____

_____

_____

Why is this person's image of you not important?

_____

_____

_____

Why does one person's comment bring you pain and the other person's comment not bother you?

_____

_____

_____

How do you think this affects your self-esteem?

_____

_____

_____

Pretend that a person you consider contaminated did say this to you and you decided to take a drive just to clear your mind. As you're driving, your negative self-talk creeps in and says, *Maybe they're right. I am stupid.* How would you silence your inner critic? How would you justify your abilities and competencies to this inner critic?

Activity: The Stupidest Person I Know (continued)

In the spaces following, list as many things as you possibly can about your abilities and competencies in every area of your life including career, family, friendship, finance, spirituality, talent, physical ability, mental ability, social ability, and so on.

_____

_____

_____

_____

_____

_____

_____

_____

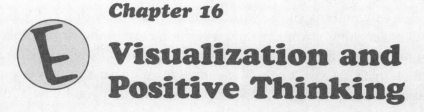

Chapter 16

Visualization and Positive Thinking

Abraham Lincoln once said, "I will work and prepare, and soon, my day will come." This came from a man who lost scores of elections; suffered through a nervous breakdown, his wife's nervous breakdown, and the death of a child; and went bankrupt. Optimism and positive thinking in the face of tragedy and distress have seen many a person go from tragedy to triumph.

The Power of Optimism

You've heard the question a thousand times: "Is the glass half full or half empty?" Researchers suggest that the way you answer that question is an indication of the way you look at life, either through optimistic eyes or pessimistic eyes.

When you think of the word *optimism*, you may think of happy, smiling, laughing, joyous people without a care in the world. This is not necessarily true. Optimism does not mean that you are constantly and eternally happy; it simply means that you have an outlook on life that is generally upbeat and positive. It means that you know and value hope.

De-Mystifying Optimism

One of the most important traits of an optimist is perseverance. Optimists will last through tough times. They have enough faith in their abilities and enough self-esteem to carry them through rough patches, even if the rough patches last for quite a while.

Optimists believe that their actions matter. They do not profess to be able to *change* the world, but they do profess to *matter* in the world. Optimism is all about an outlook. It is less about how you are treated and more about how you treat.

FACT

Research data suggests that optimists have a long list of health and social benefits over the pessimist. Optimists live longer, they have better lung capacity, they survive cancer treatments at a greater rate, and they have more productive and longer-lasting relationships.

Optimism is not innate. You are not born optimistic or pessimistic. Both are learned qualities. Both may very well date back to your early childhood or to later events in your life that shaped your attitudes.

Optimistic people tend to pay closer attention to their general health and health issues than the pessimists. They blame themselves less, work through setbacks more effectively, and are better able to eliminate contaminants (people, events, situations) from their lives.

How Does Optimism Come About?

Harmony! It's all in that one word. Harmony means a coming together of the elements, a blending of time and tide, a simultaneous combination of all that you've worked for and believed in. Harmony is unison in full grandeur.

However, harmony cannot and does not just happen. Harmony is the result of your mindset, your actions, your thoughts, your experiences, your education, your luck, your goals, and your work all coming together in one space and time. Harmony is a result of what you have done in the past to open the door to good fortune. Yes, it involves the way that you think and the attitude you have about your possibilities in the world. Harmony is the result of optimism.

How Optimism Can Help

Optimism is not a panacea for world peace, a cure for cancer, or ending hunger. But optimism has its advantages. Optimists are better able to cope with the ins and outs of daily living. They are able to take failures and setbacks with a grain of salt and not let them ruin their lives or self-esteem.

Optimists are better able to receive and grow from constructive criticism. They take the advice and see it for what it is worth and for how it may help them live better and more abundantly.

Optimists are more responsive to the challenges that life can bring about. They are the people who have the most options. They look at a challenge and are not crushed by it because they know that nothing is forever.

Optimists seem to be more creative and work harder for positive outcomes. They are not afraid of the unknown, the past, or what lies ahead. They are levelheaded about most events and are usually not deterred in their resolve.

Optimists understand that not everything can or will be changed. They accept that fact, do what they can, and move on. They do not spend needless energy fighting battles that will never be won.

Finally, optimists are contagious, and so are pessimists. Optimists are good at helping others see brighter possibilities, silver linings, happier endings, creative solutions, and enduring relationships. Their attitudes, like most attitudes, can catch on and spread.

Getting the Optimism Fever

If you've asked yourself, *How do I bring optimism into my life?* you're already halfway home. Just wanting to know more about optimism and having a willingness to try being more optimistic are important elements in your journey. Optimism is akin to the self-fulfilling prophecy; what you believe is what you get, what you do is what you are, and what you think is who you are. The following strategies will help you better understand optimism and bring it into your life.

QUESTION?

What is the primary difference between an optimist and a pessimist?
The answer is *attitude*. The optimist and the pessimist may try out for the softball team. When informed that he or she did not make the team, the optimist will volunteer to work on the sidelines with bats, balls, water, uniforms, or other duties. The pessimist will go home and complain about how unfair the world is.

Understand the Theory of Temporary

The theory of temporary means that you understand the old quote, "This too shall pass." Even the worst of times pass. Optimistic people see minor setbacks, failures, bad times, and yes, tragic times as temporary. Nothing, good or bad, lasts forever.

Seek Solutions

Optimistic people look for an amiable ending to every situation. Optimistic people ponder how to solve a problem or bring about a solution instead of focusing on who is at fault or who is to blame.

Expect Excellence

Optimists expect the best out of life and of themselves and they usually get it. They are not afraid to expect excellence from coworkers, family, friends, and partners. They understand that expectations are contagious. If you expect little, you get little. If you expect greatness, you just might get it.

Learn at Every Turn (LET)

From ruined relationships to miserable mistakes, the optimist takes every opportunity to learn from his or her mistake, misfortune, and misunderstanding. What is crushing to others will be a valuable life lesson to an optimistic person.

Avoid Aimlessness

So much of this book is about goals, and optimism is no different. Optimists routinely set, update, and revise their goals. They have a plan A, a plan B, and often a plan C. They are not tripped up by the unexpected because they have planned options.

Balancing Blame

If the blame belongs with John, an optimist will put it there and then help John learn from his error. If the blame belongs in his own hands, the optimist will embrace it, correct it, apologize for it, learn from it, and move on. Needlessly blaming yourself or improperly blaming others is not the optimist's way.

Jump on Joy

Optimists find joy in small things. They enjoy sunsets, a good conversation with a close friend; and they enjoy life in general. They are more concerned with having many small joys rather than having one huge joy.

Depersonalizing Poison

The optimist has learned not to take things so seriously. There is enough poison floating around to kill a nation, and the optimist knows how to let it roll off of his or her back. Optimists don't internalize pain or criticism. They take it for what it is worth and carry on.

Giving Greatness

Optimists take every opportunity to spread joy and kindness. From writing positive letters to businesses that offer great customer service, to writing a two-line "thank you" to a colleague, the optimist looks for ways to help others feel better.

Opt for Optimistic People

That's right; optimists seek out and associate with other optimists. No, it is not a private club—anyone can join, but the only rule is that you have to be an optimist (or an optimist in training). In a world filled with negativity, it is important to hang around those who enjoy happiness and high points in life.

Posture Positively

Optimists act like optimists. They are not closeted about their feelings and attitudes. They walk like optimists, they talk like optimists, they negotiate like optimists, they dress like optimists, and they carry the aura of optimists. Walking the walk and talking the talk have never meant so much.

Manage Movin' On

There is an old saying that goes, "You can only beat a dead horse so long until it begins to stink." How true. The optimist knows when to move on. They know what can be changed and what cannot be changed and they are unafraid to admit that it is time to move on. To end with an optimist's quote, "When the horse dies, dismount."

Conquering Pessimism

You've probably heard the old saying, "It is always darkest just before dawn." The pessimist's saying is similar: "It is always darkest just before it goes pitch black." Wow, what a difference.

Pessimists are not bad people. Some are not all gloom and doom, and many times it may surprise you just who considers herself an optimist or a pessimist.

Pessimists simply have a different worldview. Sometimes they do take the stance that things are never going to get better and most everything is evil. They sometimes plan for the worst and expect it. Life tends to respond in kind—their expectations are fulfilled.

Are You a Pessimist? Take the Test

Do you consider yourself a pessimist or an optimist? Answer the following questions truthfully to determine your perspective. Put a check beside the statements that match your attitudes and actions.

❐ 1. Someone dents your car at work and you become angry.
❐ 2. You consider constructive criticism as a helpful tool.
❐ 3. You love to gossip and talk about people.
❐ 4. You are not afraid to take risks and you like change.
❐ 5. You look at an old situation and are convinced it can never get better.
❐ 6. When disappointed, you regroup and move on.
❐ 7. If something gets too rough, you usually give up.
❐ 8. You take responsibility for your actions and outcomes.
❐ 9. You think that people are plotting against you.
❐ 10. You believe you can make a difference.
❐ 11. You use the phrase "I told you so" on a regular basis.
❐ 12. You can look at bad situations as temporary.

If you checked more odd-numbered statements than even-numbered ones, you tend to have a more pessimistic outlook on life. If you checked more even-numbered statements than odd, you tend to have a more optimistic outlook on life.

FACT

In several longitudinal studies, optimists and pessimists have been surveyed and studied. Over the years, researchers have determined that pessimists suffered more health- and mental-related problems, and died earlier than optimists.

Tips to Defeat the Dragon

If you are serious about changing your attitude and your outlook, consider the following tips for defeating pessimism.

- Cut off negative self-talk and pessimistic opinions before they fester.
- Work to believe in the Theory of Temporary.
- Seek out small victories and positive events.
- Take a few positive risks and plan for success.
- Forget the past; it is over and gone, and tomorrow has promise.

Visualizing Your Success

You are sitting on the bank of a small stream on a checkered blanket. A picnic of breads, cheeses, luscious fruits, a fine bottle of your favorite wine, and the person of your dreams surround you.

You are listening to your favorite music on a small portable CD player. The music only adds to the beauty and intensity of the moment. You lean back on the blanket as the other person gently kisses you on the lips and offers you a sip of wine. You are lightheaded from the moment, the music, the surrounding nature, the sound of the babbling stream, and the touch of another person's hand on the side of your face. You lie back and close your eyes and enjoy this perfect moment in time.

Were you there? Could you see yourself lying next to the stream?

Could you taste the fruit? This story is just one simple example of the powers of visualization on your attitude, your self-esteem, and indeed, your life.

The Power of Visualization

Visualization and daydreaming seem to be the same, but they are *not* the same. Visualization is a focused activity on a planned goal. It is more than just sitting back in a chair and dreaming about the clouds or the end of the workday, it is about creating a goal and seeing yourself obtaining the goal. It is about having a plan in place that is going to afford you the opportunity to reach your intended destiny.

FACT

A neurologist at Stanford University discovered that people who possess holographic memory—the ability to internally visualize the future—succeed more often and more easily than those without it.

Visualization in the "Real World"

Athletes have used visualization for centuries. They are trained to see themselves as winners. They can actually see themselves crossing the goal line, hitting the home run, skiing the perfect downhill, or swimming the fastest lap. They see it, they feel it, and they believe it. They visualize their success.

While mental practice is not as widely used as physical endurance preparation and strength training, many coaches use it. They suggest that creating positive mental images help them see themselves as successful.

Not only do athletes use visualization to help them succeed, but businesspeople, public speakers, physicians, salespeople, writers, and a plethora of other professionals do as well. Imagining yourself achieving the thing that you want as if it already exists helps make it possible for it to actually happen.

Putting Visualization into Action

Visualization and optimism have close ties with goal setting. It is hard to have either if you don't know what you want or what you're going after.

When working to use more visualization in your life, consider the following guidelines:

- Set a realistic goal that you really want.
- Plan your objectives so that they are doable and reasonable.
- Focus on that goal's outcome every second of every day.
- See that goal coming to fruition—visualize it happening.
- Talk to your goal and give it power—let it know you care about it.
- Take time every day to see yourself reaching this goal.
- Focus on your spiritual nature to assist you in reaching the goal.
- Be willing and able to accept the goal's fruition.

Optimism can change the course of your life. By using techniques such as positive thinking and visualization, the abundance of the world can come to you. You have to believe that every person is created to share in the miracles of life, happiness, abundance, and fulfillment. You have the energy, the mental power, to make this happen. When you give yourself the gift of optimism, you will see your self-esteem flourish and prosper.

Activity: Twenty-Four Hours

Directions: For twenty-four hours, think and talk optimistically, positively, and hopefully about *everything* in your life. *Everything!* To begin this process, examine the following categories. For each one, list at least three positive, optimistic, hopeful statements.

Your career: _____
_____
_____

Activity: Twenty-Four Hours

Your spouse/partner:

Your best friend:

Your worst foe:

Your abilities:

Your health:

Your future:

Your faith:

Your livelihood:

Activity: Twenty-Four Hours (continued)

Your mental well-being: --

Your physical well-being: --

Your finances: --

Your opportunities: --

Once you have completed this list, begin your twenty-four-hour experiment. Be completely positive for a full twenty-four hours about everything in your life. After that, try it for two days, a week, a month, and keep a journal of how your life has changed because of this positive outlook.

Chapter 17
Integrity

Personal integrity—doing what is right and what fits with your moral beliefs—is essential to self-esteem. Integrity plays such an important part in who you are as a person and how you feel about yourself and your actions. It cannot be bought, it cannot be borrowed, it cannot be negotiated, and it cannot be just an empty promise.

A Personal Definition of Integrity

Integrity is always possible. It is not easy, but it is very possible. There will always be people who lie, cheat, steal, use, abuse, and betray, but integrity is possible within yourself. Think back in history (and you won't have to think too far) and examine the number of people who were at the height of their careers when they failed their integrity. From Richard Nixon to Enron's Kenneth Lay, you can examine the multiple causes and reasons of integrity failure.

You can also think back in history to the people that you personally know who have lived an entire life of integrity and wholeness. Their beliefs were solid and their actions matched their beliefs.

Self-esteem and integrity are incalculably intertwined. It is difficult to respect yourself when you know that you are undermining another person, event, or situation. It is hard to feel good about yourself when you know that you have taken the low road to get high.

Just What Is Integrity?

Integrity comes from the Latin word *integri,* which means "wholeness"—wholeness of character, wholeness of action, wholeness of standards, and wholeness of thought. The strange thing about integrity is that it is more than a thought or an attempt; integrity is about your actions and how they match what is morally and justly right. Integrity is about fairness, faithfulness, respect, sound judgment, humility, reputation, and character. Integrity is not about winning and being on top. It is not about money and material possessions; it is about choosing right over easy, fairness over special interest, and principals over monetary gain.

Your Reputation

Years ago, reputation, specifically the reputation of young women, referred to sexual behavior. If a girl were promiscuous in high school, she would "ruin her reputation." Today, reputation encompasses much, much more.

Not only are people concerned with reputations, but businesses, industry, school systems, hospitals, hotels, and scores of other service industries are as well. Reputation has become a prized commodity. For either businesses or individuals, reputation cannot be purchased. It is not something that can be negotiated, bartered, or created from verbiage or marketing campaigns. Reputation, like true power, must be earned.

> Remember these words by Harvey MacKay: "Repairing a reputation is considerably more difficult than keeping a good one. It is like putting toothpaste back into the tube."

Your reputation speaks when you cannot or do not. It goes places even when you are stationary. Your reputation is literally bigger than you are. You do not carry it; it carries you.

Moral Bankruptcy

Integrity is more than meeting the demands of the written law and what is legal; it is about living a life that is beyond reproach regardless of the legal system. Integrity, according to author Robert Grudin, also involves continuity. It is not something that you profess one day and abandon the next. Integrity is about doing what is right through thick and thin, day-in and day-out, year after year.

People who have abandoned their integrity have common characteristics. There is no standard mold in which all morally bankrupt people fit, but you can look at the behaviors of those who have questionable integrity issues and discover much about the person and their actions.

Following, you will find how those who are morally bankrupt handle the following issues of integrity.

Self-Esteem

People with questionable integrity are usually those who care very little about themselves; thus, they are not able or willing to care about others. They have no true moral center on which to base their actions and judgments. Their self-esteem is so unhealthy that they literally cannot see how their actions damage their reputation.

Courage

Courage is a quality of the strong. People who have integrity issues are those who have very little courage to stand up for what is right. Instead, they stand up for what is right for them—their careers, their gains, and their quest for power. Cowardly behavior is a trait of morally bankrupt people.

Money and More

Nothing is ever good enough and there is never enough of "it" to the morally bankrupt person. They want more and more and they will do anything to get it. They do not concern themselves with others' feelings or desires; they are simply out for the kill and out for the hunt of more.

It has been said that money drives morality. Many a man and woman have fallen into the relentless quest for more money. Once the morally bankrupt person is infected with the "money bug," they throw all moral judgment and integrity out the window. Getting their hands on more money drives them, and their every decision is made with this goal in mind.

Judgment

Morally bankrupt people make judgments based on what will benefit them and their personal economy. They do not make sound judgments based on right and wrong as much as they make judgments based on gain and loss.

Truth

The truth is an expendable commodity to the morally bankrupt person. They do not care about the truth; they care about winning, gaining, and defeating the competition. The truth to them is as useless as day-old dishwater.

Personal integrity has become one of the characteristics that employers now seek in new associates. It is so important to some companies that they have begun giving integrity and personality assessments before they hire even the most qualified applicant.

Self-Interest

This is perhaps the most important trait of morally bankrupt people. They can only see the world through their own eyes. They have never even thought about walking in another's shoes, much less asking about another's needs. They are self-centered and have only their interest and well-being at heart.

You might think to yourself, *But isn't self-interest or looking out for yourself a positive quality?* Self-interest is a double-edged sword. Yes, it is very important to look out for yourself and guard your well-being. However, self-interest becomes dangerous when your every thought and action is based on a self-interested perspective. You begin to lose sight of what others need.

Betrayal and Trickery

People with integrity issues are prone to breaking their promises and seldom keep their word. They are skilled in the art of quiet betrayal. They know how to manipulate the situation so that it never looks as if they are at fault, but they are masters at underhanded deals, behind the scene arrangements, and shady transactions that benefit their cause.

Morally bankrupt people are great at deception. They put others in situations so that they can take the fall for their poor judgments, lies, greed, and betrayals. They are not above providing false information to cover their tracks and they are skilled at placing blame other than where it belongs.

Jealousy and Arrogance

Jealousy is a driving force of morally bankrupt people. They see that you have something that they want, and they are going to get it from you at all costs. Their jealousy drives them to the point where nothing matters but "winning." Jealousy is such a beast and so powerful that it tests even the strongest moral character.

Morally bankrupt people love to brag about what they have and what you do not have. They use power unnecessarily and abuse their status to make others look small, incompetent, weak, or foolish. They always see themselves as better than you and will tell you so at any given moment.

Fairness

The morally bankrupt person can't even spell the word *fairness*. They are driven by what is best for them, not what is best for the good of the whole. They can usually justify any action as being fair, because they are more skilled at deception than at being fair.

Developing a Personal Integrity Plan

An integrity plan is your personal mission statement. It is the words by which you plan to live, act, treat others, and interact in the world. It is necessary to have an integrity plan for your life because it is a statement that guides you when things get dark and confusing.

You can begin to develop your plan by making a list of the things that you value in your life. Your list may include things such as:

- Truth
- Honesty
- Fairness
- Spirituality
- Friends

After you have completed your list, you can begin to create a statement that incorporates your ideas for moral living, the things you value, and what you plan to do to protect your value system.

Your integrity plan or statement is much like the goal statements on which you have been concentrating. It will have a forceful action verb to give the statement power, it will have objectives that guide you, and you will symbolically sign your name to this statement.

An integrity statement might read something like this:

I believe in truth and fairness. In my actions, I will not do any deed that will jeopardize my integrity or the integrity of my friends. I will never compromise truth and fairness for personal or professional gain.

Understand that if you write an integrity statement based on what you truly believe and value, your self-esteem will suffer drastically should you go against your personal code of conduct.

"I am not bound to be true. I am not bound to succeed, but I am bound to live by the light that I have. I must stand with anyone who stands right, stand with him while he is right, and part with him when he goes wrong."

—Abraham Lincoln

Fitting Integrity into Your Life

Integrity gives your life meaning. It gives you the opportunity to look at what you value, what you cherish, what you hold most dear, and ask the question, "What am I willing to do to protect the things that give my life meaning while protecting my integrity?" That is sometimes not an easy question to answer.

Integrity gives you a chance to see how much courage you have. Are you willing to make the hard decisions and speak the hard truth to protect your integrity? Integrity gives you the opportunity to act. It is not a philosophy of only words; it is a philosophy of action. You can't profess to have integrity vocally and disregard the way you treat others. Integrity gives you the opportunity to prove your resolve. On a daily basis, you are given the opportunity to answer the question, "Am I really a person of integrity?"

Many people see integrity as a way of life while others see it as a way of life when others are looking. You can't have it both ways. Integrity is about consistency in word and deed. It is about who you are inside and how your values and ethics manifest themselves in the world.

When Your Integrity Is Threatened

Your integrity is threatened on a daily basis. Some of the threats are huge while some are as simple as taking the extra candy bar from the vending machine that fell in addition to your purchase. Yes, that candy bar is a threat to your integrity.

Your integrity is threatened most when wanting and needing are involved. Wanting more is a larger threat than needing more. When you want more, you tend to allow your hunger to swell for this thing (money, new car, bigger home, fancier clothes, etc.) and you make sacrifices of integrity to feed the hunger.

When someone begins to focus more and more on satisfying an appetite for something just for its own sake, he or she is in danger of becoming more obsessed with it. There is a real risk of letting it take over his or her character. If you think about it, most of the people that you know who have integrity problems are people who hunger for something and sacrifice everything of value to get more of it. They are not void of integrity just because they are bad; they are void of integrity because their hunger has become so great that they lose sight of the price they are paying to feed the hunger.

So, how do you keep your integrity intact when the elements of life are threatening it all the time? Consider the following tips when faced with threatening situations.

- **Keep the faith.** Faith in what you know is just and right is a monumental tool in fighting threats against your integrity. Stick to your standards of what you know is the proper thing to do. Resist the opportunity to take advantage of situations just because you can.
- **Trust yourself.** The heart may be a lonely hunter, but it is not a stupid hunter. You know your heart and you must trust in your own ability to do what is right. Do not rely on what others have done in the past, especially if you can see their errors or misjudgments.
- **Know right, and do right.** The best way to fight a threat to your integrity is to understand what is right before the threat comes. This way, you will not have a clouded view of what is right when the threat arrives. Look around at how John Doe is treated and at how

others treat John Doe. This is the greatest teacher for learning the lessons of "right."

- **Keep your hunger in check.** Don't let your desire for more or bigger or better or faster or prettier steal your integrity. Your hunger can be overpowering and can cause you to abandon your integrity in pursuit of fulfilling the hunger. Keep a close watch on what you want. It could cost you dearly.

- **Choose fairness**. The word fair means that you are consistent with the rules of ethics, principles, and morality. It means that you will choose what is morally and ethically fair over what is easy and clean. Integrity is not easy work sometimes, but it is harder work to regain your reputation once integrity is gone.

- **Practice loyalty.** Being loyal to others is certainly important, but being loyal to yourself matters just as much. One of the most painful lessons learned is when you are disloyal to your own value system, moral code, and ethical standards. It is damaging to your self-esteem to betray yourself.

Integrity is all about how you act and how you carry yourself in the world. Integrity involves your wholeness as a person, your words, your actions, your beliefs, and your attitudes. Integrity is about taking the road that is right versus taking the road for personal gain.

"The person of superior integrity does not insist upon his integrity; for this reason, he has integrity. The person of inferior integrity never loses sight of his integrity; for this reason, he lacks integrity."

—Lao Tzu

Activity: What If?

Directions: Think back on your past. Think about your career, your friends, your family, and even distant acquaintances. What do you most regret having done to a person in a time when you had a lapse in integrity? Did you lie to them? Did you cheat them out of something? Did you betray them? In the spaces following, answer the following questions.

Who is the person who suffered during your integrity lapse?

What was their relationship to you at the time?

What did you do to them?

Why did you do it?

What justifications did you give yourself for having done it?

Looking back, what could you have done differently?

Activity: What If?

What would you do differently today if the situation happened again?

_____

_____

_____

_____

How did this action affect your relationship with this person?

_____

_____

_____

How did this action affect your personal self-esteem?

_____

_____

_____

Get out a nice piece of stationery and write this person a confessional letter. Tell them what you did, why you did it, how you've suffered because of it, and then apologize to them for having caused them pain during a lapse of integrity on your part. You don't have to mail it. Only you can make the decision of how important this confessional is to your self-esteem and your ability to heal the past.

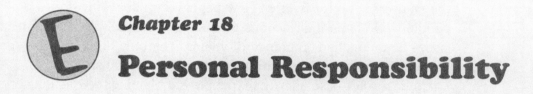

Chapter 18

Personal Responsibility

Taking responsibility for your actions can be difficult to do, but it is yet another important aspect of healthy self-esteem. Acknowledging what you have done—good or bad—is key to being in control of your life. You make the decisions about your behavior; you must be prepared to accept the responsibility for the results.

Owning Your Actions

A public school teacher was discovered to have been having sex with his students over an eleven-year period. The encounters took place in the school auditorium, the press box, his home, and his car. He blamed it on the school administration, society in general, and the parents of the students. The list is long. Newspapers are filled with stories of people who blame their actions on society, other people, environmental issues, and coughed-up mental problems. The only thing that has more girth than our newspapers are the nation's courtrooms.

In case after case after case, people are blaming their actions on someone or something other than themselves. The lack of personal responsibility has become an epidemic.

Imagine for a moment that you take no responsibility for any action in your life. How does this affect your self-esteem? Basically, it erases your self-esteem. You cannot think well of yourself if you refuse to take responsibility for your actions.

Further, if you refuse to take responsibility for your mistakes, errors, and misjudgments, you cannot rightfully take responsibility for your triumphs, successes, and accomplishments. This further damages your self-esteem.

The law of cause and effect suggests that for every action, there is a reaction. This means that for everything you say, everything you do, and everything you think, a reaction or effect is caused. Ignoring this reality causes people to shirk their responsibilities because they do not believe that their actions really cause reactions.

"What lies behind us and what lies before us are tiny matters compared to what lies within us."

—Ralph Waldo Emerson

Cause and effect can be very simple. If you eat rotten chicken, you get sick. If you jump into a deep lake with no one around and you can't swim, you drown. If you eat an entire box of donuts, three cups of coffee, and two cookies for breakfast, the effect may be sickness to your stomach, a sensation of being very full, a feeling of guilt, and—if you did it often enough—weight gain. These are effects of an action.

Therefore, because of the law of cause and effect, you must concede that your actions toward yourself and others *will* have an effect. If you do "a thing" there will be "a reaction." If you accept this law of nature, then you can begin to see how irrational it is to deny responsibility for your actions.

Failure to Accept Responsibility

You may ask yourself, *Why would anyone* not *take responsibility for his or her actions?* The answers, while often irrational, rest with the individual. All people who neglect to accept responsibility for their actions have justified the neglect in their minds. The refusal to accept responsibility is usually based in self-survival.

Some people refuse to take responsibility because they may lose money if they admit the truth about an action or mistake that could get them fired. Some people refuse to take responsibility because they may have to suffer physically at the hands of others if they admit their mistakes. Still others fear more harsh "punishments" if they accept responsibility, such as jail or prison time, divorce, or the loss of something valuable.

They become so blinded by the fear of the punishment that they refuse (or simply cannot) take the responsibility that could lead to the punishment. They are like the child who lies when he or she breaks the priceless antique Tiffany lamp. To accept responsibility for that action is too frightening to face.

The Twinkie Defense

A perfect example of neglect of responsibility came from California in the 1970s. One of the first public trials to use the "I'm not responsible for my actions" defense was the trial of San Francisco County Supervisor Daniel White. In 1978, White murdered Mayor George Moscone and Harvey Milk, a member of the board of supervisors.

A year earlier, Harvey Milk had become the first openly gay politician in America. White was staunchly antigay and clashed with Milk on numerous occasions. White became so disgruntled that he resigned his position as supervisor after continued clashes with Milk. A short while later, White went to Mayor Moscone to rescind his resignation, but Moscone refused. This enraged White, a highly decorated Vietnam soldier, policeman, and fireman. He went to city hall, found Moscone and Milk, and shot them both to death with a .38 caliber revolver.

White's lawyers used the defense that his junk-food craze had led him to murder the two. They claimed that his senses had become clouded because of too much sugar. White became known as "the junk food assassin," and his defense was called the "twinkie defense." He served only five years in the Soledad State Prison before being released.

The "Stop Me Defense"

Another growing trend seems to be the "You should have stopped me" defense. Lawyers and defendants trying to shirk responsibility or pass the blame have used this more and more in court.

The illogical and irrational arguments go like this, "You knew I had a weakness for children, so you should have stopped me from being around any child." "You knew that I was angry with John Doe and had rage toward him; therefore, you should have known that I was going to kill him, and you should have stopped me."

The "stop me defense," both in and out of the courtrooms, causes incalculable damage to all parties. It damages the real victims by negating their hurt or death, it damages the legal system because it forces a judge or jury to make the decision of responsibility for another person, and it damages the person using the argument because if they win, they will never be able to accept responsibility for their actions again.

The "twinkie defense" and the "stop me defense" are only two of the strategies used to force others to take the blame for someone else's actions. Your self-esteem rests in knowing who you are, what you value, and how you take responsibility for your own life and actions.

Handling Blame

Have we become a nation of victims? Have we passed the buck so often that we don't know how to accept responsibility for our own actions? The hardest part about blame is knowing where to place it, when to place it, how to place it, and what to do once it has been placed.

Why Blame Matters

Blame only occurs when something goes wrong. You never hear of anyone being blamed for something going right. You seldom hear of anyone blaming themselves, and rarely do you hear of anyone happy to take the blame for anything major or minor.

Blame matters because it has a direct effect on your self-esteem. If you are improperly blamed for something, it could have a damaging effect on your self-esteem and thus your future performance. If you are to blame and you do not accept responsibility for that blame, your self-esteem suffers. If you do not accept what you did wrong, you can never accept responsibility for it, you can never own it, you can never learn from it, and you can never grow from it.

"When you cast blame, you disempower yourself and relinquish control of your destiny."

—Kirk Charles

Blame matters because when you get caught up in the blame game, problems cannot be solved, solutions cannot be found, and peace is just a dream. When you spend time trying to find the person to blame, you could be spending that time correcting the problem or finding a solution to make sure the problem never happens again.

The blame game is usually the work of negative or pessimistic people. They can only see the dark side of the issue and find fault. They fail to see that for every situation in which blame can be placed, there is a situation in which learning and growth can occur. Blaming costs you time, money, effort, energy, resources, and most importantly, relationships, and maybe your personal dignity. Few things get better with blame.

The Case of Lee and Michelle

Lee and Michelle had been married for over a year when they decided to purchase their first home. It was a lovely place on a quiet street with diverse neighbors and a few children. It seemed to be the perfect place for them. Shortly after moving in, they decided to build a pool in their backyard.

A four- to five-foot cinder block wall surrounded each backyard in the neighborhood. In order to have more privacy in their backyard, Lee and Michelle asked their adjoining neighbors for permission to raise the wall to six feet. Two neighbors agreed, but the neighbor directly behind their home did not. Lee and Michelle took their case to the homeowner's association to ask for their permission. The owners of the home behind them were present at the meeting. After much heated discussion, the association *and* the backyard neighbors agreed to the proposal.

Work began on the pool and when it was completed, a separate contractor was hired to raise the wall. In order to cut costs and speed up the process, Lee and Michelle decided not to get a permit to build the wall; they already had the agreement with their homeowner's association and the neighbors, which seemed sufficient.

Shortly after the pool and wall were completed, the landscape planted, the Malibu lighting and outdoor sound system installed, a letter arrived from the county inspection office notifying them that there had been a complaint about the wall, that no permit had been issued, and that the wall had to be removed if a permit was not sought.

Lee and Michelle were furious. They knew exactly who had "turned them in." They could not believe that someone could be so cruel, so backstabbing, so petty, and so mean-spirited. Their anger swelled like a river after a three-day rain.

They went to the inspection office to begin the paperwork to permit the wall. They found that the hurdles were monumental and expensive. Engineers had to be hired, contractors had to be brought in, inspectors had to come to the home on five occasions, and the cost for retrofitting the project eventually ran over $16,000.

During the process, Lee and Michelle's anger grew. They blamed the backyard neighbors for breach of their word. They blamed them for snooping in their business. They blamed them for calling the county inspector, and they blamed them for having to spend the money to repair the project. They swelled with hatred and bitterness and only vile words came from their mouths when speaking about "the backyard neighbors." The anger was eating them both alive. They suffered physically and mentally. They had trouble sleeping, eating, and functioning at their jobs.

"The belief that we are not responsible sabotages all the power that can be found in taking responsibility for our lives."
—Jeff Herring

It was not until they sat down one evening and thoroughly examined the situation and looked at the cause and effect that their healing could begin. They finally took the blame for what had happened. They were at fault, not the neighbors. Sure, the neighbors were petty and manipulative, but that was not an issue for Lee and Michelle anymore. The only issue for them was healing and the healing could not begin without placing the blame properly.

When they accepted the responsibility for not having gotten the permit for the wall in the first place, they were able to move past the anger and frustration.

Personal Criticism

No one is going to tell you that taking or giving criticism is easy. But it is a part of personal responsibility. The ability to take and give valid criticism is important to your self-esteem. Your self-esteem and the self-esteem of others suffer when criticism is not given properly. Often, people just dive into a diatribe of critical assaults and impersonal comments without considering how the other person is going to feel, or how they will feel afterward.

Criticism and blame are different because proper, valid, constructive criticism offers not only a statement of cause, but solutions for improvement. Blame only places the cause and offers no advice. Valid criticism in not a part of the blame game.

When giving criticism, consider the following tips:

- State the criticism in a positive manner; don't attack.
- Look at the situation objectively, not personally.
- Let the other person know you care about them as a person.
- Be specific and precise in your criticism; avoid vagueness.
- Plan what you are going to say before you say it.
- Don't attack the person; focus on his or her actions.
- Try to remain unemotional; do not criticize when you are angry.
- Allow the other person to apologize and explain.
- Limit the time that you focus on the criticism; don't go on and on.
- If at all possible, end on a positive note.

When you are accepting valid criticism, consider the following:

- Try to learn from the comments and advice given.
- Listen objectively and open-mindedly.
- Don't try to blame others; accept the constructive criticism with grace.
- Own your actions and accept responsibility.
- Do not attack the person giving you criticism.
- Ask questions if given the opportunity.

Letting Go of Perfection

It may seem strange, but personal responsibility, blame, and criticism do have common traits with perfection. They may seem distant and abstract to each other, but they are not. Sometimes, perfectionism is the reason that blame is placed, and the reason that responsibility is not taken.

If you have perfectionist tendencies, you are less likely to take the blame for something gone wrong at your hand. It is out of your nature to be wrong or to have caused a problem, and thus, you may tend to pass the blame on to others to avoid the appearance of being imperfect.

If you have perfectionist tendencies, you may be more likely to place blame on others to deflect the situation from you. Perfectionists have a hard time admitting wrong or accepting responsibility for misjudgments, and this can cause them to avoid blame or place it improperly.

People with perfectionist tendencies have common traits such as the relentless pursuit of unrealistic goals, never being satisfied with the work done, believing that the less than perfect task accomplishment equals the less than perfect person, an unrealistic fear of failure, and the false impression that perfection is tied to self-worth.

Studies suggest that people who are perfectionists are less successful, less productive, suffer from greater amounts of stress and other medical problems, and have a hard time achieving healthy self-esteem.

If you feel that you are a perfectionist and want to work on being more realistic and kind to yourself, consider the following tips:

- Review your goals and make them more realistic.
- Understand that perfect is just a word, not a possibility.
- Enjoy your daily accomplishments and successes.
- Learn to celebrate mishaps of mood, action, and deed.
- Acknowledge your weaknesses as well as your strengths.

Personal responsibility can return to our society if we are willing to do our part. Accepting responsibility for your actions and deeds, refusing to place unnecessary blame, learning to take and give effective criticism, and moving away from the ideal of perfection are ways to begin the movement. It is an individual choice to accept responsibility for your life.

Activity: Past Responsibility

Directions: This exercise is not intended to make you focus on negatives, but rather look back at situations where your lack of personal responsibility may have produced less than desirable results.

Following, you will find several categories listed. Take some time with each category and identify at least one negative thing that happened in this category because of your inability to accept responsibility.

Your family:

_____

_____

Your career:

_____

_____

Your social life:

_____

_____

Your education:

_____

_____

Your relationships:

_____

_____

Your spirituality:

_____

_____

Your overall happiness:

_____

_____

Activity: Past Responsibility

Now that you have identified at least one thing that was less than positive in each category, think about what you could do to rectify the situation at this date and time.

Your family:

_____

_____

Your career:

_____

_____

Your social life:

_____

_____

Your education:

_____

_____

Your relationships:

_____

_____

Your spirituality:

_____

_____

Your overall happiness:

_____

_____

Activity: Past Responsibility (continued)

Finally, think about and write down how rectifying the situation could affect your self-esteem.

Your family:

Your career:

Your social life:

Your education:

Your relationships:

Your spirituality:

Your overall happiness:

Chapter 19

Forgiveness and Reconciliation

Time does not heal all wounds. It cannot. Often, time needs help from you. Time may soften the blow, erase some of the scars, and even cloud your memory of the hurt, but without your active participation, time cannot, and will not, heal the wounds of betrayal.

Making Peace with the Past

Perhaps the only thing harder than accepting that betrayal happened and healing from that betrayal is finding the courage to forgive others (or yourself) and move on. Moving on is impossible without making peace— peace with the person who betrayed you, peace with yourself, peace with the circumstance that led to the act, and peace with time. Your self-esteem is dependent on your ability to forgive, let go, and move on.

Letting go of the past can be dreadfully scary because you may have lived there for so long that you have no place else to go. Leaving the past behind may put you at zero, but the beauty is that zero is a beginning.

There is an old saying that you probably have heard for years and years, "Forgive and forget." The first is possible, the second is not, and that is okay. You don't have to forget the act that caused anguish. Few people, if any, can realistically forget. It can be damaging to you to pretend that you have forgotten when you know in your deepest soul that you have not. It may be psychologically and physically impossible to forget the act, but you will need to forgive, or your self-esteem will be forever flawed.

To forget the act or words that caused you pain may even be harmful. It is in remembering the act or words that you make a commitment to yourself to never repeat that act or utter those words to another person.

The most wonderful thing about the past is that you can leave it at any instant of your choosing. You are allowed a fresh start right now, and can begin moving toward forgiveness at any moment. You don't have to wait until the first of the year, or next Monday, or tomorrow morning; you can begin letting go immediately. You have that freedom; you have that power.

Making Peace with Those You've Hurt

"I've never hurt anyone," you might be saying right now. It may be true that you have never *intentionally* hurt anyone, but few people, if any, can accurately claim that they have never hurt another person. Human relationships are exceptionally delicate, and often other people in your life are hurt by your small actions and inadvertent neglect rather than by large, obvious means.

Think back to the last time that someone hurt you. What was the source of the pain or betrayal? Was it a major and planned attack by the other party, or was it a small act by her or him? Did the other person consider it significant? Did that person even know he or she hurt you? Now, turn the tables. Have you ever done the same thing to another person? As you begin to make peace with events of the past, you may find it difficult to explain the event, because looking back, it may seem so small.

Making Peace with Those Who Hurt You

Some people say that the pain of hurting another person is much worse than being hurt. Others will say that there is no worse pain than being hurt by someone for whom you care. Which is correct? Some would say it all depends on the hurt. The answer is in your heart, not in this chapter. Either way, forgiveness must be involved if you are to truly move on with your life. You either have to forgive the other person, or forgive yourself.

Forgiving those who have hurt you does not mean condoning their behavior. It does not mean that you approve of what they said or did, but rather that you are making a conscious effort to move on from that act.

What Is Forgiveness?

Forgiveness is the business of the heart. It is that simple and that complex. Forgiveness is about letting go of your own arrogance so that you can move on with the affairs of living. Forgiveness is about admitting your own shortcomings and failures so that you can more clearly see both sides of the story. Forgiveness is about no longer allowing other people to control your emotions, for when you hold hatred and bitterness in your heart, the person for whom you harbor that hatred and bitterness controls you. Forgiveness is about accepting that people make mistakes, costly mistakes, and that you make them, too. Forgiveness is about making a decision to never use the other people's acts or comments against them in any fashion; it is about never bringing the act or comment up again. Forgiveness is a canceled check.

"To forgive is the highest, most beautiful form of love. In return, you will receive untold peace and happiness."

—Robert Muller

Forgiveness is not about speed. It can, and may, take much time, but true forgiveness can't be rushed or forced. Forgiveness is not about showdowns or final confrontations. It may happen in the privacy of your own mind. You may never again see the person whom you are forgiving. Finally, forgiveness is not about weakness. Weak people are the people who cannot forgive. Forgiveness is the work of the strong. It takes strength and paramount courage to change the heart.

Forgiveness is not simply for the other person; it is for you as well. Researchers at Hope College and Virginia Commonwealth University found that apologies and restitution have an immediate and positive impact on the mind and body. Their study found that apologies reduced heart rate and lowered tension.

Some of the positive benefits of forgiveness include:

- Stress relief
- A sense of freedom
- A feeling of finding "right"
- Release from hatred and anger
- A move toward healing
- Deep joy
- A feeling of inner peace

Forgiving by Communicating

The first step is yours. If you wait for "the other person" to reach out to you, you may never find the peace you need and deserve. Time is of the essence when reaching out. True, you can reach out at any time, even decades later, but the longer you wait, the harder it will be to take that first step.

The first step in reaching out is to ensure that the lines of communication are open and that the other person knows this. Communication is the essence of any relationship; without it, the situation becomes nearly hopeless, and the thought of reconciliation and forgiveness is even direr. Listening is perhaps the most important thing that you can do when reaching out to another person. You will need to understand the other person's side of the story, and oftentimes the only way to do this is to stop talking and start listening.

Following, you will find some helpful hints to aid you in becoming a more effective listener:

- Stop talking.
- Listen for what is *not* said.
- Listen between the lines.
- Listen to how something is said.
- Give the other person your undivided attention.
- Leave your emotions behind.
- Don't jump to conclusions.
- Ask the other person questions.

"Know how to listen, and you will profit even from those who talk badly."

—Plutarch

Forgiving by Resolving Conflict

At first, conflict and forgiveness seem at different ends of the spectrum. "How can I forgive if there is conflict?" you might ask. Conflict is the struggle between people who have opposing views, opposite goals, conflicting values, and inappropriate communication. Conflict does not necessarily mean that hatred and condemnation are involved, although both can be. But rather, most conflict and estrangements occur over misunderstandings and different points of view.

The most serious interpersonal conflicts occur between people who truly care about each other. If you have a misunderstanding with a person whom you do not know or whom you care very little about, then the conflict will not be as painful because there is less to lose. It is only when you have conflict with those you love and admire that pain and betrayal come into play. Forgiveness is most important only with those you love and care about. If a complete stranger hurts you, forgiveness is not as important.

What is the best way to resolve a conflict? The stages in conflict resolution involve developing multiple solutions, evaluating each solution carefully, choosing the best solution, trying the solution, and then evaluating the solution to see if it worked.

Following, you will find several ways to resolve conflict and begin the healing and forgiving process:

- Let the other person tell her or his side of the story.
- Listen more carefully than you have ever listened before.
- Don't try to be right; try to be fair.
- Tell the other person what you need.
- Ask them what they need.
- Try to meet in the middle.
- Get away from assumptions and talk about facts.
- Look at multiple solutions instead of one solution.

All relationships, whether with family, friends, or spouses/partners, will have conflict. Communications experts suggest that conflict can actually help a relationship because it can clear the air and relieve stress. The most important factor is not whether you fight, but how you fight.

Learning to Trust Again

There are two types of people in the world—those who trust everyone until it is proved that they can't be trusted, and those who trust no one until it is proved that they can be trusted. The former are the most likely to be hurt, betrayed, and dismayed.

If you are a trusting person, you know how easily hurt can come. You put your heart and soul out on the table for everyone to see. You give of yourself and disclose things about you that are personal and sometimes private. You do so with open arms hoping that others will take your rare gifts and use them to create good. Then, *wham!* Betrayal. *How could they do that?* you ask yourself. *How could someone take my deepest fears or most honest love and see it as expendable?*

Forgiveness cannot involve tradeoffs. You must forgive completely without the promise of retribution. To say, "I'll forgive you if . . ." is as useless to your quest for healthy self-esteem as not forgiving at all.

Learning to trust again after being betrayed is one of the most difficult aspects of being human. It is like being a severely wounded soldier and walking haggardly in front of the stern enemy, empty-handed, arms extended toward them, and pleading for a cease-fire. However, you know that trust is essential for forgiveness and healing. It is essential to the interpersonal process. It is essential for you to be able to move on. It is essential for healthy self-esteem.

Trust involves risk, and retrusting involves even greater risk. It means putting yourself "out there" again, sometimes with the same people who betrayed you in the first place.

Trust is a self-fulfilling prophecy. If you let others know that you have full faith in them and trust them in earnest, they are less likely to betray that trust. Don't be afraid to say to a person, "I trust you completely. I have faith in you."

In order to forgive and make peace with those who have hurt you, you must learn to trust again. The following steps can help you in restoring trust:

- Talk openly and honestly about your pain.
- Ask why the person betrayed your trust.
- Express your intentions to trust again.
- Start with something small and less significant.
- Be a person worthy of trust.
- Establish and communicate the ramifications of future betrayal.

Understanding Differences

If you are truly interested in making peace with a person who hurt you, you will need to make every effort to understand that person's culture, background, environment, and attitudes. Understanding what makes people tick can help you understand that a comment or an action may not have been intended to hurt you; it may just be their custom.

Many people from the South think that people from the North are rude and insensitive. They think they are pushy, impolite, and opinionated. Many people from the North think that people from the South are ignorant, lazy, and uneducated. Why? Because this is the stereotype that each culture has been trained to believe. It is not until a native of Atlanta goes to New York City that he or she fully understands the magnitude of a New Yorker's heart. And, it is not until a person from New York City goes to Birmingham that he or she fully understands the nature of Southern hospitality.

Learning to forgive means learning to understand that everyone is uniquely different and is reared with different morals, values, customs, norms, and sanctions. Many conflicts can be avoided if you simply understand other cultures more deeply. Only by understanding that religion, age, race, sex, sexual orientation, education, environment, economic status, and innate factors all play important roles in who we are as people can you fully understand the other person's point of view.

The Case of Doris

Doris, a woman in her early sixties, works in retail in a major mall located in the South. She has worked for the store for over fifteen years. Everyone loves Doris because of her caring nature, her charm, her wit, and her devotion to her family and friends. If you asked anyone, you would be hard-pressed to find a single person who does not like and admire her.

During the busy holiday season, the department store hires temporary help to assist with customer service. This year, Cindy is hired to work in Doris's department. The two hit it off well and the training goes off without a hitch. It is not until Doris makes a comment about having to work Christmas Eve that the two first discover a difference in their lives. Doris wants to be off on Christmas Eve so that she can be with her family, open gifts, and get ready for services on Christmas day. Cindy says that she does not care about Christmas Eve because her family is Jewish.

Doris has never met a Jewish person before and really can't understand how someone could not care about Christmas Eve and Christmas. She invites Cindy over to her home after they finish work on December 24. Cindy declines, stating that she really has no interest in the holiday and that she would not be comfortable. Doris is incensed that Cindy is shunning her religion and her holiday. Cindy is put off because Doris refuses to acknowledge that Judaism celebrates the season with different traditions and customs. The conflict grows until neither Doris nor Cindy will speak to each other. They both feel betrayed for having revealed so much about themselves to each other only to have it used against them.

Doris and Cindy Revisited

Had Doris and Cindy taken the time to understand the other's faith, this conflict could have been easily avoided. With a more thorough understanding, neither would feel betrayed, neither would feel hurt, and neither Doris's nor Cindy's self-esteem would have been damaged by the unfortunate incident. Understanding where others are coming from can help you avoid conflict, and if conflict arises, understanding others' cultures can help you forgive.

Take Action Now

It is up to you. Do you have it in your heart to pick up the phone and make the call or pick up the pen and write the letter or turn on the computer and send the e-mail? Your self-esteem can be greatly enhanced by selecting just one person to whom you would like to reunite or one person to whom you just want to say, "I'm sorry."

Forgiveness is not an easy road, but it is a road that can begin to make you whole again. It is an act that is born out of a rare and true desire to make the world in which you live a better place. It is an act born out of necessity for emotional survival, but carried out as a need to be whole again and to aid in the quest for healthy self-esteem.

Activity: Finding Goodness

Directions: The following exercise is intended to help you come to terms with two people in your life—a person in your past that you harmed and a person who harmed you.

First, list someone that you hurt in years past and to whom you have not apologized or forgiven. Then list a person who hurt you in years past and from whom you have not had an apology or felt forgiveness.

Person 1: --

Person 2: --

A major part of forgiveness is being able to recognize valuable qualities and gifts in other people. People with healthy self-esteem are not only able to recognize these gifts and qualities in others, but also learn from them and acknowledge these gifts. In the spaces following, list at least two positive qualities about these people.

List the positive, valuable qualities that you see in person 1:

List the positive, valuable qualities that you see in person 2:

Activity: Finding Goodness

Now for the hard part, or maybe the easiest thing you've done in years. Find two nice notecards or pieces of stationery and write each of these people a handwritten note acknowledging these positive qualities. You can offer apologies or statements of forgiveness if you like, but your notes must concentrate on the positive.

EXAMPLE: (TO SOMEONE WHO HAS HURT YOU)

Dot,

I know that we have not seen eye-to-eye on some things over the past few years. We never really gave each other a chance. We both said some things that were very hurtful, and for that I am sorry. I also want you to know that I forgive you for the comments you made to me. I know in my heart that you are not that kind of person.

I also wanted to let you know that I admire the way I saw you treat your family when they were visiting, and I also admire your total sense of independence and persistence.

I hope that you and I can sit and talk some day soon.

Robb

Use this space to jot down a few positive statements to person 1.

_____

_____

_____

Use this space to jot down a few positive statements to person 2.

_____

_____

_____

Activity: Finding Goodness (continued)

Now, it's *your* turn. Spend some time reviewing what you said about the people you listed and write your notes. Don't go any further until you have written both notes.

Was writing the notes easy?   ❒ Yes   ❒ No
Why? --

Can you bring yourself to mail the notes?   ❒ Yes   ❒ No
Why? --

What could this do to your self-esteem?

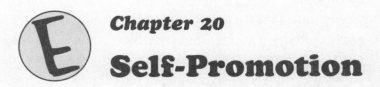

Chapter 20

Self-Promotion

"Wanted: A loving, warm, compassionate, strong, caring, determined, flexible, open-minded, healthy, honest, friendly person with a hearty soul, a keen sense of humor, and the ability to live and let live." Could this be you? Could you have written this ad about yourself? Have you ever thought about self-promotion?

It's Healthy to Self-Promote

Self-promotion may sound far-fetched and conceited, but in actuality it is healthy. Self-promotion is simply a blueprint of how you see your life. Your self-promotion is not for others to see or hear; it is for you to work with, understand, wrangle over, and build upon.

There is a difference between self-promotion and affirmations. Self-promotion is something that you do to better understand the inner qualities that you possess. It is a journey by which you write to yourself, speak with yourself, and remind yourself of your successes, your triumphs, your friends, your loves, your desires, and your goodness.

An affirmation is when you say to yourself, "I will think positively today." Self-promotion is when you speak to yourself about the many, many times that you have been positive and what it did for you. An affirmation is when you say to yourself, "I'm a good person." Self-promotion is when you open a drawer full of letters and cards and photos that are evidence that you have been, and continue to be, a positive person.

Self-promotion has nothing to do with conceit. Conceit is when you have too high of an opinion of yourself and you let others know it. Conceit has to do with vanity. Conceit is public, but self-promotion is private.

Self-promotion has to do with validation—not validation from others, but validation from yourself. It has to do with physical, tangible things that remind you of your worth and your value. It's about encouragement—not encouragement from others, but encouragement from yourself. It suggests that you look at what you have done, what you are doing now, and how you plan to do things in the future. It suggests that you look back, in order to look forward.

"There is nothing as easy as denouncing. It don't take much to see that something is wrong, but it takes some eyesight to see what will put it right again."

—Will Rogers

Self-promotion is about looking at what is right and good and solid in your life. It is about calling up the past to remind you of those things. It is not about living in the past or dwelling in the past needlessly, but it is about letting the past tell its story.

Discovering You

In our fast-paced society, it is easy to lose sight of not only where you are going, but also where you have been. It is easy to forget the things that have brought you to this point in your life.

In self-esteem research and theory, there is a term called *self-disclosure*. This means disclosing things about you and your life to other people. It means that you find someone that you trust enough to know the truth about you. Simple self-disclosure is not enough, though, because it is near impossible to disclose the truth about yourself to other people when you have not even disclosed the truth about yourself to *you*. Without giving yourself a chance to hear the good news first, it is impossible to give others the good news.

With self-promotion, you will focus on *self* self-disclosure. This means letting yourself know some things about you. It means trusting yourself enough to let you disclose your joys, your triumphs, and your successes to yourself.

Self self-disclosure will take some work. It is hard to think of talking to yourself and writing to yourself without thinking that you have a mental problem. Relax; it is perfectly healthy to remind yourself of who you are and what you have to offer. People with healthy self-esteem have the ability to reveal themselves to others *and* they have the ability to reveal themselves to themselves.

Renewing Your Relationship with Yourself

In your quest to master self-promotion, take some time now to think about yourself. Do not let any negative thoughts, feelings, or past actions come into play. Think about the good things in your life, your heart, your actions, and take the time to reflect on the following questions that can help you start your journey:

- What is your favorite activity?
- What is your favorite song?
- What is your all-time favorite movie?
- Where is your favorite place?
- What is the best thing you have ever done for yourself?
- What is the best thing you have ever done for another person?
- What is your biggest success?
- Of what are you most proud?

Don't stop there. You know yourself better than anyone. Keep on. Think about your life as a joyous story needing to be told. No one need be there, so don't be ashamed or afraid—tell it to yourself.

Mementos of the Heart

If you've been good to yourself, you have saved cards, letters, gifts, invitations, Post-It notes, napkins, and other mementos that remind you of happy times, good people, and loving moments. If you have not done this in the past, today is the day to start.

Think back to the birthday card that had a message from a friend that stopped you in your tracks. Remember? It said a few things that shocked even you. Remember that simple memo from your supervisor last year that congratulated you on your creative work in solving that problem in the office? Where are they? Where did you put them?

Letters, Cards, Memos, Photos, and Stories

If you do not already have a box or some type of safe container in which to place your letters, cards, and memos, go out today and find something in which to keep these memories.

In this box, you will begin to keep your birthday cards, anniversary cards, holiday greetings, personal letters, memos from colleagues at work, newspaper clippings, quotes, and inspirational stories that make you feel good.

> "The memory is a treasurer to whom you must give funds if you ever want to draw on it in time of need."
>
> —Anonymous

Every time your receive something that brings warmth to your life, put it in the box. This could be a family photo, photos you find in magazines or newspapers that remind you of something wonderful, or photos that friends send of their families. Your box can contain stories, quotes, poems, and essays that made you stop and think about positive things. Perhaps you read a moving one-line quote that really provoked a strong image. Cut it out, tape it to a sheet of paper, and stick it in your box.

Remember, your box is not necessarily for today; your box is a gift to yourself for tomorrow. It is a place to stick things that otherwise would be lost or not kept at all. It is a place that you can visit weeks, months, or even years later. It is a hope chest for your soul.

Your Funny File

In addition to your box, you may want to keep a file in your drawer of funny cartoons, humorous sayings, and happy stories that just make you tingle all over when you read them. Keeping a sense of humor helps enhance your self-esteem, promotes creativity, relieves stress, and in general keeps balance in your life.

You've seen funny quotes and cartoons for years. But when you try to remember what they said or what the caption of the cartoon was, your memory fails you. Your funny file should be a place where you can go on bad or depressing days to just look over things that have brought you laughter and joy in the past.

You will be amazed at how quickly your funny file or memento box can take away the negative and sad moments of the day.

Your Victory File or Wall

Your victory file is a place to keep every commendation, positive comment, certificate, degree, award, or comment from your professional and personal life.

This file may contain certificates from high school, the Boy or Girl Scouts, places where you volunteered, or awards from work. Basically, your victory file is a file of your recognition of accomplishments for your service to humanity and to yourself.

Where is your high school diploma? Where is that certificate you got for five years of service at work? Where is that "World's Greatest Mom" poster your child bought or made for you years ago? These are the types of things that go in your victory file.

A victory wall will contain the same types of accolades as your victory file, except that you can display your things so that you can see them on a daily basis. Your victory wall may contain photos of friends, framed certificates and awards, framed diplomas or degrees, framed newspaper clippings in which you may have been mentioned, placards with positive quotes, or photos of your friends, family, or pets.

This wall is a mosaic of your past. It is a mural of your life's work. It is a visual reminder of the good, positive, loving, warm, caring things that you have done and that you have in your life.

Your victory wall does not have to be "designer" perfect. It is a work in progress. The frames do not have to match, the lines of design need not apply; this is a wall that is alive with all that you have been and all that you will do.

"He is a wise man who does not grieve for the things which he has not, but rejoices for those which he has."

—Epictetus

Your victory wall should be in a part of the house where you sit to think, work, meditate, and/or relax. It should be in a place where you feel comfortable adding things and moving things around.

Letters to Myself

Journaling is an ancient act. Cave drawings from history prove that humans have always had a yearning to record their actions, thoughts, and deeds. Journaling is a way to preserve your personal history.

When you begin journaling, understand that the words you are writing are just for you. They will not be shared or published. You don't have to worry about spelling, grammar, or punctuation. Write what you feel about a situation, an event, your present state in life, or your desires, wishes, and hopes.

Journaling is therapeutic. It allows for reflection on and healing of the past, projections for the future, and allows you to talk with yourself. Expressing your emotions on paper can help you feel less anxiety and depression.

Your journal does not have to be a pricey leather-bound book with gold embossed letters. It does not have to be a formal diary with lock and key. It can be a spiral-bound composition book, loose-leaf notebook paper, or a legal pad.

Journaling should be a stress-free event. You should not feel pressured to write anything. You don't have to worry about writing once or twice a day, but once you begin, you'll welcome the time in late evenings, early mornings, or quiet lunches to have a conversation with yourself.

The content of your journal can be anything from your thoughts on the day, to a letter to an old adversary that you never plan to mail. It can be a letter to your child who is moving away or a letter to a child not yet born. The topics are limitless and completely of your choosing.

When beginning your conversation with yourself, consider the following tips:

- Don't pressure yourself to write; it must be of your free will.
- If you have trouble beginning, comment on a quote or article you read.

- Use dialogue writing (a conversation with you and someone else).
- Date your entries.
- Keep your journal in a private place.
- Don't censor your own words; what comes out, comes out.
- Reread your journal from time to time.

By speaking with yourself on a regular basis, you will create a positive way to keep track of your feelings, your thoughts, your desires, your frustrations, your setbacks, your successes, and your innermost workings. This is your history; write it for you.

Thoughts of Worth

There is an old exercise called "How Much Is It Worth to You?" In this activity, you are approached by a multibillionaire. He has more money than you could ever spend in a lifetime. He approaches you and asks to buy one day of your life, *just one day—twenty-four hours.*

He signs a promise that he will never use the day for anything. He is going to "lock" it away in a vault never to be seen, touched, spoken of, or used again. He only wants to buy one *future* day. You can even choose the day in the future that you sell to him. The sky is the limit. What would you charge him for one day of your life? What is one day of your life worth?

Common responses range from $10 billion to $10,000 to $100 to nothing. Some people say that they would not sell a day of their life for any price. They give the reason that it may be their last day. (But remember, you can choose the day that you sell.)

Think about this for a moment. How could $10 million or $100 million change your life? What could you do? How could you help others? All you are giving up is twenty-four hours. Think about this for a while. What would you charge the multibillionaire for a day of your life?

Your Answer

Do you have an answer? Did you choose a dollar amount or did you convince yourself that you would never sell a day of your life. What is a day of your life worth to you?

Whether you sold your day for $10 billion or if you did not sell your day because it is priceless to you, ask yourself this: Was today a *$10 billion day?* Was today *priceless for you?* Tonight, when you go to bed, did you have a $10 billion day? Did you get all of the gusto, all of the joy, all of the living out of today? Was today priceless? Was today worth a day of your life?

Some people reflect back on today and they would pay someone to take it from them. These are the people who have not yet learned to bask in the small and wonderful gifts that every day brings. These are the people who do not know themselves well enough to make twenty-four hours work for them. These are the people who battle with who they are and what they are worth.

"If you are ever going to enjoy life, now is the time, not tomorrow or next year. Today should always be our most wonderful day."

—Thomas Dreier

If you had trouble answering the question about how much a day of your life is worth to you, perhaps self-reflection will be of assistance to you. Perhaps this is a journal entry for you. Perhaps this is the time to begin spending quality time with yourself to think through questions such as "What is a day of my life worth?" or "What am I worth?" or "How do I value my worth?"

Being Alone

In your quest for healthy self-esteem through self-promotion, think about the time that you spend alone with yourself. Many people do not like the idea of spending time alone because it forces them to think too much, or they simply do not enjoy their own company. Being alone and spending that time in self-promotion is a way to begin to look at your inner qualities and discover what it is that you enjoy about yourself and your own company. Self-promotion is, in effect, a way to have a relationship with yourself.

Perhaps you are always searching for the other "half" of you to make you a whole person. Self-promotion allows you to move toward acceptance of yourself as a whole person without having to have another half. There are many worse things than being alone. For example, being with someone and feeling alone is worse than being alone by yourself. Being in an abusive relationship is worse than being alone and being in a one-sided relationship is worse than being alone.

It is not encouraged to spend day after day, week after week alone; other people certainly add to the quality of your life, but it can be healthy to take some time for yourself and use your alone time to establish closer ties to you.

Self-promotion is an important step in building healthy self-esteem. It allows you to spend time with yourself without any judgment from you or anyone else. If you have not yet begun to develop a humor file, victory wall, or letter/photo/card box, take time today to begin each of these. They are inexpensive, yet invaluable when it comes to taking care of your own soul. Don't let the old notion that you can't take care of and spend time with you impede your progress in the quest for healthy self-esteem.

Activity: Self-Advertisement

Directions: In the space following, pretend that you have to write an advertisement about yourself for the local newspaper. This advertisement must detail all of your strengths, abilities, competencies, and positive qualities. You are the only person who will ever write this ad. No one else knows you like you know yourself. It is up to you. Imagine that your ad will be seen by tens of thousands of people. What will it say? Promote yourself. You may use *only* positive comments.

TO BE RELEASED IMMEDIATELY

Activity: Self-Advertisement

Chapter 21

Unconventional and Creative Thinking

Fire. The wheel. The automobile. Electricity. Running water. Space travel. A cure for polio. The Eiffel Tower. Mona Lisa. Mt. Rushmore. All of these and countless other uncommon innovations, events, and talents have come from pushing the envelope, reaching beyond what was thought possible, and relying on creativity instead of convention.

What Is Unconventional and Creative Thinking?

Creativity is not new, but it is still a thing of mystery for millions. Creative people have been called everything from whack-cases to avant-garde geniuses.

When you think of creative and unconventional thinking, you probably begin to focus on art or sculpture or gardening or decorating. This is only a small part of creative thinking. Creative thinking can be used to solve problems, do strategic planning, make exceptional decisions, and evaluate projects from new points of view, and it can assist you in working with an open mind. Creativity can also assist you in thinking of new solutions to old problems. It can help you brainstorm your way through tough issues that have plagued a company, school, organization, or situation for years.

Creativity and self-esteem are great companions. Think of the times that you have tried something completely new and it worked. Think of the times that you painted a room or made a pair of pants or built a bookcase or landscaped the yard and things worked out beautifully.

Remember how that made you feel. You felt like you were winning. You felt as if you had created something new, and your self-esteem soared because of it. Creative thinking and unconventional thinking can help you greatly, especially if you have the courage to put your new ideas into action.

"A great many people think they are thinking when they are merely rearranging their prejudices."

—William James

Creative thinking requires that you let go of conventional wisdom and saying things like, "We've always done it that way." That theory is out the window. "We've never done it that way before so we can't do it now" has no place in creative and unconventional thinking.

Many people think that creativity must be innate. However, creativity can be learned and polished. Sure, there will always be people who are on the cusp of genius with their creative efforts, but everyone has the propensity for some creativity.

Characteristics of Creative Thinkers

Creative and unconventional thinkers have many traits in common. Following, you will find those traits and examples of how each trait has played a role in moving humanity forward.

Compassion

Creative and unconventional thinkers have compassion. They see a problem in society and they try to solve it in ways that are new *and* helpful. They have a great deal of respect and compassion for others.

In 1980, a little boy with a terminal illness told of his wish of becoming a police officer. Through a friend of the family, he was allowed to be a "policeman" for a day with the Arizona State Police. The boy died not long after, but his special day had planted the seed of an idea in the minds of the police officers, and the Make-A-Wish Foundation was born. The mission is "to grant the wishes of children with life-threatening illnesses to enrich the human experience with hope, strength, and joy." Today, the foundation has served over 97,000 children and operates with the help of over 25,000 volunteers. It is the result of creativity and compassion.

Courage and Risk

Courage and risk are major requirements for unconventional and creative thinkers. They are not afraid to take chances and try new things. They stretch the boundaries of what is known and acceptable. They understand that new frontiers have dangers.

In the early 1980s, a researcher named Barry Marshall bucked the trend of modern medical thought when he refuted the theory that ulcers were caused by stress or excess stomach acid. He staunchly believed that the *H. Pylori* bacteria caused them. He presented his theory at scientific meetings, but no one paid much attention or even gave his idea a chance. Everyone felt his theory was too unconventional. So, finally, he decided to prove his theory on himself. He swallowed the *H. Pylori* bacteria and gave himself ulcers and was able to provide enough evidence to convince the scientific world that he was right. Today, many treatment plans for ulcers are based on Marshall's work.

Truth

Creative and unconventional thinkers are not satisfied with "maybe" or "I think so." They are truth seekers and work hard to prove and stand by what is not only unpopular, but what is true as well.

Around 1530, the astrologer and scientist Copernicus began to quietly circulate his theory that Earth was not the center of the universe and that the universe did not revolve around Earth. This was a very unpopular view because most philosophical and religious study had been written and executed based on the theory of Ptolemy. His theory was that Earth is a fixed body and that all celestial bodies moved around it. For anyone to deny this theory was near heresy. He died never knowing how much controversy his theory would cause.

Later astrologers who supported Copernicus's theory, such as Galileo and Bruno, suffered greatly at the hands of religious and political leaders. The astrologer Bruno was burned at the stake for touting the Copernican theory. In 1633, Galileo was brought before leaders of the day and at the threat of death and relentless torture, he was forced to renounce all belief in the Copernican theory. As you know, modern astrology and science later proved all three, Copernicus, Galileo, and Bruno, to be correct. They sought truth.

Dreams and Imagination

Creative and unconventional thinkers are not afraid to take time off and just think. They are not afraid to lie under a shade tree and ponder new avenues, uncommon methods, and uncharted paths. They have trained themselves to practice the gift of "What if . . ."

The Great Depression of the 1930s reshaped the American landscape. Millions were unemployed and most had lost their life savings. Few programs existed that could help anyone. President Franklin D. Roosevelt dreamed of a way to help Americans so that they, and the country, would never have to suffer this way again. He examined the few programs available and in 1935, he proposed to Congress a legislation program of social insurance. These programs, a part of the New Deal, would later become known as Unemployment Insurance and Social Security. His dream of helping in a way that had never been known before still exists today.

Individuality

Creative and unconventional thinkers do not concern themselves with fitting in. They are more concerned with "what is possible" than "how would I look doing it." They are not concerned with being just like other people.

If you have ever seen the fictional movie *Billy Elliot*, you understand the power of individuality. Billy Elliott is an eleven-year-old boy in strike-ridden England. His mother has died and he, his father, and his much older brother live in a flat together. Billy is in school and is supposed to be taking boxing when he discovers a dance class. He secretly begins taking ballet instead of boxing. His teacher takes a keen interest in his innate talents and encourages him to audition for the Royal Ballet School. When he misses the audition, she comes to his home, and this is the first that his father and brother know of his ballet interests. They are ashamed and embarrassed by his acts, but Billy is undeterred. He practices and later gains his father's consent to audition. His is accepted and later goes on to join the Royal Ballet. Though fictional, Billy Elliott embodies the individuality in all of us; he was just strong enough to keep his alive.

Stick-to-it-ness

Perseverance is a prime trait of people who are creative and unconventional. They do not give up easily, or at all. They have the courage to see things through to fruition.

The Reverend Dr. Martin Luther King Jr. was a person of perseverance. He knew that civil rights for African-Americans would not come overnight and that it would not come easily. He understood that the battle was bigger than he was and he understood that the price for equality might very well be death. He was undeterred by setbacks, violence, jail time, verbal slurs, and threats. For years and years, he fought the good fight knowing that he might never see equality in his lifetime. But, he understood that the fight had to begin and he was willing to be the person to carry the torch.

FACT

Creativity involves taking risks and not worrying about what others might think of you or your ideas. By taking risks, you are more likely to engage in creative projects than if you simply do what others think is "right" or safe.

The Fear of What Others Think

It is a fear that is sometimes paralyzing: *What will they think of me?* It has driven many a creative person into the doldrums of common living. This fear has squashed more dreams and damaged more people's self-esteem than most other fears combined.

Think back to a time in your life when your efforts or dreams have been hampered by your fear of popular opinion. When this happens, you are caught in the middle of true self and public self. For many people, public self wins most every time.

The court of public opinion is a very strong entity. It can try you and convict you before you know what hit you. Can you imagine the number of inventions, cures, artistic creations, literature, and social programs that have gone untried because of fear of what others would think of the idea?

Censoring Yourself

The fear of what others think can cause a frightening phenomenon in your life. It can cause you to censor what you think, what you feel, what you really want to do because someone may think it is foolhardy or inappropriate.

Censoring means that you did not say what you wanted to say at that meeting last week because no one else had ever said it before. Censoring yourself means that you decided not to take that class in sculpting because none of your friends had ever done it before. Censoring means that you chose not to follow your dream of opening your own little café because so many people told you that it would not work.

Censoring yourself is basically a death sentence of sorts. You literally kill off parts of your most creative self and, little by little, your self-esteem and your true self dies alongside it.

The Case of Catherine

Catherine was never a traditional girl. She played in trees, refused to wear dresses, enjoyed cars more than dolls, and would rather spend time with her father at a ballgame than anything else in the world. She was the classic "tomboy."

When she grew older, she knew that her love of cars was going to turn into her life's work. She took auto mechanics in high school, much to the chagrin of her mother and many of her friends. She was constantly called names and often harassed in class by her male counterparts.

She persevered and decided to attend the community college in her town and major in auto/diesel repair. She faced roadblock after roadblock. Although her grades were excellent, she found that most scholarship programs denied her money because of her gender.

Some of her professors were less than happy to see her in class and did not help her as much as they helped the male students. She was determined that she would not let them win. She was determined to break the glass ceiling and follow her dreams. She was determined not to censor her life's dream to satisfy the prejudices of narrow-minded people.

Today, Catherine owns her own auto repair and parts business and employs twenty-three people, nine of whom are women. Think about the tragedy of what could have happened to her (and twenty-three others) had she censored her life for the sake of fear.

Doing What Others Dare Not Do

After you have conquered your fear of what others may think and have made the decision to live your true, creative self, you may find yourself on the cusp of greatness. Living in true creativity will allow you to go, see, think, do, feel, and experience what others have not.

Start with the Question

Perhaps you want (or need) to be more creative at work or at home and you're stuck; things will just not come to you. A great tip to jump-start your brain is to think backward. Instead of trying to find a creative answer, you may need to start with a creative question. Great philosophers have long known that the question is often more important than the answer.

Pretend that you are at work and you have been asked to help resolve an internal interpersonal conflict. You've looked at the situation and tried to develop a plan to resolve the issue. No good ideas have come to you yet.

"A lot of things happen on the back of a cocktail napkin. You have to be very open, and everyone has to feel their ideas are welcome."
—Gina Day

Turn the situation around. Instead of trying to find a solution to the conflict, try to ask questions that will get at the heart of the matter. Try to think of questions that have not yet been asked, let alone answered. If the questions are accurate and well planned, they may resolve the conflict quicker than a solution.

Giving Creativity a Chance

You may have tried to be creative and feel that the more you tried, the worse it got. This can be frustrating and damaging to your efforts. Creativity should not be a forced issue. Try a few different things to spark your creativity. First, determine if your most creative time of day is in the early morning, at lunchtime, or late into the night. It may be that you are most creative in your office during your lunchtime. It may be that you are most creative when you first get up in the morning—most people say this is their most creative time.

Creativity cannot be tied to a timeline. Deadlines and schedules impede creativity, and often, when working under stress and pressure, your creativity suffers. Therefore, try to use your stress-free time as creative time.

Just because you have tried creativity before, maybe unsuccessfully, don't give up on your creative self. Creativity and self-esteem are great partners and need each other.

Trying Different, New, and Scary Things

So, you've decided to give it a first try or another try. You have decided to let go of your fears of what other people may think and you're ready to live your true, creative self. Congratulations.

As you begin your journey to healthier self-esteem through creativity, keep the following strategies for creative success in mind. Remember, creativity is a natural part of who you are. You just have to work to find the best way to bring it to light.

- Keep an open mind to all possibilities, large and small.
- Never think that something is too crazy or stupid.
- Involve yourself in many different activities and projects.
- If you get stuck, leave it alone and move on to something else for a while.
- Use brainstorming to open up your senses.
- Be flexible and let an idea or project flow in its own way.
- Let work become play and play become work.
- Always think beyond what is in the present.
- Let music, art, and nature be your muse for creativity.

Creative and unconventional thinking can assist you in building a life that is beyond common. It can help you find your true self. It can assist you in building healthy self-esteem through discovery, fearlessness, curiosity, and maintaining a sense of individual style. Once you let yourself begin to experience the world of creative thinking and doing, you will understand how important this one thing is to your self-esteem.

Activity: Being Unconventional

Directions: A major part of creativity is knowing that you don't have to "follow the crowd" or think in a bandwagon fashion. This activity asks you to think in an unconventional way about common activities. Think about what you could do to make the following activities unique to you and unconventional to anyone. Write a description of some of your ideas.

EXAMPLE: DINNER WITH FRIENDS

I would remove all of the furniture from the living or dining room, except for the plants (fake or real). I would bring in all the plants from the other parts of the house so that the room looked very lush. I would make a semicircle around the fireplace and spread out a blanket and put pillows all around the semicircle. Dinner would be served from the center of the blanket and would consist of breads, cheeses, fruits, and such that could be eaten with the fingers. Soft music would be playing in the background. In essence, we would have an indoor picnic complete with plants and a campfire. People could lounge around and have a very leisurely meal with good friends in an intimate, unusual atmosphere.

A vacation for adults

Activity: Being Unconventional

Choosing a topic for a book and a plan for writing that book

A homemade toy for a child

Redecorating a room

Improving self-esteem

_____

_____

_____

_____

_____

_____

_____

Solving a problem (Think about the times you have solved problems or witnessed others solving problems and do something completely different. Be creative.)

State the problem:

_____

_____

_____

_____

_____

_____

_____

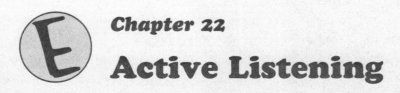

Chapter 22

Active Listening

Although listening is the very first language skill developed by those who have the gift of hearing, it is often the least regarded. Seldom does anyone have a class or formal training in listening. Most people, educators included, take listening for granted and assume it is automatic. Nothing could be further from the truth.

Listening versus Hearing

There are weighty differences between listening and hearing. Hearing is an automatic response while listening is a voluntary action. Hearing has little to do with choice, while listening has everything to do with choice.

Think of it in this light: Just because you have hands, this does not make you a painter, sculptor, or carpenter. Just because you have feet, this does not make you a dancer or marathon runner. Thus, just because you have ears, this does not make you a listener.

Stop reading for a moment and listen to the sounds around you. What are they? Do you hear traffic? Do you hear the buzz of a florescent light? Do you hear children playing, neighbors talking, or music in the background? If you can answer this question, you were listening. Yes! It is that simple. If you stopped to focus on the sounds around you, it was a voluntary decision and your hearing went a step further and turned into listening.

Test Your Listening Abilities

The only real test for listening is to listen. The following assessment will, however, help you understand if you are using your listening skills to best advantage.

Review the following statements. Put a check by the statements that most closely match your listening traits.

☐ 1. I tune out when something is boring to me.
☐ 2. I listen to the whole story before making a decision or coming to a conclusion.
☐ 3. I often begin formulating a response in my head as the other person talks.
☐ 4. I really try to understand the other person's point when listening.
☐ 5. Sometimes, I start listening on a negative note.
☐ 6. I objectively evaluate all information, regardless of the source.
☐ 7. My mind wanders to unrelated material when the speaker is talking.
☐ 8. I can tune out distractions such as noise when I am listening.
☐ 9. I judge the information before I truly understand what the speaker means.

❏ 10. I leave my emotions outside when listening. I listen with an objective mind.

❏ 11. I often interrupt the speaker so that I can say what I want to say.

❏ 12. I force myself to never mentally argue with the speaker when he or she is speaking.

❏ 13. I answer questions that are asked of other people.

❏ 14. I usually accept information as true from people I like and respect.

❏ 15. I eliminate some information from the message to simplify what I am hearing.

❏ 16. I force myself to be silent during conversations so that I can focus on what is being said instead of what I am going to say.

If you checked more odd numbers than even numbers, you have created some monumental barriers to effective listening. If you checked more even numbers than odd numbers, you have learned how to eliminate many barriers to the listening process.

The Listening Process

Listening does not just happen. There is a process that takes place in the brain that allows us to become more active listeners.

The process involves four parts:

- Receiving
- Focusing
- Understanding
- Reacting

If you hear a car horn blowing behind you, you have *received* the sound. This does not mean that you were listening; it simply means that you were within the range of the sound.

If you turn down the radio to see if the horn is blown again (or if it was a horn at all), you have begun to *focus* on the sound. This is the beginning of the listening process. You have made a voluntary decision to begin doing more than hearing.

If the horn blows again and you recognize the sound as definitely being a horn, you have begun to *understand* the sound. Your brain relates this sound to sounds it has heard before and lets you know that the sound is indeed a horn, not a baby crying.

Research suggests that twenty-four hours after you hear something, you will only remember about 50 percent of the information. After forty-eight hours, you only remember about 25 percent.

Finally, you will have a *reaction* to everything you hear. The reaction may be to speed up or slow down or pull over if a horn is blowing. The reaction may be to change the baby's diaper if the baby is crying, or the reaction can be to do nothing. Doing nothing is still a reaction.

These four steps can take place in less than a second. Think of the last time that you heard someone scream loudly or if you heard something fall, crash, and break right behind you. What was your reaction? You probably screamed and jumped. This took place almost immediately. This is how quickly these four steps can happen.

The Importance of Listening

Listening is, by far, one of the most important aspects of communication. So often, you pay attention to your speech, your words, your dialect, but neglect your ability to listen.

Your self-esteem can be greatly enhanced by learning how to be a more effective listener. Effective listening helps create more positive and productive professional and personal relationships. Effective listening allows you to be in control of the information that is disseminated.

When you are an active listener, you are able to more accurately pinpoint potential problems on the horizon and possibly stop them before they fester. Active listening helps you obtain more information, thus helping you make more effective decisions.

Lastly, active listening demands that you become a part of the communication process. If you are listening, truly listening, you are involved in the process of two-way communication.

FACT

You listen at a much faster pace than people talk. You *speak* at a rate of 90 to 200 words per minute, but you *listen* at a rate of 400 to 600 words per minute and *think* at a rate of 500 to 1,000 words per minute. The difference in the speed of speech, listening, and thought can be an obstacle to the listening process simply because your mind can begin to wander.

The Benefits of Listening

The benefits of being an active listener are incalculable. They range from increased knowledge to being able to have more compassion. Listening (and yes, deaf people can listen, too) is a hallmark of successful people. It is a skill practiced by so few that to be able to do it well sets you apart from the pack.

Some of the benefits of listening include:

- You are better able to help others.
- You have more power and influence in the world.
- You are able to understand things on a deeper level.
- You are able to understand more about different cultures.
- You have the resources to make more informed, rational decisions.
- You have the tools to avoid conflicts and reduce problems.
- You are able to participate in life more because you know more.
- You can become a more effective leader.
- You will become more popular because people admire good listeners.
- Your self-esteem in greatly enhanced.

Listening with an Open Mind

Open-minded! What a word. So many people profess to be open-minded, when in actuality, they are only open to things that they already know and like. Things from cultural barriers to ignorance cause people to not listen to ideas, concepts, desires, and frustrations of others.

Open-minded listening is a tall order. It requires that you shed your fears, your inhibitions, your prejudices, your own knowledge, and your judgments. It is not an easy thing to do, but it is a necessary and important thing to do.

If you are an American Caucasian female, you will never know what it is like to be an African-American male in this country. There is no way that you could possibly understand what it is like. You can imagine, you can read, and you can pretend, but you will never know.

The only way that you will ever come close to knowing what it is like to be African-American, Hispanic, Asian, gay, poor, disabled, or anything that you are not is to listen to the people who are. This is your only hope for ever having the tiniest clue as to what happens in the daily lives of people who are different from you. The only way to ever begin to understand *what you are not* is to listen, really listen to *those who are.*

"We were all given one mouth and two ears. The wisest people use them in that proportion."

—Anonymous

The Chinese Verb "to Listen"

The Chinese verb "to listen" is perhaps the simplest, yet most comprehensive, example of open-minded, active, complete listening known. The Chinese character that means "to listen" is made up of the characters that mean "eyes," "ear," "undivided attention," and "heart." The Chinese view listening as a whole-body experience that involves all of these things.

The Ears

Listening with your ears means that you understand and employ the parts of the listening process including focusing, understanding, and reacting. It means that you have moved past the hearing stage and made a voluntary decision to listen.

The Eyes

Listening with your eyes means that you look at the person who is talking. It means that you observe his or her facial expressions, mannerisms, and nonverbal communication. It means that with your eyes you begin to see what that person is saying, even if he or she is not speaking.

Undivided Attention

This is perhaps the most difficult of actions. Your undivided attention means that you have eliminated all distractions and all barriers that may cloud your ability to listen. It means that you have moved beyond the prejudices and biases that you hold about a person, an issue, or a topic. It means that the person speaking to you is the only thing on your mind.

The Heart

It has been said that empathy is *your* pain in *my* heart. This is what listening with your heart entails, sympathy and empathy. It means that you are able to put yourself in other people's shoes, inside their head, inside their life, and listen to them from their point of view.

QUESTION?

Is listening really that important in the world of work?
Listening is one of the top skills for which employers look when hiring new associates. Poor listening skills in the world of work can cost a company millions, can create havoc and conflict, and in some cases, such as emergency rooms and hospitals, can even cause death.

Learning to Become an Active Listener

While listening is a voluntary act, it is not an easy voluntary act. It takes time and effort and much practice to become an active listener.

First, you must work to overcome the biggest barrier to listening—the urge to talk too much. It is a physical impossibility to listen and talk at the same time. Active listening requires that you learn the art of silence.

When practicing this skill, you can begin by forcing yourself to be silent in places where you might normally be a very talkative person, such as parties, gatherings of friends, lunch with colleagues, or on a date. You might also work on this skill by learning the art of asking questions and waiting for answers. Let the other person talk as long as he or she wishes. Your job is to listen.

Another major obstacle to listening is prejudging the situation even before the other person or persons begin to speak. Prejudging means that you have already made up your mind about the outcome before you give the person or the information a chance.

It may be that you do not like the information or idea being presented and you judge this unfairly, or it may be that you do not like the person communicating the message and you automatically judge the information based on who is giving it. Remember, active listening requires that you listen to the message and not judge the messenger until all of the cards are on the table.

When working on your skills to become a more active listener, consider the following tips:

- Work hard to give your complete attention to the person communicating.
- Avoid jumping to conclusions.
- Listen for how something is said.
- Listen for what is not said.
- Do not overreact; give the communicator a chance.
- Look for nonverbal signs in the message.
- Leave your emotions and prejudices behind.
- Give the communicator eye contact.
- Stop talking.

By practicing these simple techniques, you will be amazed at how quickly your listening skills begin to improve. You'll also begin to see a major difference in how you feel about yourself and your communication abilities.

Overcoming the Obstacles to Listening

As you begin your journey to active listening, you will encounter some barriers and obstacles along the way. Don't worry; this is normal and natural. Learning to listen actively and objectively will require some work on your part.

Some of the more common barriers can be overcome with practice, dedication, and a commitment from you to become a better listener.

- **Noise and distractions.** Learn to tune out common noises and distractions by focusing solely on the person communicating. Giving them your undivided attention can help you do this.
- **Emotions.** Leaving your emotions aside while listening will allow you to listen with a "clean slate." It is hard to listen to someone when you are angry or frustrated or sad.
- **Prejudices.** Your prejudices can cause you to tune out information that may be helpful to you. Your prejudices may extend beyond the message, to the person speaking.
- **Information overload.** It is difficult to judge how much information may come from a certain situation. Ways to deal with information overload include listening for the main issues, taking notes while listening, and asking questions if the opportunity arises.
- **Language and dialect barriers.** When a person speaks a language other than your own, you may have trouble with certain sounds and dialects. One way to combat this is to listen intently to the person communicating and to look at his or her lips. Sometimes, watching a person's lips can help with translation.
- **A.D.D.** If you have attention deficit disorder, this may be a hard barrier to overcome. You can get medical advice and/or prescription medication to assist you in focusing your attention.
- **Nonverbal communication.** It may be that a person's body language is so distracting that it is difficult to listen to them because of this nonverbal communication. Try to be patient and focus your attention on the message, not the messenger.
- **Impatience.** This is another difficult barrier to overcome, but it can be overcome with work and concentration. Don't let your immediate

need for satisfaction cheat you out of information that may be needed later on. If you feel yourself becoming impatient, use positive self-talk to relax yourself and bring yourself back into focus.

- **Lack of interest.** There are few things worse than a person who is boring. However, just because the person may lack communication skills, this does not mean that their message is unimportant or trivial. Try to focus on the information that you need and try to ask yourself, *How can I use this information to help others and myself?*

Conquering these barriers will assist you in becoming a more dynamic, active listener in almost every situation, from work to love, from business to friendship.

Active listening will help you in more ways than you can imagine. It allows you to be more active in your own life, and in the lives of those you love. It allows you to be able to help others on a level that you never dreamed you could. It allows you to garner information and data that will be helpful to you for the rest of your life. Most importantly, however, listening can help you build stronger, more productive, more caring, and compassionate relationships. Everyone loves a person who speaks well, but a person who listens well endears herself for eternity.

Activity: Listening with Questions

Directions: For this listening exercise, you will need to log on to the following Web site hosted by the History Channel: ✍ *www.historychannel.com/speeches.*

Once you have logged on, click on the icon for Political and Government Speeches, then scroll to the bottom and click on the small alphabet icon [K–O]. Scroll down until you find the "I Have a Dream" speech by Dr. Martin Luther King Jr.

Listen to the entire sixteen-minute speech delivered in Washington, D.C., in August of 1963. Listen carefully to his vocal tones, his inflections, and his passion. Listen for *how* he says certain words and phrases. Listen for details in the content of his message.

Do not read any further in this exercise until you have listened to his famous speech. Stop reading and log on to the History Channel Web site.

Activity: Listening with Questions

After you have listened to his speech, return here to answer a few questions.

After having listened to his speech, answer the following questions without going back to relisten. You can check your answers by listening to the speech a second time.

1. He says that America has written a bad check marked _____
   _____

2. He says that 1963 is not an end, but a _____
   _____

3. He says that the Negro must meet physical force with _____
   _____

4. He dreams of this nation living up to the true meaning of its creed: "We hold _____
   _____"

5. He dreams that this nation will judge his children by_____
   _____
   _____

6. Name one place from where he wishes freedom to ring.
   _____

7. "Free at last, free at last . . ." are words taken from an old _____
   _____

Check your answers by listening to the speech again, this time with these questions in front of you.

Activity: Listening with Questions (continued)

Was it hard to remember the details of the speech? ☐ Yes   ☐ No
Why?

Was it easy to tune out all distractions and listen with your ears, heart, and undivided attention? ☐ Yes   ☐ No
Why?

What was the hardest part about listening to this speech? Why?

What would have made this speech easier to listen to?

When you answered the previous questions correctly, how did this make you feel?

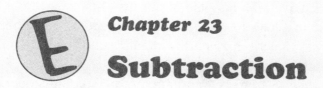

Chapter 23

Subtraction

It is strange to think that math plays a role in self-esteem development, but it does. Subtracting means that you are ready to take away the negative powers that others have over you. It means that you are strong enough to admit your shortcomings, thus taking away the power from those who would use these shortcomings against you.

Admitting Your Weaknesses

In the movie *Fatal Attraction*, Michael Douglas has an extramarital affair with Glenn Close. When she discovers that he is married, she begins to use this information against him. She knows that she has information that will be damaging to his personal and professional life. It is not until he actually tells his wife about his affair that the character played by Glenn Close loses the power of negotiation. When Douglas told his wife that he had had an affair with Close, he took away her tool of destruction.

If you ever tell a lie to someone and another person finds out that you lied, that person has power over you until you admit the lie yourself. In doing this, you take the power away from the person who knows about the lie. You strip that person of his or her negative tool of persuasion. Once you admit the lie, his or her power is gone.

This is how subtraction works. Many people will find your weaknesses, your fears, your shortcomings, and once discovered, will use this knowledge against you at every turn. They become relentless in using this weapon to manipulate you.

The *only way* to combat this is to be comfortable in admitting your own shortcomings, thus taking the power away from other people to use this against you.

QUESTION?

What is a weakness?

A weakness is something that you are not as adept at as others may be. It's a flaw that you might have. Your weakness may be that you lack patience, that you have a temper, that you don't particularly enjoy being around children, or that you talk too much. Weaknesses are not permanent, but they are deeply engrained in your personality and will take a concerted effort to overcome.

Parents

Perhaps the very first people to use this tool against you were your parents. They may not have known what they were doing, but they may have unwittingly used the power of your weaknesses to damage your self-esteem.

It may be that they were using the power to try to help you. Imagine the parent who has watched his or her child struggle and struggle with math. Then, the parent finds out that his or her child has voluntarily registered for a math competition at school. The parent may say to the child, "You know you have trouble in math and you should really rethink this. I really don't think you're going to be able to do it."

The parent is trying to help the child avoid embarrassment, when in actuality he or she has used the child's weakness as a tool to damage the child's self-esteem. On the other hand, some parents would say this to keep the child from exploring new options or engaging in new activities. They would use the knowledge of the child's math problems to deliberately hurt the child's esteem.

Friends

Just because you call them your friends does not mean that they always are your "friends." Sometimes, your friends can be the most vicious people you know.

Suppose that your friend found out that you were not very good at volleyball and a group of friends wanted to go play. Your friend may use this information against you in order to feel better about his or her own abilities. This person may jokingly cut you down in front of other friends just so that everyone knows your weakness.

"It is well, when judging a friend, to remember that he is judging you with the same godlike and superior impartiality."
—Arnold Bennett

However, if you admit that weakness up front, make light of the fact that you don't play very well but say that you'd love to try, you have taken the power of hurt away from that "friend" to embarrass you.

Coworkers

Perhaps the most damaging relationship you can have is when your coworkers know your weaknesses. Often, they will use this power to advance their own career over yours. They may take every opportunity possible to let others in the environment know what your weaknesses are.

Suppose that a coworker finds out that you do not like to deal with conflict and that you have a very hard time being around people who are in conflict. Your coworker may use every opportunity to let others know this, thus planting the seed in people's minds that you would not make a very good manager because you can't deal with people in conflict.

Once that seed is planted, you will have a hard time addressing the issue unless you admit it up front, work to overcome it, and learn from those who do it well. By admitting the shortcoming on your own, you have taken the power away from that coworker.

Subtraction and Self-Esteem

Your self-esteem can be greatly enhanced or greatly damaged by this subtraction technique. If you discover that someone is using one of your weaknesses against you and you do nothing about this, your self-esteem, and maybe your career and relationships, may suffer.

However, if you become the first to admit that you don't like conflict, or you don't play volleyball very well, or that you don't know how to use PowerPoint, then no one can use that information against you, because it is already public knowledge.

It is okay to relinquish the thought that you are perfect. You are not, and no one else is either. Everyone has strengths, and everyone has weaknesses. The key is to acknowledge both. In doing so, you begin to understand the essence of being human. You begin to understand that life is a series of "haves and have nots," of "can do and can't do," and "knowing and not knowing."

It is only when you refuse to admit your shortcomings and faults that another person can use them over you. By having the courage and the self-esteem to say, "You're right; I'm not perfect and never will be," you have taken a monumental step in subtracting negative power away from others.

Overcoming Weakness

Weaknesses are personal. What you perceive to be your weakness, others may perceive to be a gift. What one person sees as a weakness in his or her life, the next person may see as a blessing.

Many people have marvelous gifts and incredible talents but focus on one or two of their shortcomings. They have a hard time moving past their weakness and focusing on their strengths. People with healthy self-esteem are usually those who have learned that their weaknesses are not death sentences and that they have other qualities to compensate for their deficiency.

"In the midst of winter, I finally learned that there was in me an invincible summer."

—Albert Camus

Shortcomings are just that, short. They are not massive-life-threatening-impossible-comings. Often, our shortcomings, or perceived shortcomings, can be a result of comparisons to other people and their lives.

As discussed earlier in this book, comparing your life and talents to other people is a dangerous thing, especially when working to build healthier self-esteem. Other people do not have your life, your successes, your setbacks, your triumphs, your family, your friends, your struggle, or your soul.

To compare yourself and your shortcomings to another person is to invalidate all that you are in every other area of your life.

Nurturing Yourself

Overcoming your weaknesses may seem impossible, but it is not. People do it every day. You have probably overcome many weaknesses and not really even noticed it. Moving past your shortcomings requires that you love yourself enough to nurture yourself.

If you had a friend who needed help and assistance, physically, emotionally, or mentally, you would go to that friend in an instant. Now, you must move toward the view that *you are a friend of yours, too*, and you must go to yourself sometimes for nurturing.

Some ways to nurture yourself include:

- Find what you love to do and make time—schedule time—to do it.
- Meet the basic needs of your body (food, shelter, rest, intimacy).
- Get a massage, learn yoga, or meditate to relax your body more.
- Surround yourself with positive, supportive friends.
- Allow yourself to grow emotionally, spiritually, and intellectually.
- Give yourself a break from self-criticism and negative self-talk.
- Give yourself a break from others' criticism and negative feedback.

By following these simple yet monumental tips, you can begin to feel better about yourself, thus allowing you to focus on your strengths rather than your weaknesses.

Weaknesses Be Gone!

Another part of nurturing yourself is allowing yourself the opportunity to properly identify and work toward minimizing your weaknesses. You may never rid yourself completely of them, but if they disturb you and are obstructing your self-esteem development, it is important to identify them correctly and work toward improving or eliminating them.

The first step in this process is to stop procrastinating. You may have complained and griped about these weaknesses for years, but now is the time to act. Procrastinating will not eliminate the problem, nor will it allow you to work successfully to overcome it.

The next step is to stop avoiding your weak spots. If you really want to work on them, you must face them head-on. You will need to be relentless in your pursuit of elimination or reduction.

Fighting your weaknesses will require that you are mentally and emotionally aware at all times. It means that you are going to literally "stalk" your shortcomings until you change them or until they no longer concern you.

Avoiding the task or putting the task off until a later date can only serve to damage your attempts and your self-esteem. You will need to make a dedicated decision to work on your weaknesses every day.

Other ways to reduce or eliminate your weaknesses include:

- Visualize your life without the perceived weakness.
- Set realistic goals to overcome the weakness.
- Work toward that goal with every action and interaction in which you engage.
- Talk to others about your attempts to overcome this weakness.
- Catch yourself actually not doing the "thing" and reward yourself.
- Do not become compulsive about this shortcoming.
- Do not engage in self-defeating habits to eliminate the weakness.

Remember that every person in the world has weaknesses. Those who proclaim that they do not are sadly mistaken. Don't let this shortcoming overwhelm you or consume you. Remember, just admitting that you have it is half the battle in eliminating it.

Putting It into Perspective

You've heard the old expression before, "For what it's worth . . ." and then the person begins to unload on you all of the criticism and negativity that they can find. Well, "for what it's worth," you don't have to take it. "For what it's worth," you can choose to have your own method of evaluating your life, work, and performance. "For what it's worth," you can learn to let unconstructive criticism wash away with the water.

The Desire to Improve

Everyone wants to improve in one fashion or another; it is human nature. Everyone has small and large habits that need breaking, attitudes that need adjusting, and weaknesses that need strengthening. One way to do this is by garnering feedback from people you trust.

You should recognize up-front, however, that not all people, not even your friends, are accomplished in the art of feedback and criticism. Although they may mean well, they may choose words and phrases that are inappropriate and they may choose a time to give you feedback that is inappropriate.

Some people, even your friends, will use criticism as a way to put you in your place. Once again, they have found a weakness and they may use that weakness to exploit your inadequate feelings. When seeking to improve your actions and behaviors through feedback, understand that you may not always get the response that you want. Some people may be more honest than you would like them to be. Therefore, you have to be prepared to hear what they have to say. It goes back to the age-old expression, "If you have the courage to ask the question, you must have the courage to hear the answer."

Hearing other people's negative opinions about you can be very bad for your self-esteem. Their criticism causes you to have self-doubts—fueling doubts you already had and even causing you to worry about new ones. You must be careful to listen to what they are really saying and realize that you control how you react and deal with that information.

Do remember, however, that not all feedback is true. You need to look at feedback as a means to help improve your weakness, not as an end-all and be-all. Other people's opinions are just that—their opinions. You may value their opinion, but you will still need to look at their feedback through a sifter.

You will need to take what they say, evaluate if they are being fair, look at the perspective in which it was given, and then decide if you will accept and act on that feedback. It is healthy to seek feedback on habits, behaviors, attitudes, and activities that you wish to improve. It shows that you have enough courage to seek the advice of others. However, keep in mind that you have the final word in what is true and untrue in your life.

The Case of Luanda

Luanda fished for feedback more than most people. She seemed to need it to function. However, Luanda was not really looking for feedback as much as she was looking for praise and affirmation. Feedback can certainly include praise, but Luanda needed praise more than most, so when feedback came that was less than sterling, she did one of two things—she got angry or she got hurt. No one could predict which was coming.

One day at work, Luanda made a presentation about a project on which she and her team had been working. They had spent over three weeks putting together a training program for a new client. When she presented the new program to her counterparts at the consulting firm, the feedback was, on a whole, excellent. However, there were suggestions coming from a few senior members on ways to strengthen the project. Maurice, one of her associates working on another team, made a number of positive comments, but also made a number of constructive, helpful suggestions. He based his suggestions on his work with a similar client in a similar situation. He prefaced his remarks by saying that he and his team had worked with a similar client and that he offered the comments so that Luanda and her team might learn from his team's mistakes. When he completed his comments, most everyone in the room agreed that his points for improvement were valid. The manager asked Luanda to make the necessary changes to her team's program to strengthen it. She agreed.

Once the meeting was over, Luanda stopped Maurice in the hallway. He thought that she was going to thank him for his assistance, but instead, she began to berate and attack him in front of other colleagues.

"How could you do that to me in front of everyone?" she questioned angrily. "I thought we were friends. I never expected this type of treatment from you." She continued on for over five minutes about how unfaithful he had been and how he just wanted her and her team to fail. She even suggested that he was out to get her fired. Maurice was in complete shock. He did not know that Luanda would respond this way. He did not realize that she presented the project for praise, and that she didn't really want anyone's suggestions for improvement.

Learning from Others' Comments

Both Luanda and Maurice learned a valuable lesson. Luanda learned to expect honesty if you ask for it, and Maurice learned that not every person who asks for honest feedback really wants it.

We can learn much from other people. We can learn from their experiences, their failures, and yes, their successes. We can learn, however, only if we are willing to listen to their feedback on an honest level. We can learn only if we give them the chance to honestly be critical of our work without the threat of retaliation, violence, anger, or loss of relationships.

People with the healthiest self-esteem are those who welcome the comments of others for improvement. They know how to distinguish between positive, constructive feedback, and useless, self-serving, destructive comments and feedback.

Remember that feedback that is useful centers on your work, your actions, your progress, and your projects. Feedback that attacks you as a person is useless and unproductive. By learning to accept feedback, you can begin to admit and work on your shortcomings. You can begin to improve your behaviors, attitudes, and actions if you decide that this is the right thing for you.

By learning to admit your weaknesses, you will soon realize how liberating it is to know that no one can use this information against you anymore. You have the power to eliminate this worry from your life. You also have the power to begin working to eliminate this weakness or shortcoming from your life if it is of great concern to you. Just remember, the boat is full of people just like you, imperfections and all.

Activity: I Am Certain

Directions: There are few things in life of which we can be certain. However, your talents and skills are one of the things you can be sure about. You have the power to determine the things about which you are certain in your own life. Forget about any weaknesses you feel you have at the moment. List ten things about which you are certain with regards to your own abilities, skills, and talents.

Activity: I Am Certain

EXAMPLE:

I am certain that I can build a wooden deck.
I am certain that I can plant trees and shrubs.
I am certain that I can detail a car.
I am certain that I can type.
I am certain that I am a patient person.
I am certain that I am a good listener.

I am certain that I

_____

I am certain that I   .

_____

I am certain that I

_____

I am certain that I

_____

I am certain that I

_____

I am certain that I

_____

I am certain that I

_____

I am certain that I

_____

Activity: I Am Certain (continued)

I am certain that I

I am certain that I

Of which statement are you most proud? Why?

What one thing do you wish was on your list that is not there? Why?

What would this one thing do to help your self-esteem?

Using the goal sheet from the back of the book, devise a goal plan to bring this ability into your life.

Chapter 24
Giving

When you mention the word "giving," many people automatically assume that you are speaking of money or possessions. Giving can include money and material gifts, but it also encompasses a much larger array than tangible goods. Giving of yourself, your time, your talents, and your soul are some of the most nourishing acts in building healthy self-esteem.

Service to Others

When you give to another person, you are, in essence, admitting that you have an understanding of the grand scheme of human kindness. You are living on a level beyond selfishness, beyond greed, beyond your personal needs. You are living in your higher self. According to educator, writer, and speaker Leo Buscaglia, "You want to be the most educated, the most brilliant, the most exciting, the most versatile, the most creative individual in the world, because then you can give it away; and the only reason you have anything, is to give it away."

Service to others is about giving something that no other human on earth could possibly give—you! It is about finding what is rare and divine in your soul that you would like to share with the world. Service to others is about digging deep into the caverns of your abilities, your talents, and your personality and finding the gift that you want to share with humanity.

"Everyone has the power for greatness, not for fame, because greatness is determined by service."

—Dr. Martin Luther King Jr

Humanity and Empathy

Humanity is used to describe the human race, but it is also associated with the word *humane*, which encompasses kindness, compassion, and mercy. Your self-esteem is tied directly to your humanity and how you treat other people. It has been written and spoken by religious leaders, philosophers, educators, therapists, and countless others that those who do not love and respect themselves cannot love or respect others.

Service and humanity begin with empathy. Empathy is when you put yourself in the lives of others. It is when you truly understand their pain, joy, fears, and actions on an internal level. Empathy at its highest level is when you are involved enough to know what other people need and how you can help them with their needs. Empathy is when you forego judgment for understanding, when you move beyond reacting and learn to take action, and when you help find the answers instead of blaming. Most of the time, people with the greatest empathy are those who know how to listen to what is spoken *and* to what is not spoken.

To become a giving person, it will be important for you to cultivate your sense of empathy. Giving is most appreciated when you give what is truly needed, not what you *think* is needed. Understanding what is truly needed can come from learning to listen with an empathetic ear.

By learning to listen more carefully, you can begin to hear the needs of humanity. You can begin to understand more fully how your hands can be the hands that can change a human life.

An Investment in Human History

There is an old saying that goes, "Teachers touch the future. They never know where their influence ends." This is true not just for "formal" teachers in the school systems, but for you as well. As a person who gives of yourself, you never know where your influence ends, or if it ever does.

When you give of yourself, you can think of it as an investment in the future. You can look at it as leaving a piece of yourself with humanity. You can think of it as your living monument when you are gone. By giving to one person—just one other person—you could have a profound influence upon that person and upon history.

Visualize for a moment that you helped John Doe, who lives in a homeless shelter, by allowing him to rake the leaves in your front yard for $10. John Doe, whom you have never met before, takes the $10 and goes to the Salvation Army Store and buys a pair of pants, a shirt, and a newer pair of shoes.

By buying this outfit, John Doe is able to approach the manager of a local landscaping business to ask for employment. The manager agrees to hire him on a trial basis. After one month, John Doe is hired full-time with benefits. John Doe, grateful for a second chance, moves out of the shelter, rents a room that he found listed in the paper, saves his money, and decides that because he got a second chance, he wants to help someone else.

After six months, he has saved over $400. He approaches the local community college and gives the money to a student fund to purchase textbooks for struggling college students. Because of John Doe, two students are able to purchase their books to work on their degrees, one in social work and the other in education. Five years later, these two students are employed. One is a special-education teacher in high school; the other works as a marriage and family specialist at the local Department of Human Services. Their daily actions help the lives of hundreds each year.

When volunteering for any organization or project, think about the new golden rule: Do unto others as they would have you do unto them. Volunteers should never try to force their help on anyone nor should they try to "rescue" anyone.

Just think, because some leaves fell on your lawn and you chose to spend $10 on a "wanderer," the course of human history changed for thousands of people. Because you took a chance and gave just a little, you played a part in this miracle called the circle of life.

Altruism and Giving

Altruism and giving both deal with selflessness. Altruism means having a genuine concern, compassion, and kindness toward humanity, genuinely caring for the welfare of your fellow citizens. Those who have deep altruistic qualities find ways to help their fellow citizens on any level; they do not need a formal outlet such as volunteering to be able to do so.

Altruism does not concern itself with reward, status, money, or power. Altruism is about doing good deeds and helping others simply for the sake of doing it. It comes from a total abandonment of ego and remuneration. It is rooted in a desire to move humanity forward.

By discovering your own altruistic goals and by serving others, you are, in essence, helping yourself. The more you give, the better you feel. Those who give to others live longer and healthier lives, and have a stronger immune system.

You may say to yourself, "I'm just not a very altruistic person." This may be true, but altruism can be learned. It is innate in some people, but others have to work at it. One way to work at becoming more altruistic is to actually be more altruistic. By doing more altruistic work, you can become "hooked" and, in turn, continue to do and give more.

> "Practicing the *Law of Giving* is actually very simple: if you want joy, give joy to others; if you want love, learn to give love; if you want attention and appreciation, learn to give attention and appreciation; if you want material affluence, help others to become materially affluent."
>
> —Deepak Chopra

Study after study on altruism, giving, and volunteerism suggests that the people who are more involved in these activities report an increased quality of life for themselves. In giving, the gifts are returned tenfold.

Volunteering

Giving does not have to involve volunteering your time, but that may be one way that you can give back to the community. Volunteering is a more structured, formal means by which to offer your services, talents, and energy.

When you volunteer as your method of giving, you will be asked to donate a certain amount of time each week or month. You should treat this service as you would treat a formal job. If you volunteer to serve in a certain capacity and you are unable to physically be at the place of service, it is not like a place of employment where the "boss" may find someone to fill in. In volunteering, if you are not there, it is likely that the service will not be done.

Are you wondering if volunteers are really needed or if you can help at all? Consider this: Every night in America, 750,000 people sleep on the streets; 11.6 million children wake up in poverty; a child is arrested for a violent crime ever five minutes; suicide is the ninth leading cause of death in America; the number of hate crimes increase every year; worldwide, 40 million people are living with AIDS; 19,000 children die daily from malnutrition; and a quarter of the world's population lives on $1.08 a day.

THE EVERYTHING SELF-ESTEEM BOOK

When thinking about volunteering, consider why you are doing it, what others are gaining from it, what you are gaining from it, how much you enjoy the volunteer work, and how well you think you can perform the tasks at hand.

Why People Volunteer

People volunteer for a variety of reasons—some altruistic, some not. Some people actually see volunteering as their civic duty, while others do it to gain job experience or to network for future employment.

Volunteering does not have to be completely one-sided. You do not, and should not, volunteer to do something for which you have no interest, no aptitude, no desire, and no passion. Volunteering, while rewarding and stimulating, can also be trying, frustrating, and full of political hurdles, not to mention grueling work.

"You cannot do a kindness too soon, for you never know how soon it will be too late."

—Ralph Waldo Emerson

However, volunteering can also be filled with rewards beyond imagination. It can be more rewarding than any job or career track on which you have ever embarked. Some of the most common reasons that people volunteer include:

- They are asked to do so by a friend or colleague.
- They believe (and know) that their efforts make a difference.
- It is their way to fight against a social ill such as abuse or poverty.
- They see it as a part of the political process.
- They see it as an outlet for expressing their compassion and successes.
- They have a genuine need and deep desire to help others.
- They understand that they can help change a human life.
- They see volunteering as fun and enjoyable.
- It builds character and healthy self-esteem.

Why People Do Not Volunteer

Just as there are countless reasons for why people volunteer, there are just as many reasons for why people would rather not volunteer. Some feel that volunteering doesn't really help at all. Others see that some organizations have abused their public image for the personal gain of board members and leaders, and they are skeptical.

Volunteering is something about which you have to feel good. If you are made to feel guilty or made to volunteer out of pressure, this is not volunteering for the right reasons (and isn't likely to help your self-esteem one bit, either).

Some additional reasons that people do not volunteer include:

- They can't find the time or it is too time-consuming.
- They don't see the benefits or any positive outcomes.
- They are jaded by past scandals and abuses of power.
- They don't think there is a place for them.
- They tried it at one place and it did not go well, and they won't try it again.
- They believe that the people being served should be doing more to help themselves.
- They are apathetic.

Giving through volunteering is the work of your heart. It is work on which you cannot put a price tag. It is work that can help you realize a dream, network, improve your self-esteem, share your talents, and make a difference through your positive attitude. Volunteering, however, must be right for you.

Finding Gifts in Everyday Life

Even the poorest citizen in the United States can give. Giving has so little to do with money. Every person on earth has some gift worthy of being offered. Perhaps it is performing something as simple as changing a tire for someone broken down on the roadside. Maybe it is complimenting the outfit of a coworker.

Everyday gifts are not rare, they are not expensive, they are not hard to do, and they are not steeped in formality. However, they are priceless to the person on the receiving end. And, they can be priceless to you and your self-esteem.

Some of the simple, everyday gifts that you can offer may include:

- Write a note of "thank you" to someone once a week.
- Call a store manager and praise an employee who did well.
- Compliment a stranger.
- Go to yard sales and buy books to donate to prisons.
- Volunteer your pet for a "petting program" at a nursing home or hospital.
- Save all of your loose change all year and buy a child's Christmas presents.
- Spend time with an Alzheimer's victim to allow the family some free time.
- Start a phone book recycling program at work or in your neighborhood.
- Start a graffiti removal program in your neighborhood.

These acts of selfless giving cost very little, or nothing, but the returns for those who receive them are enormous.

Giving to Yourself

Finally, you must not forget to give to yourself. If you are not nurturing your own needs, desires, and passions, you will not be able to do so for others.

Giving to yourself means that you identify your basic needs for a quality life. Is it that you need good friends around you? Do you need your family? Do you need quiet time for reflection and contemplation? Do you need a good book, a glass of wine, and some great music?

Or, do you need to be working and giving and helping others? You can have it all. But you must develop a plan for having it all. Perhaps you will decide to volunteer one week and spend time on yourself the next week. While volunteering and altruistic deeds are about others, the decisions and the passion must be about you.

Good luck on finding and sharing the passion of your heart.

"Giving to the world" sounds so monumental that the mere words can overwhelm you. But, hopefully, you understand now that giving to the world can be accomplished through giving to one person. Service to humanity begins by stopping to find out who needs help, and helping those you can. You don't have to save the rain forest; you don't have to feed the entire homeless population. You don't have to give your life's savings. Service to humanity begins in your heart and ends in the heart of another person.

Activity: What Can I Do Today?

Directions: Following, you will find a series of categories that you will need to evaluate to help you decide what talents you have and where best those talents might be used to help other people. Write down the things that you can do in each of these situations. Some of the categories are abstract and intangible, while other categories are very concrete and tangible. Some of the categories require physical things like time and resources, while other categories require nothing but you! Take your time. This exercise can change the way you look at giving to humanity.

WHAT CAN I DO *THIS WEEK* . . .

To help someone smile

To help someone remember better times

To help someone laugh heartily

Activity: What Can I Do Today? (continued)

To help restore someone's confidence

To help someone believe in friendship again

To help invigorate a child's imagination

To help someone believe in love again

To help someone who is struggling with a health issue

To help someone who is lonely

To help an organization that assists others

To help someone spiritually

Activity: What Can I Do Today? (continued)

To help turn around the life of a troubled teenager

....

....

To help restore a damaged relationship

....

....

To help someone come to terms with a tragedy

....

....

To help the environment

....

....

To help my neighborhood

....

....

To help in the political arena

....

....

To help someone cope with major stress in his or her life

....

....

To help someone find her or his purpose in life

....

....

Activity: What Can I Do Today? (continued)

To help someone who is struggling financially

To help a library

To help a public school

To help a complete stranger

To help my best friend

Astonishingly, if you did just one of these things each week, this one exercise would allow you to give of yourself for six months. That's right, half a year's worth of service in this one activity! It is that simple. Enjoy the ride.

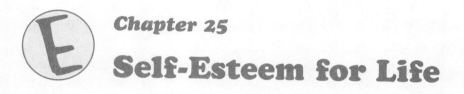

Chapter 25

Self-Esteem for Life

You've read and worked and toiled and debated and evaluated and maybe even cried and laughed some. Hopefully, you've looked at your life from many angles and made some decisions that are going to carry you forward on your quest for healthy self-esteem. Now, the job will be to sustain the progress that you've made. The job will be keeping the new life you've honed for yourself out of the broken edges of the past. Now, the job is for life.

More Work Ahead

Nothing, unfortunately, lasts forever, self-esteem included. Without working to keep up habits that reinforce a healthy self-esteem, you're likely to end up back where you started. Once acquired, self-esteem is not a permanent, everlasting thing. It must be nurtured, guided, fine-tuned, and revisited frequently. Your self-esteem should be treated as an infant child—watched carefully, loved much, but also given enough room to flourish.

As discussed throughout the book, there are countless influences on your self-esteem. From your parents to your friends to your colleagues to strangers to your field of work to your innate desires, the influences come in every shape, size, and origin. It takes a strong person to fight the urges of negative self-talk, negative and unsupportive people, and critics who would use the power of words and office to condemn you at every turn. However, you now know that you have the authority to make your self-esteem decisions for yourself. You know that you have the power to sustain positive feeling about your life.

Only Champagne and Caviar

Yes, you've had moments that you would just as soon never remember. You've had to pick yourself up and brush yourself off more times that you care to imagine. But, you did it. You made it. You're standing.

Today is the day that you will make choices that will affect the remaining days of your life. Today is the day that you are going to stand up and demand freedom from the past, demand freedom from all that has been negative and unfulfilling in your life, and demand that your soul be allowed to explore and expand.

You are going to demand this from yourself. You are going to stand up to your past and say, "No more." You are going to stand up to your past and say, "I will not allow you to chain me down ever again." You are going to stand up and say, "I have a right to be happy, I have a right to feel good about myself, and I have a right to feel joy and pleasure in my life."

"I was always willing to take a great deal of the burden of getting along in life on my own shoulders, but I wasn't willing to give myself a pat on the back. I was always looking to somebody else to do that. That was all wrong."

—Raquel Welch

You are the only person on earth who can do this for yourself. You are the only person who can make this happen. You are the only person who can serve yourself the champagne and caviar that you deserve. If you leave it up to others, you'll only get warm water and Cracker Jacks. You deserve more.

Standing Up

The previous chapters have shown you how to stand up and take control of your self-esteem and your life. Standing up means that you may have to readjust your stance, find new shoes, and walk more carefully this time around. Standing up means that you have made the decision to be equal in the world and not allow anyone to take that equality from you. Standing up means that you are now ready to walk forward.

By standing up, you are now ready to ask yourself, "What are my possibilities?" "What great things are in my future?" "What path will I take that will lead me to myself?" "What goodness can I do for others?" These questions would not have been possible with unhealthy self-esteem.

By standing up, you are ready to walk toward a life of service, a life of your own choosing, and a life of healthier choices. By standing up, you are ready to face the challenges that might have crippled you before.

Strategies for Life-Long Improvement

As you read through this chapter, you will be reminded of tips and strategies for looking ahead while working toward healthier self-esteem. You will not be able to work on every tip every day, but it is suggested that you return to this chapter anytime you feel weak, down, challenged, threatened, sad, or confused by the events of life.

Healthy self-esteem is a lifelong challenge and everyone needs help along the way. Let these strategies be your guiding voice.

Make Wellness a Priority

Today, you will pass by the donut shop and feel good about it. Today, you will make an appointment to see your physician. Today, you will stop by the local gym and inquire about a membership. If you don't like gyms, you will put on a pair of comfortable walking shoes and you will walk around your neighborhood and see it as the street to your health. Today, you will begin to eat more healthy foods, exercise more, smoke less, reduce your stress by positive thinking and meditation, and you will embrace this new energy with arms of passion.

Make Choices That Directly Affect Your Well-Being

From today forward, you will begin to make career, financial, emotional, physical, and mental decisions that only affect your life in a positive way. You will no longer let guilt, aimlessness, fear, or sorrow be your guide. You will begin to put your well-being first. This may sound selfish, but without taking care of you, you can't give proper attention to those you love.

Do Not Ignore Your Personal Needs

Today, you will begin to develop a Personal Needs Plan and you will begin to act upon this plan. You Personal Needs Plan will be developed based on what you feel is important and essential to your happiness, your self-esteem, your livelihood, and your mental well-being. You will post this plan in a conspicuous place and you will work daily to assure that you are meeting your personal needs.

Replace Aggression with Assertion

Today, you will make the commitment to never use aggression again. You will do everything in your power to win and succeed by assertion and intelligence rather than by aggression and ignorance. Today, you will begin reading and studying how to become a more assertive individual and you will use this newfound power at work, at home, with friends, with family, and even with strangers. Today, you will make the commitment to never be taken advantage of again. You will do this through assertiveness, not aggression.

Communicate with Yourself

Today, you will sit with yourself in the quiet hours (yes, you can have a quiet hour if you really want one) and you will talk with yourself about the goals and dreams of the day. You will allow yourself to listen to your soul, your inner navigator, and you will listen with passion unfurled. Today, you become your own best friend. You will talk to yourself about your past, your present, and your future. You will allow yourself the freedom to explore new avenues and you will grant yourself the privilege of your own company. Today, you will discover the power of your own inner voice.

"No one can make you feel inferior without your consent."
—Eleanor Roosevelt

Practice Integrity in Every Action

Today, you will re-evaluate your actions, your words, your behaviors, and your treatment of others and determine if you have been a person of integrity. Today, you will write an Integrity Statement, post that statement in a place where you can see it daily, and you will begin to sift your thoughts, actions, deeds, and treatment of others through this integrity plan. Today, you will make the decision to never worry again about whether right or wrong is important to you. Today, you will begin walking a path of ethical, moral, and just truth.

Accept Responsibility for Your Life and Your Actions

Today, you will begin to accept praise for what you do well and the consequences for what you neglect or pass off to others. Today, you will begin to take full responsibility for the good, bad, ugly, positive, rewarding, crazy, fulfilling, devastating, negative, and glorious things in your life. Today, you will admit to yourself that every action has a reaction, and you have the power to change both.

Practice Altruistic Giving and Sharing

Today, you will let the altruistic nature of your life come to fruition. You will begin to offer gifts of gratitude, gifts of friendship, gifts of hope, and gifts of abstract origin to those around you. Today, you will find some way to share a piece of happiness with one other person. You will bring your favorite song to work and play it while you and your colleagues eat lunch. Today, you will share with someone the title of a great new book that you read. Today, you will send a thank-you note to a person who helped you. Today, you will begin to experience the enormity of receiving through giving.

Be True to Yourself

Today, maybe for the first day in your life, you are going to make a commitment to be yourself. You will not face the day wearing the costume that was created by your parents or your spouse or your "friends" or your coworkers. Today, you will hold your head high and proclaim your individual nature, your individual style, and your individual aspirations. Today, you will stop living the life of someone else and you will begin having what you want instead of taking what others give.

Leave Shoulda, Woulda, Coulda Forever

Today, you are going to bury the triplets, shoulda, woulda, coulda. You will never again use the phrase, "I should have . . . ," or "I would have . . . ," or I could have . . ." This set of triplets have cried and moaned since you gave birth to them in the doldrums of your lowest days. It is time to say goodbye to what should have been, what would have been, and what could have been. If it really shoulda, woulda, coulda been—it would have been. It wasn't. Move on.

Forgive Your Past

Today, you will begin the process of healing old wounds, closing past trials, and ending bitter remembrances. You will make a concerted effort to begin by forgiving yourself for carrying this baggage for so long. Today, you will admit to yourself, truly admit, that the *past is over* and no degree of anguish or torture can change it. You will learn to admit that tomorrow, this current day will have become the past, and that only you can change *today* so that your past can be looked upon with fondness.

Move On

Today, you will make a commitment to yourself to move on with your life, with or without the support, advice, or permission of anyone else. While it would be nice to have the support of those you love, today, you will understand that you do not need it. If you want to return to school to better yourself, move on. If you want to begin looking for another place of employment, move on. If you want to eliminate negative and contaminated people from your life, move on. You have that power, you have that authority, and you have that right. Today, you will make the commitment to never wait for another person to grant you permission.

Remove Contaminated People from Your Life

Today, you will give John and Jane Doe the last opportunity to ever hurt you. You will let them know how much their negative behaviors and attitudes have hindered your growth and esteem, and if they are unwilling to change, today, you will walk away knowing that your life is better served without the contamination they brought. Today, you will forgive yourself for allowing others to contaminate your life and your dreams. Today, you will move on.

Live in Your Spiritual Nature

Today, you will return to the part of your soul that is most aligned with the mysteries and majesty of the universe. You will begin to see your life as a connected entity to every living thing. You will begin to understand that your life is a part of human history and you have a choice as to how your pages will read. You have a choice as to how your life will matter. Today, you will begin to make decisions that are based, in part, on your spiritual nature. You will begin to consider your ethical and character development as importantly as you consider your career and financial development.

Journaling is a creative way to keep track of your efforts to keep up your healthy self-esteem. Make lists of compliments you gave or received each day, or jot down some of the positive thoughts you had—about anything!—as you went through your day. This will help reinforce those positive aspects of your day and give you something to look back to on a day that you're feeling down.

Make an Effort to Grow in Some Way Every Day

Today, you will step outside your comfort zone and experience the joys, thrills, uncertainty, and fears associated with growth and change. You will find some way to do something new, something useful, and something worthwhile that brings you closer to your dreams and helps another human being. Today, you will set your sights on a new path both emotionally and spiritually. You will take every opportunity to seize challenging risks, uncertain opportunities, and mysterious adventures. Today, you will begin to walk out of the stagnation that has engulfed you.

Spend Time Being Creative and "Out There"

Today, you will begin to look at every single action that you do in a new light. You will begin to ask yourself, "Is there a better way to get this done?" "Is there a more interesting way to make this happen?" Today, you will make a commitment to yourself to rediscover the creative part of your personality. You will re-establish wonder and mystery in your life. You will take the steps necessary to polish your creative and industrious nature. Today, you will give yourself permission to be a child again.

Learn to Live on the Light Side

Today, you're going to laugh at yourself, your family, your friends, and your work. You are not going to take things so seriously. Today, you're going to admit that there is drama, and then there is *real drama*. Today, you are going to concern yourself only with real drama. Everything need not be a tragedy or a major stress-event in your life. You will learn which war to fight and which battle to smile at and move on. Today, you are going to find humor in things that have brought you pain in the past.

Practice Optimism

Today, you will see only good. You will think only good. You will act only good. Today, you are going to allow yourself the luxury of not thinking one negative thought, not criticizing, not judging, not evaluating. You are going to find only what is right about the world. Perhaps it is the turning leaves, the man on the news who returned a dog to its rightful owner, the young child who saved his mom from a burning home, or the minimum-wage worker who squirreled away enough money to send four children to college. Today, you will allow yourself to have the best that life has to offer—and tomorrow, you'll do it all over again.

Visualize Your Life as You Would Have It

Today, you will begin to see a picture in your mind about how you want your life to look. Do you want more friends? Do you want to feel better physically? Do you want to feel better mentally and emotionally? Do you want a new job? Do you want a better-looking body? Do you want to be known as a person with a giving, altruistic nature? Today, you will see this person, this new life, in your mind, and you will begin to visualize having it. You will set your goals on paper, and never lose sight of what you need.

Strive for Some Joy Every Day

Today, you will find a small piece of joy in the snow falling, the birds singing, the colorful rainbow after the storm, the petting of your cat, the washing of dishes, the run on the treadmill, the work that you do, and the smallest of things that make up your everyday life. Today, you will begin to not expect joy to come to you, but you will begin the day by seeking joy in things, large and small. Today, and each day hereafter, joy will be your calling card.

Find People Whom You Love and Who Love You

Today, you are going to make a commitment to strengthen your relationships with those you love. You are going to set goals to keep them close in your life by cards, letters, e-mails, visits, and phone calls. You are going to begin scheduling time to be with loved ones just as you would schedule time to go to work. Today, you are going to move out of your comfort zone and begin to seek new friends through organizations, volunteering, going back to school, joining a crafts club, or any other means by which you can expand your circle of friends. Today, you are going to bring love closer to your heart.

Build People Up

Today, you will find some way to help another person feel better about himself. It may as simple as a compliment to a stranger or a formal letter complimenting a coworker, but today, you will begin to understand the raw power of what it feels like to build up other people. Today, you will use this power to help someone less fortunate, someone less able, and someone less willing. Today, you will begin to reap the rewards associated with building up other people.

If Someone Applauds You, Don't Ask Why

Today, you are going to accept praise, applause, honor, appreciation, ovations, and approval with the mindset in which they are intended. Beginning today, you will *never* allow yourself to *ever again* make light of compliments that are rightfully yours. You will hold your head high, listen intently to what is offered to you, accept it with grace and class, and store it away in your soul's hope chest. Today, you are going to realize that compliments have been coming your way for years; you were just not healthy enough to hear them gently calling you home.

"Be such a person and live such a life that if every person were as you, and every life as yours, this earth would be God's paradise."
—Phillip Brooks

Set Goals for Your Personal Success

Today, and from this day on, you will never face another day without at least one goal. From this time on, you will take a few moments in the evening to set one goal for the next day. That goal will not have to be major or life altering, but you will not face another day of aimlessness and wandering. Today, you are going to begin to live a life of purpose and a life that moves toward your success. Today, you are going to plot a course that allows you the flexibility and freedom to seek your passion.

Find Passion and Purpose in Your Work

Today, you will begin to look at your life's work in a different frame. You will either find what is good and right and just with your career choice, or you will begin to move toward other work-related ventures. Today, you will approach your work as if it were your first day. Anew with promise and dreams of change, you will step toward the light of your vocation with the attitude of giving and receiving. Today, you will find some degree of passion in your work.

Allow Yourself to Listen with Empathy

Today, you will begin putting yourself into the hearts of those to whom you are listening. You will move away from just hearing people talk to really listening to the words of their life. You will begin to associate their lives with yours, their trials with yours, their joys with yours, and their pains with yours. Today, you will begin listening empathetically and objectively to all you encounter. You will not argue mentally with them, you will not formulate opinions about them or their message until you have the entire story, and today, you will force yourself to be silent long enough to hear the stories in the wind.

Let Go of Perfection

Today, you will let go of "practice makes perfect." It does not and never will. You will begin to work toward improvement, realizing that improvement is the only possibility, because perfection is just a word. Today, you will give yourself permission to laugh at your mistakes. You will begin to find lessons from errors and misjudgments. Today, you will understand how wonderful it is to live a life free from the pressures of perfectionism.

Learn to Say No When You Want to Say No

Today, you are going to put your personal needs before those of others. You are going to learn how to say no to things that are damaging to your self-esteem. You are going to learn to say no to the things that that you do not want to do. You are going to learn to say no to the things that go against who you are as a person of integrity, altruism, and spirituality. Today, you are going to say no to all of the activities and self-defeating behaviors that have crippled you and your aspirations.

Find What Brings You Harmony and Stick to It

Today, you are going to begin your search for harmony. You are going to look for the proper mix of fun and laughter and giving and work and risk and wellness and history and future and forgiveness. You are going to find the elements that bring you to your own true self, your own harmony. Today, you are going to begin to understand that no one thing can bring you peace and comfort. You are going to go on a journey to find the balance that will create harmony in your soul.

Bringing It Home

Self-esteem will always remain a slippery slope. But now that you possess the tools to nurture yourself and protect yourself, the slope has become much less steep. The slope has become manageable. You, and only you, have the power, the clout to make your life work for you.

Only you can control what you allow to influence your feelings, your actions, your attitudes, and your thoughts of worth. Choose happiness, choose peace, choose challenge, choose love, choose giving, choose laughter, choose growth, choose integrity, choose forgiveness, choose wisely. The choice will change your life forever!

"Happiness comes only when we push our brains and hearts to the farthest reaches of which we are capable. The purpose of life is to matter—to count, to stand for something, to have it make some difference that we lived at all."

—Leo Buscaglia

Appendices

Appendix A

The Self-Esteem Assessment Inventory

Appendix B

Additional Resources

Appendix C

Goal-Planning Worksheet

Appendix D

Bibliography

The Self-Esteem Assessment Inventory

Do not take this assessment if you do not have at least a half-hour of uninterrupted quiet time. Answer the following questions as truthfully as possible. You should answer these questions based on how you actually feel and behave, not how you *think* you should feel and behave. Remember, there are no right or wrong answers, and you are the only person who will see your responses.

True or False

❒ T ❒ F   1. I am as physically attractive as most people.

❒ T ❒ F   2. I do not think I am as intellectually capable as most people.

❒ T ❒ F   3. I definitely feel that I can make it on my own, financially, emotionally, and socially.

❒ T ❒ F   4. I engage in activities that promote my personal growth.

❒ T ❒ F   5. I deal well with most situations.

❒ T ❒ F   6. If I could change lives with someone else, I would do it.

❒ T ❒ F   7. I enjoy going to social settings such as mixers, work-related events, and parties.

❒ T ❒ F   8. I am not a very optimistic person most of the time.

❒ T ❒ F   9. I have many things in my life of which I am proud.

❒ T ❒ F   10. When someone criticizes me, I take it in context and move on with my day.

❒ T ❒ F   11. My family seldom understands or supports me.

❒ T ❒ F   12. There are times when I feel completely worthless.

❒ T ❒ F   13. I do not embarrass easily or worry about "looking like a fool" very often.

❒ T ❒ F   14. I usually try to fit in with "the group" even if I have to be untruthful to myself.

❒ T ❒ F   15. I set personal goals and stick to a plan to reach those goals.

❒ T ❒ F   16. I meet people very easily and make new friends quickly and easily.

❏ T ❏ F 17. Losing bothers me greatly.

❏ T ❏ F 18. Most of the time, I doubt my abilities.

❏ T ❏ F 19. When I make a mistake, I admit it and move on.

❏ T ❏ F 20. I am a procrastinator.

❏ T ❏ F 21. I am better off than most people around me.

❏ T ❏ F 22. I enjoy telling other people about my accomplishments and do it often.

❏ T ❏ F 23. I ask for help when I need it.

❏ T ❏ F 24. I will do whatever it takes to succeed at any cost.

❏ T ❏ F 25. I need the praise of others and sometimes seek it out.

Scoring

Compare *your* "true" or "false" responses with this key and add up the number of points corresponding to each of your responses. Enter the corresponding score on the blank line. (For example, if you answered *true* to question 1, you score 1 point. If you answered *false* to question 1, you score 0 points.) Then add your total points and multiply by 4 to get your score. Check the following chart to determine what your score means.

1.	T=1 F=0	_____	15.	T=1 F=0	_____
2.	T=0 F=1	_____	16.	T=1 F=0	_____
3.	T=1 F=0	_____	17	T=0 F=1	_____
4.	T=1 F=0	_____	18.	T=0 F=1	_____
5.	T=1 F=0	_____	19.	T=1 F=0	_____
6.	T=0 F=1	_____	20.	T=0 F=1	_____
7.	T=1 F=0	_____	21.	T=1 F=0	_____
8.	T=0 F=1	_____	22.	T=0 F=1	_____
9.	T=1 F=0	_____	23.	T=1 F=0	_____
10.	T=1 F=0	_____	24.	T=0 F=1	_____
11.	T=0 F=1	_____	25.	T=0 F=1	_____
12.	T=0 F=1	_____			
13.	T=1 F=0	_____			
14.	T=0 F=1	_____			

Once you have completed the score transfer, total the right-hand column.

RIGHT-HAND COLUMN TOTAL = _____ × 4 = _____

What Your Score Means

80–100   You have very positive, healthy self-esteem
60–79   You have a moderate to resonable level of self-esteem
40–59   You have a low to moderate level of self-esteem
39–BELOW You have severely low, unhealthy self-esteem

If you took the time to answer the questions truthfully, your score should closely reflect your level of self-esteem. Measuring self-esteem is a tricky and sometimes inaccurate task. To get the most accurate reading, the person taking the assessment should be completely unaware that her or his self-esteem is being assessed. Since you picked up a self-esteem book, this is not completely possible. If you look back at the assessment, you will see that nowhere is self-esteem mentioned. This was done to try to elicit the most honest response from you.

Most people who take the assessment score in the 60 to 79 range. If you scored higher, the score reflects that you have a healthy view of yourself and that you may only have one or two areas on which you would like to work. If you scored lower, the score reflects that you may not have a healthy view of your abilities, your gifts, your accomplishments, and your dealings in the world. Do not despair. *The Everything Self-Esteem Book* is written to assist you in the journey to building healthier self-esteem.

Appendix B

Additional Resources

Web Sites

The National Association for Self-Esteem
✐ *www.self-esteem-nase.org*

The Self-Esteem Learning Foundation
✐ *www.selfesteem.org*

OneStepAtAtime.com
✐ *www.self-esteem.com*

More-Selfesteem.com
✐ *www.more-selfesteem.com*

SelfGrowth.com
✐ *www.selfgrowth.com*

The Self-Esteem Theme Page
✐ *www.cln.org/themes/self_esteem.html*

Books

Branden, Nathaniel. *Self-Esteem at Work: How Confident People Make Powerful Companies* (San Francisco: Jossey-Bass, 1998).

Branden, Nathaniel. *The Six Pillars of Self-Esteem* (New York: Bantam, 1994).

Burns, David. *Ten Days to Self-Esteem* (New York: Quill, 1993).

Buscaglia, Leo. *Living, Loving, and Learning* (New York: Fawcett, 1982).

Chopra, Deepak. *The Seven Spiritual Laws of Success* (San Rafael, CA: Amber-Allen Publishing, 1994).

Gawain, Shakti. *Creative Visualization* (Novato, CA: Nataraj Publishing, 2002).

Glass, Lillian. *Toxic People: 10 Ways of Dealing with People Who Make Your Life Miserable* (New York: St. Martin's Press, 1995).

Hafen, Brent, Keith J. Karren, Kathryn J. Frandsen, and N. Lee Smith. *Mind/Body Health: The Effects of Attitudes, Emotions and Relationships* (Boston: Allyn and Bacon, 1996).

McKay, Matthew and Patrick Fanning. *Self-Esteem, 3rd ed.* (Oakland, CA: New Harbinger, 2000).

Palmer, Parker. *Let Your Life Speak: Listening to the Voice of Vocation* (San Francisco: Jossey-Bass, 2000).

Schiraldi, Glenn. *The Self-Esteem Workbook* (Oakland, CA: New Harbinger Publications, 2001).

Sorensen, Marilyn. *Breaking the Chain of Low Self-Esteem* (Sherwood, OR: Wolf Publishing, 1998).

Sorensen, Marilyn. *Low Self-Esteem Misunderstood and Misdiagnosed* (Sherwood, OR: Wolf Publishing, 2001).

Williamson, Marianne. *Illuminata* (New York: Riverhead Books, 1997).

Self-Esteem Inventories

The Coopersmith Self-Esteem Inventory
Carried by Mind Garden
1690 Woodside Road, Suite 202
Redwood City, CA 94061
(650) 261-3500
✐ *www.mindgarden.com*

The Self-Esteem Self-Evaluation Survey online from the National Association for Self-Esteem
✐ *www.self-esteem-nase.org/jssurvey.shtml*

Goal-Planning Worksheet

Sample Goal-Planning Worksheet

Goal Statement: I will (Notice the action verb *will*. Never write a goal that states, "I want to . . ." or "I plan to . . ."; always begin with "I will" or "I am going to.")

‗‗‗‗‗‗‗‗‗‗‗‗‗‗‗‗‗‗‗‗‗‗‗‗‗‗‗‗‗‗‗‗‗‗‗‗‗‗

by ‗‗‗‗‗‗‗‗, 20 ‗‗‗‗‗‗‗‗ . (You must set a deadline for reaching this goal.)

I plan to do this by (These are your *action* steps. How do you plan to set this goal into action?)

1. ‗‗‗‗‗‗‗‗‗‗‗‗‗‗‗‗‗‗‗‗‗‗‗‗‗‗‗‗‗‗‗‗‗‗‗‗‗‗

2. ‗‗‗‗‗‗‗‗‗‗‗‗‗‗‗‗‗‗‗‗‗‗‗‗‗‗‗‗‗‗‗‗‗‗‗‗‗‗

3. ‗‗‗‗‗‗‗‗‗‗‗‗‗‗‗‗‗‗‗‗‗‗‗‗‗‗‗‗‗‗‗‗‗‗‗‗‗‗

4. ‗‗‗‗‗‗‗‗‗‗‗‗‗‗‗‗‗‗‗‗‗‗‗‗‗‗‗‗‗‗‗‗‗‗‗‗‗‗

5. ‗‗‗‗‗‗‗‗‗‗‗‗‗‗‗‗‗‗‗‗‗‗‗‗‗‗‗‗‗‗‗‗‗‗‗‗‗‗

Narrative Statement (The picture of what your life will look like when this change is made):

‗‗‗‗‗‗‗‗‗‗‗‗‗‗‗‗‗‗‗‗‗‗‗‗‗‗‗‗‗‗‗‗‗‗‗‗‗‗

‗‗‗‗‗‗‗‗‗‗‗‗‗‗‗‗‗‗‗‗‗‗‗‗‗‗‗‗‗‗‗‗‗‗‗‗‗‗

‗‗‗‗‗‗‗‗‗‗‗‗‗‗‗‗‗‗‗‗‗‗‗‗‗‗‗‗‗‗‗‗‗‗‗‗‗‗

‗‗‗‗‗‗‗‗‗‗‗‗‗‗‗‗‗‗‗‗‗‗‗‗‗‗‗‗‗‗‗‗‗‗‗‗‗‗

Use another sheet if necessary.

Sample Goal-Planning Worksheet (continued)

I deserve this change in my life because --

I commit to this change in my life this ------------------------------------ day of

------------------------------------ , 20 ------------------

    Signature (This is an important step in this process. Your signature binds you to this goal.)

Appendix D
Bibliography

Alder, Robert, Lawrence Rosenfeld, and Neil Towne. *Interplay: the Process of Interpersonal Communication,* 4th ed (New York: Holt, Rinehart and Winston, 1989).

Arkoff, Abe. *The Illuminated Life* (Boston: Allyn and Bacon, 1995).

Begley, Sharon. "You're OK, I'm Terrific: 'Self-Esteem' Backfires." *Newsweek,* 13 July 1998, p. 69.

Bensimhon, Dan. "The Cheer of Living Dangerously." *Men's Health* 7, no. 2 (1992): p.56.

Benson, Herbert and Eileen Stuart. *The Wellness Book* (New York: Fireside, 1992).

Boss, Shira. "The Writer's Cure for Stress." *Good Housekeeping* 229, no. 3 (1999): p.180.

Bragg, Terry. *31 Days to High Self-Esteem* (Murray, UT: Peacemakers Publishing, 1997).

Branden, Nathaniel. *Self-Esteem at Work: How Confident People Make Powerful Companies* (San Francisco: Jossey-Bass, 1998).

Branden, Nathaniel. *The Six Pillars of Self-Esteem* (New York: Bantam, 1994).

Burns, David. *Feeling Good: The New Mood Therapy* (New York: New American Library, 1981).

Buscaglia, Leo. *Living, Loving, and Learning* (New York: Fawcett, 1982).

Carter, Carol, Joyce Bishop, and Sarah Kravits. *Keys to Success,* 4th ed. (New Jersey: Prentice Hall, 2003).

Castro, Janice. "Vox Pop." *Time,* 10 February 1992, p. 15.

Chopra, Deepak. *The Seven Spiritual Laws of Success* (San Rafael, CA: Amber-Allen Publishing, 1994).

Cooley, Charles. *On Self and Social Organization* (Chicago: University of Chicago Press, 1998).

Coopersmith, Stanley. *The Antecedents of Self-Esteem* (New York: W. H. Freeman, 1967).

Devito, Joseph. *The Interpersonal Communication Book,* 7th ed. (New York: Harper Collins, 1995).

Dinesen, Isak. *Out of Africa* (New York: Modern Library, 1992).

Dold, Cathy. "Want To Be Your Own Therapist? Keep A Journal." *Cosmopolitan* 221, no. 2 (1996): p. 115.

Dutton, Gail. "Cutting-Edge Stressbusters." *HR Focus* 75, no. 9 (1998): p. 11.

Edelstein, Michael. *Three-Minute Therapy* (New York: Glenbridge Publishing, 1997).

Eisenmna, Russell. "Creativity, Risk Taking, Sex Difference, and Birth Order." *The Journal of Evolutionary Psychology*, August 2001, p. 199.

Farley, Frank. "The Big T in Personality; Thrill-Seeking Often Produces the Best Achievers But It Can Also Create the Worst Criminals." *Psychology Today,* 20 (1986): p. 44.

Feldman, Robert. *Development Across the Life Span,* 3rd ed. (New Jersey: Prentice Hall, 2003).

Gawain, Shakti. *Creative Visualization* (Novato, CA: Nataraj Publishing, 2002).

Ghate, Onkar. "Say No to the Self-Esteem Pushers." *MediaLink of the Ayn Rand Institute,* November 2002.

Gibran, Kahlil. *The Prophet* (New York: Knopf, 1923).

Glass, Lillian. *Toxic People: 10 Ways of Dealing with People Who Make Your Life Miserable* (New York: St. Martin's Press, 1995).

Graham, Stephanie, Susan Furr, Claudia Flowers, and Mary Thomas Burke. "Religion and Spirituality in Coping with Stress." *Counseling and Values* 46, no. 1 (2001): p. 2.

Growald, Eileen Rockefeller and Allan Luks. "Beyond Self." *American Health,* March 1988, p. 51.

Grudin, Robert. *The Grace of Great Things: Creativity and Innovation* (New York: Ticknor and Fields, 1990).

Hafen, Brent, Keith J. Karren, Kathryn J. Frandsen, and N. Lee Smith. *Mind/Body Health: The Effects of Attitudes, Emotions and Relationships* (Boston: Allyn and Bacon, 1996).

Hanna, Sharon. *Person to Person: Positive Relationships Don't Just Happen* (New Jersey: Prentice Hall, 2003).

Herndon, Lucia. "Volunteers Have to Feel the Need to do Right." *Knight Ridder/Tribune News Service,* 18 March 1997, p. 318.

Hickam Jr. Homer. *Rocket Boys* (New York: Delta Trace, 1998).

Hirshberg, Eric. "What Creative Slump? Tough Times, Not Flush Times, Inspire Great Work." *ADWEEK, New England Edition* 39, no. 35 (2002): p. 101.

James, William. *The Principles of Psychology* (New York: Doven, 1995).

Jaya, S. Sundareson Petaling. "Volunteerism Is Every Citizen's Responsibility." *New Straits Times,* 3 May 2001.

Jeffers, Susan. *Feel the Fear and Do It Anyway* (San Diego: Harcourt, Brace and Jovanovich, 1987).

Khazei, Alan. "A New Citizenship for a New Century." *Brookings Review* 20, no. 4 (2002): p. 31.

Lane, Harland. *The Wild Boy of Aveyron* (Cambridge, MA: The Harvard Press, 1976).

Light, Paul C. "The Volunteering Decision: What Prompts It? What Sustains It?" *Brookings Review* 20, no. 4 (2002): p. 45.

Maslow, Abraham. *Self-Actualization* (New York: Addison-Wesley, 1987).

McKay, Matthew and Patrick Fanning. *Self-Esteem*, 3rd ed. (Oakland, CA: New Harbinger Press, 2000).

"Middle-Aged Women Are Happiest." *Marketing to Women: Addressing Women and Women's Sensibilities* 15, no. 7 (2002): p. 3.

Miller, Michael Craig. "The Benefit of Positive Psychology." *The Harvard Mental Health Letter* 18, no. 7 (2000).

Morris, Holly J. "Happiness Explained." *U.S. News and World Report*, 3 September 2001, p. 46.

Myers, Isabella Briggs and Mary McCaulley. *Manual: A Guide to the Development and Use of the Myers-Briggs Type Indicator* (Palo Alto, CA: Consulting Psychologists Press, 1985).

Neihart, Maureen. "Systematic Risk-Taking." *The Roeper Review* 21, no. 4 (1999): p. 289.

Notarius, Clifford and Lisa Herrick. "Listener Response Strategies to a Distressed Other." *Journal of Social and Personal Relationships* 5, no. 97 (1988): p. 108.

Nozizwe, Lena. "The Power of Optimism." *Vibrant Life* 1, no. 7 (1991), p. 28.

O'Brien, Tim. "You Can Take Yourself to New Heights." *Knight Ridder/ Tribune News Service,* 21 April 1995, p. 421.

O'Connell, David. "Spirituality's Importance in Recovery Cannot Be Denied." *Alcoholism and Drug Abuse Weekly* 11, no. 47 (1999): p. 5.

Palmer, Parker. *Let Your Life Speak: Listening to the Voice of Vocation* (San Francisco: Jossey-Bass, 2000).

Parachin, Victor. "Integrity—The Most Important Trait to Cultivate." *Supervision* 63, no. 2 (2002): p. 3.

Patterson, James and Peter Kim. *The Day America Told the Truth* (New York: Prentice Hall Trade, 1991).

Phillips, Bill. *Body for Life: Twelve Weeks to Mental and Physical Health* (New York: Harper Collins, 1999).

President and Fellows of Harvard College. "Placebos in the Brain." *Harvard Mental Health Letter* 19, no. 12 (2002).

Ramsey, Robert. "How an Optimistic Outlook Can Give You an Edge." *Supervision* 6, no. 9 (2000): p. 6.

Reisenauer, Tim. "Creativity, Not I.Q. Made Them Successful." *Everett Business Journal* 5, no. 9 (2000): p. 3.

Rosemond, John. "Toilets, Like Obligations, May Finally Fade Away." *Knight Ridder/Tribune News Service,* 13 October 1998, p. 101.

Seligman, Martin. *Learned Optimism: How to Change Your Mind and Your Life* (New York: Pocket Books, 1998).

Sheldon, Kennon, Andrew Elliot, Youngmee Kim, and Tim Kasser. "What Is Satisfying About Satisfying Events?" *Journal of Personality and Social Psychology* 80, no. 2 (2001): p. 325.

"Smarties: Smarter Than You Think." *Chemistry and Industry* 12 (June 2002): p. 42.

Sorensen, Marilyn. *Breaking the Chains of Low Self-Esteem* (Sherwood, OR: Wolf Publishing, 1998).

Steenland, Sally. "Two Men, Each Convicted of Sexual Crimes, Blame Everyone Except Themselves for Their Misdeeds." *Knight Ridder/Tribune News Service,* 28 September 1993, p. 928.

Syemore, Rhea. "Did You Know?" *Chatelaine* 73, no. 8 (2000): p. 30.

Taylor, Steve. "Where Is Happiness?" *www.thinkdeeply.com,* August 26, 2002, p. 2.

Thompson, Joy. "Pearl of Integrity Becoming Harder and Harder to Find." *Knight Ridder/Tribune News Service,* 16 April 1997, p. 416.

Vanzant, Iyanla. *Living through the Meantime: Learning to Break the Patterns of the Past and Begin the Healing Process* (New York: Fireside, 2001).

Veenhoven, Ruut. "Advances in Understanding Happiness." *Quebecoise de Psychologie* 18, (1997): p.29.

Walters, Brenda and Sandra Mckee. *Life Management: Skills for Busy People* (Upper Saddle River, NJ: Prentice Hall, 1997).

Watson, Charles. *Managing with Integrity: Insights from America's CEO's* (New York: Praeger, 1991).

Wegscheider-Cruse, Sharon. *Learning to Love Yourself: Finding Your Self-Worth* (Deerfield Beach, FL: Health Communications, 1987).

Williamson, Marianne. *Illuminata* (New York: Riverhead Books, 1997).

Wittman, Juliet. "Creativity is Indefinable and Inescapable." *Knight Ridder/Tribune News Service,* 3 November 1995, p. 1,103.

Woolfolk, Anita. *Educational Psychology,* 7th ed. (Boston: Allyn and Bacon, 1998).

Wurman, Richard. *Understanding* (Newport, RI: TED Conferences, Inc., 2000).

Index

Feeling trait, 71–72
Ferber, Edna, 130
Financial issues, 54–55, 73, 180
Fitness, 88, 104–6, 276
Focus, 147
Foes, 153
Forbes, 6
Forgiveness
    benefits of, 204
    and healing, 37, 201
    and past incidents, 132–33,
        136–37, 202–3, 210, 279
    of self, 28
    taking action, 209–12
    through communication, 204–5
    through conflict resolution, 205–6
    and trust, 206–8
    understanding, 203–4
Fosdick, Harry Emerson, 95
Franklin, Benjamin, 42
Friends, 24–25, 182, 183, 250–51
Frost, Robert, 28
Future-based happiness, 83
Future goals, 64–65, 78. *See also* Goals

G

Galileo, 228
Garcia, Will, 50
Genetics, 27
Ghate, Onkar, 6
Gibran, Kahlil, 42
Gifts in life, 267–68
Giving to others, 261–71, 278, 282.
    See also Volunteerism
Goals
    attaining, 145–48
    committing to, 62–64, 274–85
    failure of, 62
    for future, 60–62, 64–65, 78
    guidelines for, 61–62
    and motivation, 122–24
    for professional life, 64–65, 283–84
    setting, 60–62, 169, 280, 283–84
    stretching limits, 79–80

study on, 60
    understanding, 60–61
    visualization of, 63, 122–23, 172–74
    worksheet for, 66–67, 293–94
Goodness, 210–12
Growth, 50–51
Grudin, Robert, 179

H

Habits
    forming, 85, 90
    of happiness, 85–88
    keeping, 274
Happiness
    benefits of, 84, 285
    in career, 71–72
    defining, 82–85
    and education, 89
    finding, 41–43, 88–89, 282, 285
    habits of, 85–88
    level of, 82, 83
    limits to, 84–85
    from others, 44
    sharing, 89–90, 170
    small pleasures, 88, 89, 170
    source of, 81
    tips for, 44–45
    types of, 82–85
    understanding, 42
    worksheet for, 91
Harmony, 167, 284
Harris, Sydney, 30
Healing, 37, 158, 195, 201, 204, 206
Healthiness, 88, 103–12, 276–77. *See
    also* Wellness
Healthy eating, 106–7, 276
Hedonistic happiness, 83
Helping others, 76–77, 86. *See also*
    Volunteerism
Herring, Jeff, 195
Hickam, Homer, Jr., 32–33
Holographic memories, 173
Homophobic, 154
Honesty, 182

Hubbard, Elbert, 156
Human history, 263–64, 280
Humanity, 262–63
Humor, sense of, 213, 217, 281
Hurting others, 202–3

I

"If only," 15–16
Imagination, 228–29
Immoral people, 179–82
Independence, 41
Individuality, 229
Inferiority, 277
Inner critic, 58–60
Inner qualities, 220, 221
Inspirational mementos, 216–18
Integrity
    definition of, 177–79, 185
    of employees, 181
    importance of, 177
    lack of, 179–82, 185
    lapse in, 186–87
    plan for, 182–83, 277–78
    possessing, 184–87
    practicing, 277–78, 284
    statement of, 182–83, 277
    threats to, 184–85
    and wants, 184, 185
Intelligence, 276–77
Internal motivation, 124
Introvert trait, 71–72
Intuitive trait, 71–72
It's a Wonderful Life, 149

J, K

James, William, 3–5, 7, 226
"Jealous jokers," 156
Jealousy, 153, 156, 181–82
Job
    versus career, 70–72, 75–77
    purpose in, 69–80, 141–48, 283
    see also Career; Professional life

THE EVERYTHING TOTAL FITNESS BOOK

By Ellen Karpay

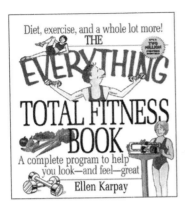

Trade paperback,
$12.95 ($19.95 CAN)
1-58062-318-2, 304 pages

*T*he *Everything® Total Fitness Book* features complete information and instructions on the best exercises for aerobic and muscular fitness, from outdoor sports for all seasons to the latest machines at the gym. The step-by-step illustrations of exercise, weight training, and stretching techniques will help ensure that your workouts are safe and effective. With dozens of helpful hints, tips, and excuse-busters, you'll quickly develop a routine that works for you. You'll learn to build time for rigorous and effective exercise into even the busiest schedule.

OTHER *EVERYTHING®* BOOKS BY ADAMS MEDIA

BUSINESS

Everything® **Business Planning Book**
Everything® **Coaching and Mentoring Book**
Everything® **Fundraising Book**
Everything® **Home-Based Business Book**
Everything® **Leadership Book**
Everything® **Managing People Book**
Everything® **Network Marketing Book**
Everything® **Online Business Book**
Everything® **Project Management Book**
Everything® **Selling Book**
Everything® **Start Your Own Business Book**
Everything® **Time Management Book**

COMPUTERS

Everything® **Build Your Own Home Page Book**

Everything® **Computer Book**
Everything® **Internet Book**
Everything® **Microsoft® Word 2000 Book**

COOKBOOKS

Everything® **Barbecue Cookbook**
Everything® **Bartender's Book, $9.95**
Everything® **Chinese Cookbook**
Everything® **Chocolate Cookbook**
Everything® **Cookbook**
Everything® **Dessert Cookbook**
Everything® **Diabetes Cookbook**
Everything® **Low-Carb Cookbook**
Everything® **Low-Fat High-Flavor Cookbook**
Everything® **Mediterranean Cookbook**
Everything® **Mexican Cookbook**
Everything® **One-Pot Cookbook**
Everything® **Pasta Book**

Everything® **Quick Meals Cookbook**
Everything® **Slow Cooker Cookbook**
Everything® **Soup Cookbook**
Everything® **Thai Cookbook**
Everything® **Vegetarian Cookbook**
Everything® **Wine Book**

HEALTH

Everything® **Anti-Aging Book**
Everything® **Diabetes Book**
Everything® **Dieting Book**
Everything® **Herbal Remedies Book**
Everything® **Hypnosis Book**
Everything® **Menopause Book**
Everything® **Nutrition Book**
Everything® **Reflexology Book**
Everything® **Stress Management Book**
Everything®**Vitamins, Minerals, and Nutritional Supplements Book**

All Everything® books are priced at $12.95 or $14.95, unless otherwise stated. Prices subject to change without notice.
Canadian prices range from $11.95–$31.95, and are subject to change without notice.

HISTORY

Everything® **American History Book**
Everything® **Civil War Book**
Everything® **Irish History & Heritage Book**
Everything® **Mafia Book**
Everything® **World War II Book**

HOBBIES & GAMES

Everything® **Bridge Book**
Everything® **Candlemaking Book**
Everything® **Casino Gambling Book**
Everything® **Chess Basics Book**
Everything® **Collectibles Book**
Everything® **Crossword and Puzzle Book**
Everything® **Digital Photography Book**
Everything® **Family Tree Book**
Everything® **Games Book**
Everything® **Knitting Book**
Everything® **Magic Book**
Everything® **Motorcycle Book**
Everything® **Online Genealogy Book**
Everything® **Photography Book**
Everything® **Pool & Billiards Book**
Everything® **Quilting Book**
Everything® **Scrapbooking Book**
Everything® **Soapmaking Book**

HOME IMPROVEMENT

Everything® **Feng Shui Book**
Everything® **Gardening Book**
Everything® **Home Decorating Book**
Everything® **Landscaping Book**
Everything® **Lawn Care Book**
Everything® **Organize Your Home Book**

KIDS' STORY BOOKS

Everything® **Bedtime Story Book**
Everything® **Bible Stories Book**
Everything® **Fairy Tales Book**
Everything® **Mother Goose Book**

EVERYTHING® KIDS' BOOKS

All titles are $6.95
Everything® **Kids' Baseball Book, 2nd Ed.** ($10.95 CAN)
Everything® **Kids' Bugs Book** ($10.95 CAN)
Everything® **Kids' Christmas Puzzle & Activity Book** ($10.95 CAN)
Everything® **Kids' Cookbook** ($10.95 CAN)
Everything® **Kids' Halloween Puzzle & Activity Book** ($10.95 CAN)
Everything® **Kids' Joke Book** ($10.95 CAN)
Everything® **Kids' Math Puzzles Book** ($10.95 CAN)
Everything® **Kids' Mazes Book** ($10.95 CAN)
Everything® **Kids' Money Book** ($11.95 CAN)
Everything® **Kids' Monsters Book** ($10.95 CAN)
Everything® **Kids' Nature Book** ($11.95 CAN)
Everything® **Kids' Puzzle Book** ($10.95 CAN)
Everything® **Kids' Science Experiments Book** ($10.95 CAN)
Everything® **Kids' Soccer Book** ($10.95 CAN)
Everything® **Kids' Travel Activity Book** ($10.95 CAN)

LANGUAGE

Everything® **Learning French Book**
Everything® **Learning German Book**
Everything® **Learning Italian Book**
Everything® **Learning Latin Book**
Everything® **Learning Spanish Book**
Everything® **Sign Language Book**

MUSIC

Everything® **Drums Book (with CD),** $19.95 ($31.95 CAN)
Everything® **Guitar Book**
Everything® **Playing Piano and Keyboards Book**

Everything® **Rock & Blues Guitar Book (with CD),** $19.95 ($31.95 CAN)
Everything® **Songwriting Book**

NEW AGE

Everything® **Astrology Book**
Everything® **Divining the Future Book**
Everything® **Dreams Book**
Everything® **Ghost Book**
Everything® **Meditation Book**
Everything® **Numerology Book**
Everything® **Palmistry Book**
Everything® **Psychic Book**
Everything® **Spells & Charms Book**
Everything® **Tarot Book**
Everything® **Wicca and Witchcraft Book**

PARENTING

Everything® **Baby Names Book**
Everything® **Baby Shower Book**
Everything® **Baby's First Food Book**
Everything® **Baby's First Year Book**
Everything® **Breastfeeding Book**
Everything® **Father-to-Be Book**
Everything® **Get Ready for Baby Book**
Everything® **Homeschooling Book**
Everything® **Parent's Guide to Positive Discipline**
Everything® **Potty Training Book,** $9.95 ($15.95 CAN)
Everything® **Pregnancy Book, 2nd Ed.**
Everything® **Pregnancy Fitness Book**
Everything® **Pregnancy Organizer,** $15.00 ($22.95 CAN)
Everything® **Toddler Book**
Everything® **Tween Book**

PERSONAL FINANCE

Everything® **Budgeting Book**
Everything® **Get Out of Debt Book**
Everything® **Get Rich Book**
Everything® **Homebuying Book, 2nd Ed.**
Everything® **Homeselling Book**

All Everything® books are priced at $12.95 or $14.95, unless otherwise stated. Prices subject to change without notice.
Canadian prices range from $11.95–$31.95, and are subject to change without notice.

Everything® **Investing Book**
Everything® **Money Book**
Everything® **Mutual Funds Book**
Everything® **Online Investing Book**
Everything® **Personal Finance Book**
Everything® **Personal Finance in Your 20s & 30s Book**
Everything® **Wills & Estate Planning Book**

PETS

Everything® **Cat Book**
Everything® **Dog Book**
Everything® **Dog Training and Tricks Book**
Everything® **Horse Book**
Everything® **Puppy Book**
Everything® **Tropical Fish Book**

REFERENCE

Everything® **Astronomy Book**
Everything® **Car Care Book**
Everything® **Christmas Book, $15.00 ($21.95 CAN)**
Everything® **Classical Mythology Book**
Everything® **Einstein Book**
Everything® **Etiquette Book**
Everything® **Great Thinkers Book**
Everything® **Philosophy Book**
Everything® **Shakespeare Book**
Everything® **Tall Tales, Legends, & Other Outrageous Lies Book**
Everything® **Toasts Book**
Everything® **Trivia Book**
Everything® **Weather Book**

RELIGION

Everything® **Angels Book**
Everything® **Buddhism Book**
Everything® **Catholicism Book**
Everything® **Jewish History & Heritage Book**
Everything® **Judaism Book**

Everything® **Prayer Book**
Everything® **Saints Book**
Everything® **Understanding Islam Book**
Everything® **World's Religions Book**
Everything® **Zen Book**

SCHOOL & CAREERS

Everything® **After College Book**
Everything® **College Survival Book**
Everything® **Cover Letter Book**
Everything® **Get-a-Job Book**
Everything® **Hot Careers Book**
Everything® **Job Interview Book**
Everything® **Online Job Search Book**
Everything® **Resume Book, 2nd Ed.**
Everything® **Study Book**

SELF-HELP

Everything® **Dating Book**
Everything® **Divorce Book**
Everything® **Great Marriage Book**
Everything® **Great Sex Book**
Everything® **Romance Book**
Everything® **Self-Esteem Book**
Everything® **Success Book**

SPORTS & FITNESS

Everything® **Bicycle Book**
Everything® **Body Shaping Book**
Everything® **Fishing Book**
Everything® **Fly-Fishing Book**
Everything® **Golf Book**
Everything® **Golf Instruction Book**
Everything® **Pilates Book**
Everything® **Running Book**
Everything® **Sailing Book, 2nd Ed.**
Everything® **T'ai Chi and QiGong Book**
Everything® **Total Fitness Book**
Everything® **Weight Training Book**
Everything® **Yoga Book**

TRAVEL

Everything® **Guide to Las Vegas**

Everything® **Guide to New England**
Everything® **Guide to New York City**
Everything® **Guide to Washington D.C.**
Everything® **Travel Guide to The Disneyland Resort®, California Adventure®, Universal Studios®, and the Anaheim Area**
Everything® **Travel Guide to the Walt Disney World Resort®, Universal Studios®, and Greater Orlando, 3rd Ed.**

WEDDINGS

Everything® **Bachelorette Party Book**
Everything® **Bridesmaid Book**
Everything® **Creative Wedding Ideas Book**
Everything® **Jewish Wedding Book**
Everything® **Wedding Book, 2nd Ed.**
Everything® **Wedding Checklist, $7.95 ($11.95 CAN)**
Everything® **Wedding Etiquette Book, $7.95 ($11.95 CAN)**
Everything® **Wedding Organizer, $15.00 ($22.95 CAN)**
Everything® **Wedding Shower Book, $7.95 ($12.95 CAN)**
Everything® **Wedding Vows Book, $7.95 ($11.95 CAN)**
Everything® **Weddings on a Budget Book, $9.95 ($15.95 CAN)**

WRITING

Everything® **Creative Writing Book**
Everything® **Get Published Book**
Everything® **Grammar and Style Book**
Everything® **Grant Writing Book**
Everything® **Guide to Writing Children's Books**
Everything® **Screenwriting Book**
Everything® **Writing Well Book**

Available wherever books are sold!
To order, call 800-872-5627, or visit us at everything.com

Everything® and everything.com® are registered trademarks of F+W Publications, Inc.